Robert Lyman was for twenty years an officer in the
British Army. Educated at Scotch College, Melbourne and
the Royal Military Academy, Sandhurst, he has degrees from the
Universities of York, Wales, London and Cranfield.

ROBERT LYMAN

THE LONGEST SIEGE

TOBRUK – THE BATTLE THAT SAVED NORTH AFRICA

PAN BOOKS

First published 2009 by Macmillan

First published in paperback 2010 by Pan Books
an imprint of Pan Macmillan, a division of Macmillan Publishers Limited
Pan Macmillan, 20 New Wharf Road, London N1 9RR
Basingstoke and Oxford
Associated companies throughout the world
www.panmacmillan.com

ISBN 978-0-330-51081-3

1 3 5 7 9 8 6 4 2

A CIP catalogue record for this book is available from
the British Library.

Maps by ML Design
Typeset by SetSystems Ltd, Saffron Walden, Essex
Printed in the UK by CPI Mackays, Chatham ME5 8TD

Visit **www.panmacmillan.com** to read more about all our books
and to buy them. You will also find features, author interviews and
news of any author events, and you can sign up for e-newsletters
so that you're always first to hear about our new releases.

For Philip and Isla Brownless

Photographic Acknowledgements

Getty Images: 1 + 11 (Time & Life pictures), 14 + 22 (Keystone), 38 (Hulton Archive)

Corbis: 2, 6, 7

Imperial War Museum: 3 (E1772), 5 (E1776), 8 (E2478), 10 (MH5568), 12 (E2887), 16 (E2872), 17 (E4792), 18 (E4800), 19 (E4814), 20 (E4946), 25 (E5128), 26 (E5512), 27 (E5547), 28 (E5559), 35 (E6442)

Australian War Memorial: 4 (100014), 9 (009589), 21 (020280), 23 (P01810_004), 24 (9493_20A), 29 (021033), 30 (040453), 31 (041859), 32 (020753), 33 (020893), 34 (041843), 36 (011006),

AP/PA Photos: 13, 15, 39

Contents

Acknowledgements

This book is dedicated to the Reverend Philip Brownless, a veteran of the siege and whose original idea this book was, and his indefatigable wife, Isla, whose extraordinary capacity for editing has been a serious loss to the publishing industry.

I wish to thank the many people who made this book possible. In no particular order they include Ben Brownless (Philip and Isla's son), who accompanied me to Tobruk; Lieutenant General A.D. Leakey CMG CBE; Mr Roderick Suddaby and the staff at the Imperial War Museum Department of Documents; the staff of the Liddell Hart Archives at my alma mater, King's College, London; the staff at the British Library and the National Archives, Kew; Major George Burns; Colonel Andrew Duncan; veterans Major R.G. Holmes MM, Peter (and Mrs) Cochrane, Frank Harrison, Alex Franks, Tom Swallow, Jack (and Mrs) Senior, Peter Bindloss and Alec Clarke; authors Colin Smith and Ian W. Walker; Hilary Pethick (for translating German texts); and Mrs Caroline Davies (for translating Italian texts).

In the United States I was assisted by veterans the Reverend Christopher Morley and Zbigniew Wolynski, and Mr Peter Guinta; in New Zealand by Alan Gray and Martyn Thompson. In Libya I wish to thank Mr Sami el-Gibany and his son Muhammad, who eased my way around the battlefield, as did Mr Abdelghader Awad Imzainy in Tobruk and the local historian Mr Fadeel Altaib, son of the Tobruk postmaster during the siege; Mr Muhammad Haneesh, keeper of the war graves in Tobruk and battlefield guide; and Professor Dr Fadhl Ali Muhammad, keeper of antiquities in Cyrenaica. In Germany I am grateful to Bernd Peitz; Rudolf Schneider, who served with Rommel's personal battle squadron, and to Klaus and Elke, his son and daughter-in-law respectively, for their warm hospitality during my visits to Germany; and to veterans Hans Werner Schmidt, Rolf-Werner Völker and Rolf Munniger.

In Australia I wish to thank my brother Bruce Lyman, Colonel Bob Breen; the Australian War Memorial, Canberra; the Oral History Collection, National Library of Australia, Park, Canberra; Eddie Marlowe; the Polish Carpathian Brigade veterans Marian Jackiewicz and Mietek Drelich; Barry York; Kristen Alexander and Alexander Staunton of the Military History Society of Australia. I am particularly grateful for the help received from Major General Gordon Maitland AO OBE RFD ED (RL), who set me right on more than one issue and was a supportive though challenging correspondent.

I wish to acknowledge the following authors and publishers for permission to quote from their works: Peter Cochrane for *Charlie Company*; Constable and Robinson Ltd for *Take These Men* by Cyril Joly and *With Rommel in the Desert* by Heinz Schmidt; Christopher Somerville for *Our War: How the British Commonwealth Fought the Second World War*; Martyn Thompson for *Our War: The Grim Digs. New Zealand Soldiers in North Africa, 1940–43*; Frank Harrison for *Tobruk*; Don West for *Warriors in the Know*; Colin Smith for *War without Hate*; Lieutenant General David Leakey for *Leakey's Luck* by his father, Major General Rea Leakey; Paul Carell for *The Foxes of the Desert (Die Wüstenfüchse*, Hamburg, 1961); Alex Franks for his delightful conversations and his unpublished memoir *Non Combatant*; Angus and Robertson (Sydney) for permission to quote from Chester Wilmot's *Tobruk, 1941* and John Devine's *The Rats of Tobruk*; Susan Travers *Tomorrow Be Brave*; Ian W. Walker for *Iron Hulls, Iron Hearts*; Weidenfeld and Nicholson for Robin Neillands *The Desert Rats*; David Irving for *The Trail of the Fox*; HarperCollins for Basil Liddell Hart's *The Rommel Papers*; William Heinemann for the Countess of Ranfurly for *To War With Whitaker*; Frank Harrison for *Tobruk: The Birth of a Legend*; and Cassel and Company for Alan Moorehead's *African Trilogy*.

To the Imperial War Museum, London, and individual copyright holders I am grateful for the use of the following material: W.A. Lewis (88/60/1); R.L. Braithwaite (87/6/1); L.A. Passfield (87/29/1); B.R. Thomas (90/26/1); E.G. Porter (82/32/1); A.C. Collins (92/1/1); H. Atkins (92/28/1); B.R. Cowles (93/6/1); R.K. Ellis (PP/MCR/388); A.O.C. McGinlay (93/11/1); A. St Clair-Ford (PP/MCR/365); S.D.H.D. Wallis (91/8/1); F.D. Franks (PP/MCR/351); W.J. Green

(91/16/1); S.C. Hankinson (91/16/1); J.A.J. Dennis (95/5/1); L.E. Tutt (85/35/1); D. Prosser (Con Shelf); R.B.T. Daniell (67/429/1–2); C.F. Shaw (67/261/1); R.A. Grimsey (78/52/1); C.M.S. Gardner (99/23/1); J.H. Parker-Jones (01/10/1); J.E.G. Quinn (P247); J.W. Kelly (P469); J.S. Parish (04/31/1); P.J. Hurman (99/85/1); H. Wiles (06/99/1); P. Cleere (67/279/1); Lamb (86/11/1); Pleydell (90/25/1); Owen (95/2/1); T. Stephanides; and H.L. Sykes.

To the BBC and individual copyright holders for use of the People's War archive, 2004–6: Tom Barker (ID A1904258); Walter Drysdale (ID A4441231); Preston John Hurman (ID A2057032); Reginald Copper (ID A4513268); David Boe (ID A3894771); Bill Harvey (ID A4569096); Bob Borthwick (ID A4544101); Alan Jones (ID A4544011); Richard Hill (IDA2051236); and Graeme Sorley (ID A2270549).

To the Australian War Memorial, Canberra and individual copyright holders, for material from the following records: PRO 0603 (16 Infantry Brigade Papers); MSS 1658 (Richard Stanton); PR91/190 (20 Infantry Brigade); PRO 0213 (Neville Parramore); MSS 1545 (D Company, 2/13th Battalion); PRO0667 (John Johnson); MSS 0868 (Frank Rolleston); PRO 0339 (Michael Kelly); PR85/250 (Francis Gorman); PR88/125 (Rowland Bourke); PR84/113 (Kevin Thomas); PR84/163 (Ron Grant); PR83/002 (W Fitzgerald); PR83/138 (David West); PRO 0186 (Andrew Nation); PRO 0303 (H Hennessey); PRO 0434 (W Bradbury); PRO 0508 (M. Chalmers); PRO 0548 (James Liddiard); PRO 0574 (Unknown Sailor); PRO 0570 (2/12th Battalion); MSS 1572 (John Haslam); PRO 0656 (Francis Pinwell); MSS 1656 (Philip Hurst); PRO 0809 (Les Perkins); PRO 1328 (Gordon Grainger); PRO 1362 (Norman Ericson); PRO 1770 (James Eagleton); MSS 1605 (Frank Pervsersi); PRO 0231 (Bayne Geikie); MSS 1587 (Leslie Watkins); MSS 1604 (Gavin Keating); and PRO 2055 (Cecil Greenwood).

The two men who made this book possible were my indefatigable agent, Charlie Viney, and my editor at Macmillan, Richard Milner, to whom I am indebted for their enthusiasm, patience and encouragement.

Abbreviations

1st AIF	First Australian Imperial Force (World War I)
2nd AIF	Second Australian Imperial Force (World War II)
ADC	aide-de-camp
C-in-C	Allied commander-in-chief (Wavell until June 1941, Auchinleck thereafter)
CO	commanding officer (of an infantry battalion or artillery/armoured regiment)
cwt	hundredweight = 100 pounds (approximately 45 kilos)
GOC	general officer commanding (major general commanding a division)
NAAFI	Navy, Army and Air Force Institutes (British armed forces trading organization)
OC	officer commanding (an infantry company or tank squadron)
OKW	*Oberkommando der Wehrmacht* (German armed forces high command)
OP	observation post (mainly for artillery purposes)
RTR	Royal Tank Regiment (British)

Maps

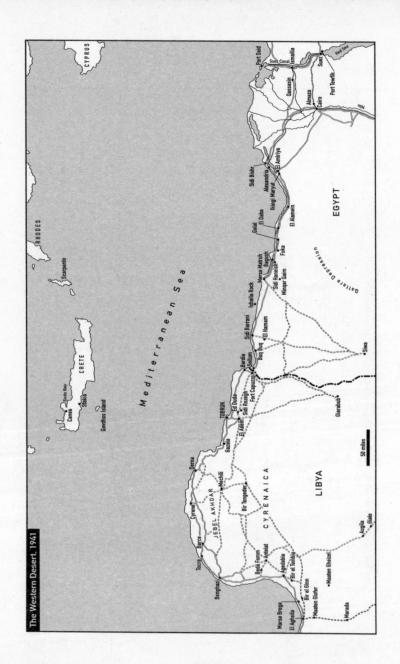

The Western Desert, 1941

The lines of advance of General Rommel's columns through Cyrenaica, April 1941

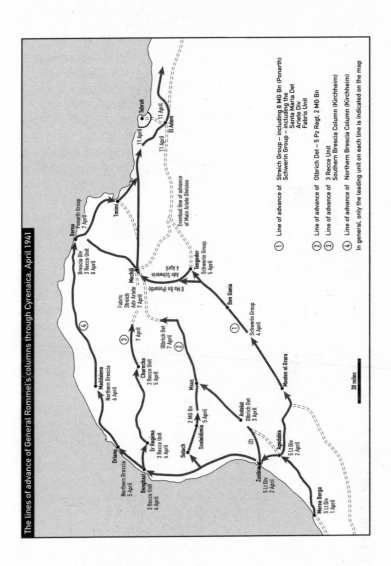

(1) Line of advance of   Streich Group – including 8 MG Bn (Ponarth)
                         Schwerin Group – including the
                                         Santa Maria Det
                                         Ariete Div
                                         Fabris Unit

(2) Line of advance of   Olbrich Det – 5 Pz Regt, 2 MG Bn

(3) Line of advance of   3 Recce Unit
                         Southern Brescia Column (Kirchheim)

(4) Line of advance of   Northern Brescia Column (Kirchheim)

In general, only the leading unit on each line is indicated on the map

30 miles

Tobruk

El Adem   11 April   11 April

Eventual line of advance
of Main Ariete Division

Tmimi

Derna
Ponarth Group
7 April

Brescia Div
3 Recce Unit
8 April

Mechili

Tengeder
Schwerin Group
5 April

Adv Schwerin
6 April

Fabris
Streich
Adv Ariete
7 April

8 Mg Bn (Ponarth)

Ben Gania

Schwerin Group
4 April

Olbrich Det
7 April   7 April

Charruba
3 Recce Unit
5 April

Maddalena
Northern Brescia
6 April

Msus

Mealtan el Grara

2 MG Bn
5 April

Antelat
Olbrich Det
3 April

Er Regima
3 Recce Unit
4 April

Soluch

Sceleidima

Driana
Northern Brescia
5 April

Benghazi
3 Recce Unit
4 April

Agedabia
5 Lt Div
2 April

(2)

Zuetina
5 Lt Div
2 April

Mersa Brega
5 Lt Div
1 April

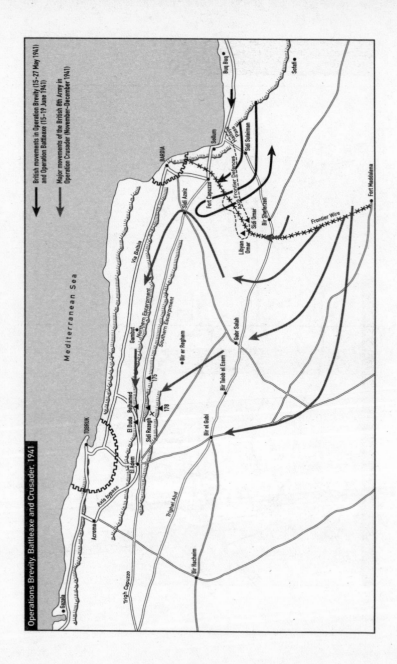

Operations Brevity, Battleaxe and Crusader, 1941

British movements in Operation Brevity (15-27 May 1941) and Operation Battleaxe (15-19 June 1941)

Major movements of the British 8th Army in Operation Crusader (November-December 1941)

Mediterranean Sea

Buq Buq
Sofafi
Sollum
Halfaya Pass
Sidi Suleiman
BARDIA
Fort Capuzzo
Sidi Azeiz
Axis Frontier Defences
Sidi Omar
Bir Sheferzan
Libyan Omar
Frontier Wire
Fort Maddalena
Gabr Salah
Via Balbia
Gambut
Northern Escarpment
Bir er Regham
Southern Escarpment
Bir Taieb el Esem
175
178
El Duda Belhamed
Sidi Rezegh
Bir el Gubi
TOBRUK
El Adem
Axis bypass
Acroma
Trigh el Abd
Trigh Capuzzo
Bir Hacheim
Gazala

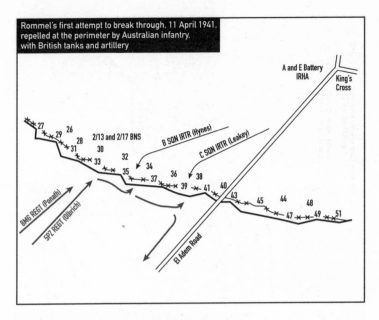

Rommel's first attempt to break through, 11 April 1941, repelled at the perimeter by Australian infantry, with British tanks and artillery

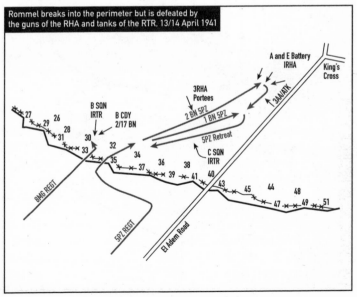

Rommel breaks into the perimeter but is defeated by the guns of the RHA and tanks of the RTR, 13/14 April 1941

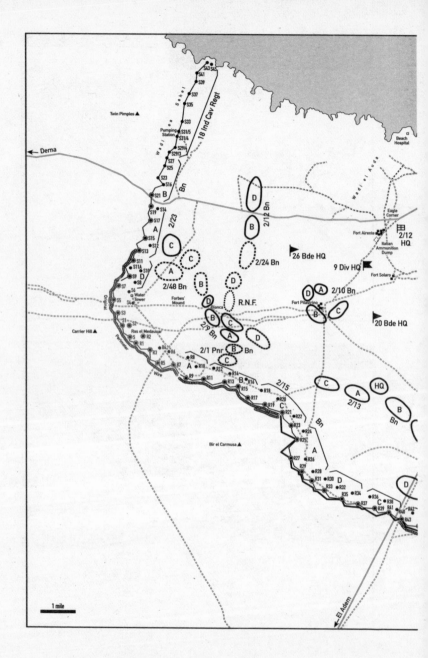

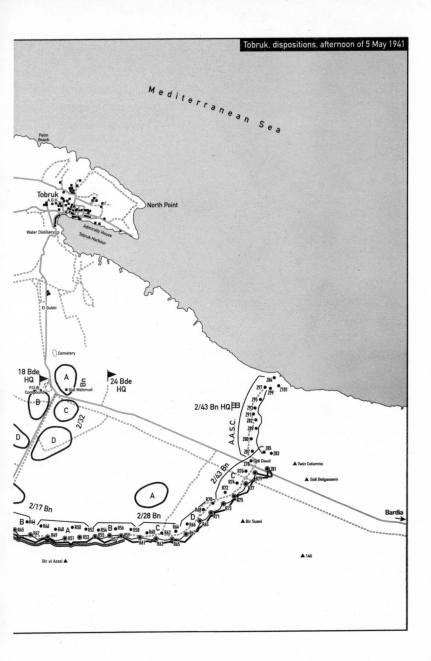

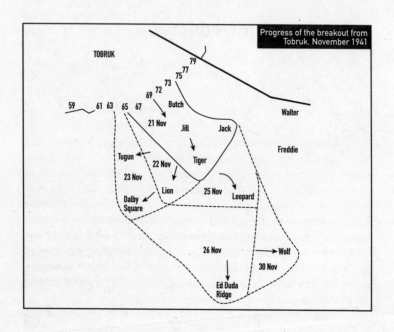

Progress of the breakout from Tobruk, November 1941

TOBRUK

59 61 63 65 67 69 72 73 75 77 79

Butch
21 Nov
Jill   Jack
Tugun
22 Nov   Tiger
23 Nov
Lion
Dalby   25 Nov   Leopard
Square

Walter

Freddie

26 Nov   → Wolf
30 Nov
Ed Duda
Ridge

Introduction

On 10 April 1941 began the 242-day siege of Tobruk, the longest and one of the most dramatic of all sieges in modern British and Commonwealth history. It easily outlasted the 147 days of the siege of Kut in Mesopotamia, which had ended in ignominy in 1916, and surpassed the 186 days of Mafeking and 188 days of Ladysmith during the Boer War. The survival of the garrison against the determined onslaught of Rommel's Italo-German legions between April and December 1941 was a staggering achievement and had significant strategic consequences for Great Britain and the course of the Second World War. Tobruk was one of the very few sieges during the Second World War that did not end in the surrender or overrunning of the fortress.

The siege was played out between a mixed force of Britons and Australians (leavened for periods by a smattering of Czechs, Poles and Indians) and the German and Italian forces of General Erwin Rommel – the fabled 'Desert Fox'. In March 1941 Rommel's Afrika Korps, together with two Italian corps, headed for Egypt in an audacious race for the Nile and the greatest prize that the Middle East could offer: the Suez Canal. If they had succeeded they would have cut the British empire in half. Rommel's brilliant attack into Cyrenaica would have been strategically decisive – nothing defended Egypt at the time – were it not for one factor: Tobruk. Drawing a perimeter around them, those troops that could scurried back to the relative safety of the port and prepared to defend themselves against the weight of the German armoured blitzkrieg launched against them in late March. There seemed little hope that they would succeed. Surely nothing could now stop Rommel rolling up the defences and using the port for his own advance on the Nile? But this ignored the extraordinary tenacity of the weak, ill-equipped and inexperienced mixed British and Australian force, which stubbornly refused to surrender. Tobruk's garrison comprised the newly formed Australian 9th Infantry Division, together with British tanks, artillery, anti-tank and anti-aircraft troops and a machine-gun battalion. Try as Rommel might – and he tried everything over those eight long months, including infantry, tanks, waves of Stuka dive-bombers, U-boats and heavy artillery – he entirely failed to eject first the Australians and then, when they had been relieved, the British 70th Division and the Carpathian Brigade of the Free Polish Army. At Tobruk in 1941 Rommel had the dubious honour of presiding over the first major German defeat of the Second World War.

*

In August 2007 I stood on Tobruk's northern promontory and looked across a yellow and rocky landscape little changed since 1941. I was with Ben Brownless, son of the Tobruk veteran who had persuaded me some years before to write the story of the siege. With my two teenage sons we had journeyed to Libya to walk over the undisturbed desert battlefields that surround this straggling little North African port. In the silence of the moment, standing under the blistering heat of the desert noon, I could picture in my mind the angle-winged Stukas as they dived on the scattered defenders; imagined I could hear the incoming shells of the huge artillery piece that the besieged dubbed Bardia Bill ripping through the air like express trains and falling into the harbour amongst the debris of nearly a hundred twisted, shattered hulks. The battles that had taken place sixty-six years before suddenly seemed less distant. And when I sat in front of veterans – British, Australian and German – and heard them relive their experiences of war it seemed not very long ago at all.

Indeed, these battles remain vividly etched in the memories of the now ageing veterans, like Ben's father, Lieutenant (now the Reverend) Philip Brownless and his erstwhile enemy Private Rudolf Schneider, once a member of Rommel's personal company. It was when interviewing these men that something of the closeness and reality of the long desert struggle became apparent to me. Tobruk was the defining moment of their lives, and remains deeply etched on their consciousness. When the siege was lifted at Christmas 1941 Lieutenant Brownless found himself put on a troopship and sent off to fight the Japanese in the jungles of eastern India and Burma, where he was to remain until the end of the war. But now, in his ninetieth year, it is to Tobruk that his mind goes when he thinks about the war. The power of memory to take one back to the midst of flying shrapnel and screaming Stukas is what makes these men (and women) still on occasions dream the sort of vivid and sometimes terrifying dreams that people who have not been in battle can only imagine. It was many years after the event that another veteran of the desert war, the indomitable Susan Travers, could write with extraordinary power about the moment that the Stukas swung out of the sky and fell on her lonely trench in the desert bastion of Bir Hacheim, far to the south of Tobruk:

> The Stukas were the worst. I could hear them several miles away, like a vast swarm of bees droning in the distance, heading directly for us across the endless desert sky. At first sight they looked like a plague of silver locusts above us . . . My heart would begin to pound in my chest as the humming got nearer. My legs would quiver as the fear rose from the pit of my stomach, clutched at my throat and squeezed tighter and tighter . . .
>
> Flying in formation in waves of up to a hundred planes at a time, without warning they would break away independently to hurtle headlong towards us, shrieking, spinning and whistling. At the exact moment when the bombs were released from their special mounts under their wings, the screaming would stop and they would soar silently, almost gracefully, back up into the sky, freed from the burden of their load.

The only female member of the French Foreign Legion, Travers would sit in her slit trench, her tin helmet clamped firmly on her head, hands behind her head and elbows thrust between her drawn-up knees, counting the five long seconds between the bomb's release and impact. One, two, three, four . . . The detonation would come with a *crump* followed by a 'blinding flash of white light', making her jump despite anticipating the blast. The trench would shudder and shake, stones raining on her and dust rising into her nose and mouth as she gasped for breath. Reading Susan Travers' experiences and listening to Philip Brownless, Rudolf Schneider and many others recount theirs brought the war along these beautiful and ancient shores to life.

Apart from rebuilding and expansion on the northern promontory, little has changed around Tobruk since 1941. Leaving the town to gain access to the southern and south-eastern defences, one follows the road from the harbour up a steep climb to the encircling escarpment, which levels out into a rock-strewn plateau fifty feet above sea level. On the left-hand side lies the German memorial to their dead, a massive circular stone ossuary overlooking the harbour. Further along this plateau lies the site of the old El Gubbi airfield. By late April 1941 this was in truth an aircraft graveyard: close to the road lay the remains of a silver Hurricane, with a sad little pile of stones alongside it, atop which sat a little cross, remembering the broken body of the pilot lying underneath. Today the airfield has disappeared. What does remain, half a mile further on, is the Commonwealth War Graves cemetery, the silent resting place of many of Tobruk's Allied dead.

Shortly thereafter the road rises another fifty feet to the next escarpment, at which point in 1941 could be found, on the right-hand side of the road, the garrison prisoner of war 'cage'. Immediately after this the road joins the junction at Sidi Mahmoud known as King's Cross. This is still a busy crossroads, on the southernmost side of which lies the Free French cemetery. At King's Cross the left-hand road continues due east towards Bardia and Egypt, leaving the Tobruk perimeter at the site of the heavily fortified (and still intact) defences at Wadi es Zettun eight miles further on. Travelling due south from King's Cross in the direction of El Adem takes the traveller gently up to a final escarpment, on top of which during the siege lay the Blue Line. Stopping at the highest point on the road, with rolls of ancient barbed wire to either side following the course of the Blue Line, one can stand and look forward the nearly three miles to the perimeter defences. Looking half right, five miles away is Fort Pilastrino, buried into the wall of the escarpment. Almost exactly south-south-west, some five and a half miles distant and just over a mile beyond the wire, lies the famous well at Bir el Carmusa, atop which sat a lone fig tree. This unsurprisingly became a landmark for Germans and Aus-tralians alike and every gun in the area ranged itself using this obvious reference point. Moving down this road towards El Adem the Red Line is shortly reached. The road here in 1941 was blocked by wire, mines and an anti-tank ditch, and ten miles beyond lay the German-held airfield at El Adem. In 2007 all these defences remain, even to the piles of rusting barbed wire and the litter-filled concrete emplacements.

*

The story of the siege of Tobruk is one of extraordinary resilience by 24,000 defenders who fought off increasingly desperate attempts by two German panzer divisions and an entire Italian corps to take an otherwise obscure Libyan port. This is a story of bayonets and grenades against tanks, of David versus Goliath. It is also a mesmerizing tale of human endurance and heroism, of persistence against overwhelming odds and the morale-sapping knowledge that, with their backs to the sea, the defenders were surrounded by the men and machines who only the year before had brought Western Europe to its knees. Yet they won through to counter-attack out of the fortress in November, creating a corridor to link up with the advancing 8th Army. By December 1941 Rommel had been beaten and forced to withdraw his forces from Cyrenaica. The siege was lifted and the exhausted defenders were able to march out in triumph. Tobruk was a dramatic success for the Allies, breaking the myth of German invincibility that had hitherto disheartened their armies. It was the battle which saved North Africa from the Nazis.

1 » MUSSOLINI'S BID FOR THE NILE

The Italian fascist dictator Benito Mussolini, who had presided over Italy's fortunes since seizing power in 1924, little knew of the vast oil wealth that sat hidden under the shifting golden sands of his Libyan colony. So far as the Duce was concerned the country was economically worthless, a drain on the overburdened Italian exchequer. In terms of the testosterone of empire, however, and with recent bloodily acquired possessions in Ethiopia and Albania complementing the long-held colonies of Eritrea and Italian Somaliland, the colony proved beyond argument to Mussolini that fascist Italy was the rightful successor to the imperial mantle of ancient Rome. In his political rhetoric Libya was Italy's 'fourth shore', its long coastal strip lapping the Mediterranean – especially the fertile hills of Cyrenaica's Jebel Akhdar – colonized by poor farmers from Sicily tempted by the prospect of free houses and low taxes. Wrested from the Ottomans in 1912, a ruthless campaign against nationalist dissent in the late 1920s (especially against the Senussi tribe in Cyrenaica, Libya's easternmost province) ensured that during the following decade Italy was left in relative peace to enjoy its North African imperial idyll.

When, in June 1940, the fall of France persuaded the Italian leader to take Italy to war against the democracies, his extravagant delusions – combined with intelligence from his extensive network of spies in Cairo informing him of British military poverty in the Middle East – persuaded Mussolini that Egypt was a ripe plum awaiting picking. The *Wehrmacht*'s explosive blitzkrieg into France in the spring of that year and the French surrender in the forest at Compiègne removed the threat from Tunisia to Italy's lines of communication in the Mediterranean and inspired Mussolini to emulate his ally's success.

1

Accordingly, he ordered his defence minister, General Pietro Badoglio, and the military commander in Libya, the larger-than-life aviation pioneer Air Marshal Italo Balbo, to prepare a swift attack along the coast into Egypt to seize Cairo and capture the Suez Canal. A successful invasion of Egypt would add glory both to Italian arms and Mussolini's personal leadership, securing fascist Italy the joy of conquest enjoyed so far only by Germany, whose string of victories across Europe had left Mussolini feeling sidelined and humiliated. It would also (assuming Sudan followed Egypt) consolidate Italian possessions in North Africa and the Horn of Africa to create a vast colony sweeping from the Mediterranean to the Indian Ocean. Benito Mussolini had long deluded himself that he was the natural leader of the Rome–Berlin Axis. However, although Hitler had a penchant for talking incessantly (a frequent complaint of the Duce at meetings between the dictators), he had also demonstrated that he could act. Mussolini now believed he could achieve a victory to compare with those of his Nazi rival and worthy of a modern Roman Caesar.

*

Between 1940 and 1941 the war in North Africa was fought along the narrow strip of Mediterranean coastline that stretches from Alexandria in Egypt in the east 1,875 miles to Tripoli in Libya in the west. This coastal strip is bounded to the south by the vast expanses of the Sahara Desert. West of Alexandria the coastline is a gently undulating rocky plain that rises sharply to a 600-foot escarpment about ten miles inland and then stretches south to the great Qattara Depression, where it falls hundreds of feet into a vast salt plain the size of a medium-sized European country. The escarpment approaches the sea at the tiny coastal village of Sollum on the border with Libya, the road running through the ridge at Halfaya.

To the west, in Libya, the escarpment virtually touches the sea along through Bardia and Tobruk. Then, as the coast reaches Derna, the ridge becomes more dramatic, rising in places to 2,000 feet in a rugged display of rock that indicates the start of the Jebel Akhdar, a vast expanse of wooded hills and ravines stretching 200 miles further to the western margins of Cyrenaica at Benghazi. Apart from the Jebel

Akhdar the terrain is almost flat, with gentle undulations providing some scope for observation and concealment. In the desert inland of Tobruk minuscule rises in the ground such as those at Point 209 (Ras el Medawar) to the south-west and Ed Duda to the south-east are sufficient to dominate the terrain for many miles. Patches of the coastal strip, particularly in Cyrenaica, are green and fertile but in the main it is rocky, and swept with jagged stones and drifting sand. Very little lives here, water is scarce and the environment unforgiving. Inland the rocky plains disappear to leave a surface of impenetrable limestone, and much further inland the limestone gives way to the endless waves of the Great Sand Sea.

All-weather roads were scarce in Italian Libya. A single tarmacked road, the Via Balbia, ran along the coast from Tripoli to Benghazi and thence around Cyrenaica's rocky headlands through Derna and Tobruk – Libya's only natural harbour – to Bardia. The ground is extraordinarily hard, making it almost impossible for troops on either side to dig slit trenches without mechanical or explosive aids, and the rough terrain played havoc with tank tracks, vehicle tyres and suspensions, while drifting sand and dust was sucked into engines, clogging up filters and penetrating working parts. Except for the Jebel Akhdar, scattered villages along the coast and the nomadic Bedouin, there were virtually no people.

*

The problem for the Italians was that their commanders in Libya were unable to act on Mussolini's offensive aspirations immediately after their declaration of war on 10 June 1940. Instead, it was Britain which seized the initiative. It had been apparent to General Archibald Wavell, the British Middle Eastern commander-in-chief, that Italian belligerence would one day express itself in action of some kind or another. From April 1940 overflights by RAF reconnaissance aircraft based in Egypt clearly indicated that the Italians were reinforcing their positions in eastern Cyrenaica.

Wavell responded by dispatching from its bases in the Nile Delta a force commanded by the diminutive Lieutenant General Richard O'Connor, a well-regarded infantry commander who in the First World

War had fought alongside the Italians and been awarded their Silver Medal for Valour. O'Connor's force dug in at Mersa Matruh, 120 miles west of Alexandria, and mounted patrols deep into 'the blue' (as the troops called the desert) to watch the border with Libya, which was marked by a barbed-wire fence six feet high and twelve feet wide stretching 400 miles from the coast a few miles west of Sollum down to the Jarabub oasis in the Great Sand Sea.

O'Connor possessed little more than 10,000 men, the grand title of his Western Desert Force hiding from few the reality of Britain's military weakness in the region. For reasons of propaganda the British garrison in the otherwise independent Egypt commanded by General 'Jumbo' Wilson was known as the Army of the Nile, although the stark truth was that it was tiny. O'Connor's force, based on the 7th Armoured Division, was virtually everything that Britain had available to defend Egypt at the time, so it was fortunate that this division, which had adopted as its symbol the desert rat – the jerboa – and which was thereafter universally known as the Desert Rats, was a superbly trained desert-hardened mobile fighting formation. It had been in the desert since 1938 and had learned how to survive and operate amid the climatic and topographical extremes of the region. The personal weapon drills, hardiness, discipline, initiative and esprit de corps of the Desert Rats more than compensated for the vast numerical superiority enjoyed by the Italian army on the other side of the fence.

The Desert Rats comprised two armoured brigades equipped with a mixture of tanks and old armoured cars. The 4th Armoured Brigade, commanded from June 1940 by Brigadier J.A.L. Caunter (nicknamed 'Blood' from his favourite phrase 'buckets of blood'), comprised the 1st Battalion, Royal Tank Regiment (1st RTR), equipped with fifty Mark VI light tanks, and the 6th RTR, equipped with forty Mark VIs and a small number of the stronger thirteen-ton A9 cruiser tanks. The Mark VIs were armed only with twin Vickers machine guns, while the cruisers boasted a 2-pounder (40-millimetre) gun in a traversable turret and were capable of a speed of 30 miles per hour. The 7th Armoured Brigade contained three cavalry regiments, two of which had only recently given up their beloved horses for chariots of iron. Horses and hunting suffused every conversation, colouring their view of the war.

Sergeant Alec Lewis of F (Sphinx) Battery, 4th Royal Horse Artillery (RHA), recalled:

> Most of the staff officers were from cavalry regiments and their off-duty conversation . . . was usually about horses and hunting . . . At Gerawla, on the Sunday before Italy declared war, a gymkhana was held on 'National Hunt lines', complete with a tote. The competitors were various units' tanks, Bren carriers, vehicles and motorcycles – an enjoyable break.

The 7th Hussars had recently converted to A9 cruiser tanks; the 8th Hussars possessed only fifteen-hundredweight (cwt) trucks and had no tanks at all; while the 11th Hussars (the famous Cherrypickers, so named after a patrol was caught by French cavalry picking cherries in an orchard during the Peninsular War) had 1924-vintage Rolls-Royce and Morris armoured cars – they had, however, the advantage of having been mechanized since 1928. Artillery support was provided by the 3rd RHA equipped with First World War 3.7-inch howitzers, and the divisional infantry consisted of a single battalion of the Rifle Brigade – 1st Kings Royal Rifle Corps – commanded by Lieutenant Colonel W.H.E. Gott, whose ancient Viking surname had long been transformed by some prep-school wag into the nickname 'Strafer', inspired by the First World War German exhortation that God should punish the British, *'Gott strafe England.'* The artillery and Gott's infantry were grouped together into the divisional support group. The doctrine of the day was that the tanks would fight fast mobile actions independent of infantry or artillery, and the support elements be allocated to whichever armoured force needed them at the time. The support group could also fight independently if required.

In addition to the Desert Rats, the newly arrived and entirely green 6th Australian and 2nd New Zealand Divisions were in the Nile Delta training and familiarizing themselves with desert conditions. The 4th Indian Division was also on its way but had not yet arrived. When it did, two months later, the Western Desert Force numbered some 31,000 men, but this was still only a fraction of what the Italians were able to field in Libya.

Across the Middle East the RAF was similarly impoverished. By early June the British boasted 205 military aircraft in the region, but the only fighters in the whole of Middle East Command were obsolescent Gladiator biplanes. The rest – Lysanders, Bombays, Valentias, Wellesleys, Vincents, Battles, Hardys, Audaxes, Harts, Hartebeests and Londons – were all overdue for the museum. The only exceptions were some Blenheim light bombers. In July 1940 a flight of four Hurricane fighters arrived in the Middle East, but these were necessarily thinly scattered, and only one was available for the entire Western Desert. This was quickly dubbed Collishaw's Battleship (after the commander of 202 Group RAF – the Desert Air Force – Air Commodore Raymond Collishaw) and became part of a complex deception in which it was moved repeatedly between forward airstrips in an attempt to deceive the enemy into thinking that Britain had a surfeit of fast modern fighters in the region.

The British were able to make up for their many material deficiencies by a marked superiority over the Italians in the quality of their military leaders. One of the brightest stars in the British firmament was General Richard O'Connor. An intelligent practical man who enjoyed an easy rapport with his men, O'Connor possessed the rare trait of being able to judge issues on the basis of rationality rather than orthodoxy. His aide-de-amp (ADC) in July 1940 described him as 'vigorous and intense, and deeply serious. Behind the friendly façade lay an expression of grim determination – of vigilance.' Embarrassed by pomp and show he had an open and enquiring mind, and, important in 1940, he was able to work at speed. Rapid action, use of surprise as a weapon, coordination of air and land forces and the taking of risks were as prevalent in his generalship as they were in those of his arch-nemesis, General Erwin Rommel. O'Connor created strong relations with Collishaw's Desert Air Force. This was no chateau general, but one who personally reconnoitred the ground over which he would have to fight. An 11th Hussars patrol operating along the frontier wire reported one day that it had encountered a lone staff car, which had appeared from the direction of the enemy. In it was Richard O'Connor.

Major Lloyd Owen, a company commander with the 1st Battalion Queen's Regiment and later a founder member of the famous Long Range Desert Group, recalled meeting O'Connor in the desert a month before the Italian invasion. His men were digging defensive positions:

'Good morning, Lloyd Owen', he said as he thrust out his hand to shake mine. There was a galaxy of brass hats in his wake. 'I see your men have dug some damned good positions. Tell them they've done well. The ground looks horribly hard. Are you sure that you can bring fire to bear all along the anti-tank ditch?'

'Yes, sir.'

'Good. I'm sure you know best. You're the chap who has got to fight this position. How are the men? Got any worries?'

'No, sir. They would like some beer if we could get it, but that's everyone's worry.'

'I'll see what I can do. Nice to see you again. I must be off now. Goodbye and good luck to you all.'

The beer arrived that evening.

*

O'Connor had little time to prepare his puny force for war. At 3 a.m. on 10 June 1940 Sergeant Patrick Cleere, the experienced, desert-hardened commander of 2 Troop, C Squadron, 7th Hussars, heard over his tank radio that Italy had declared war. To most this came as no surprise, Mussolini's earlier indecision having given way to sabre-rattling when the German victories in the Low Countries and France became certain and overwhelming. That night the desert leaguer outside Mersa Matruh in which his squadron had taken sanctuary became a hive of activity as the British rushed to prepare their first raid into Italian-held Libya.

After a few hours of feverish bustle Cleere's troop of three A9 cruiser tanks joined at daybreak an amalgam of other units from the 4th Armoured Brigade for the start of their 150-mile trek into Libya. Clouds of dust spewed skywards from each vehicle as – widely dispersed to counter the possibility of air attack – the force moved west. Their immediate target was the border garrison of Fort Capuzzo, a straggling *Beau Geste*-style complex near Sidi Omar which dominated the eastern Cyrenaican desert and protected the coast road running to Tobruk and eventually to Benghazi and beyond. The British raiding party cut through the border fence and the following day captured a convoy of trucks carrying fifty-two bemused Italians who had not been informed that their country was at war.

The journey placed severe strain on the tanks with 40 per cent of the A9s and 20 per cent of the Mark VIs breaking down en route. Patrick Cleere was in one of the 7th Hussars A9 cruisers that made it to the start line in front of Sidi Omar on 14 June, as was Captain Rea Leakey, a 1st RTR tank commander doing an unwelcome stint as a staff officer in the 4th Armoured Brigade, who contrived to find himself in a Mark VI outside the gates of Fort Capuzzo. Driving around to the rear of the fort, and thus avoiding the extensive minefield at the front, the A9s began firing 2-pounder shells at the gates, while RAF Blenheims arrived to join in the attack from the air. Leakey was soon in the thick of the fighting but unfortunately the tank's twin Vickers 0.303-inch water-cooled machine guns had not yet arrived from England. He was forced to improvise:

> So out of the gaping holes where those guns should have been, my gunner fired his rifle and I discharged the six rounds from my pistol. After some thirty minutes our tanks had silenced the enemy's machine guns, and the infantry moved up towards the walls of the fort. By this time Blood had his tank positioned some fifty yards from the main entrance to the fort, and he was pumping 2-pound armour-piercing [AP] shells through the large metal doors. This was too much for the Italians, and they gave up. The flag that fluttered from the mast in the centre of the fort was lowered, and was exchanged for a white sheet. The doors were flung open, and out marched some sixteen officers followed by over 200 men.

The next target was Fort Maddalena, seventy miles to the north. For Sergeant Major Smith of A Squadron, 11th Hussars the attack demonstrated that the British still had much to learn about coordinating operations between army and air force:

> The general plan was for the RAF to send Blenheim bombers in to soften the target; we would attack from the front and, crash-bang, the job would be done. However, it did not quite go like that. Hour X arrived – no bombers. X plus fifteen, no bombers. X plus thirty,

no bombers. So we decided to attack alone. After a struggle we took the fort and we were rounding up prisoners when the bombers arrived – and, yes, they bombed us! We tried all forms of recognition, Very lights and so on, but nothing worked. I was standing by an eighty-foot-high watchtower when I saw a plane release a bomb above me. I knew it was mine but I continued watching it fall. It hit the side of the watchtower and bounced off, exploding outside the fort perimeter. I had a fag.

Two days later a force of forty Italian L3 light tanks, obsolete vehicles largely worthless as weapons of war, mounting two fixed 8-millimetre machine guns and protected by brittle armour, together with thirty trucks loaded with 300 infantry, was engaged and destroyed on the Via Balbia at Ghirba. The Italian force from the 1st Libyan Division was surprised by a squadron of the 11th Hussars' armoured cars, a squadron of cruisers and Mark VIs of the 7th Hussars, together with 2-pounder anti-tank guns of the RHA. To British amazement Lieutenant Colonel D'Avanzo's Italian force formed up in a square, artillery in each corner, with infantry in the open and tanks in the centre, recalling an era when such tactics were used against charging dervish horsemen or Ethiopian spearmen.

The Italians were slaughtered, the British tanks and guns circling and firing into the crowded square. The British suffered not a single casualty. D'Avanzo was killed in his car. It was an unequal contest. One British trooper in an A9 cruiser tank saw 'a little L3 blazing away at us with a machine gun. He put on speed [in his A9] until his gun could be depressed on to it and then his 2-pounder wrecked it.' General Lastucci, chief engineer of the Italian 10th Army and erstwhile colleague of General O'Connor in the First World War, when Great Britain and Italy had been allies, was captured together with his mistress, another woman and more importantly maps showing Bardia's defences. 'I remember Lastucci's mistress well,' Leakey recalled, 'because she had a filthy temper and demanded to be taken back to Bardia immediately, but her boyfriend the general was determined to take her with him to enliven his days of captivity.' The second woman was heavily pregnant and gave birth in captivity shortly afterwards.

The first three months of the war consisted of a series of such measured hit-and-run attacks by the weak British forces in the Western Desert from the desert and the air. British tactics were to avoid major confrontations and not to provoke a full-scale invasion of Egypt, but to conduct pinprick raids against isolated forts, airfields and vulnerable supply lines in order to confuse, dominate and demoralize the Italians. The raids were designed to demonstrate British determination and persuade the Italians that an attack towards the Nile would be fiercely contested. These aggressive patrols, in which no fixed positions on the Libyan side of the wire were held and which roamed far and wide, harassed the Italians and gave them an exaggerated estimate of British strength. They also gave the young British soldiers confidence in their ability to navigate and fight across huge swathes of desert, by day and night.

On 3 July a 1,000-strong Italian mechanized force attempted to advance forward of their frontier defences towards the Egyptian border at Sollum. The preparations for this advance, however, had been well advertised and an ambush prepared. Leaguering at night about four miles from one ambush position, the tanks of C Squadron, 1st RTR moved quietly forward at dawn the following morning, with the sun behind them blinding any Italian observers. Captain Cyril Joly's troop of four A9 cruiser tanks moved into position on the flank of the expected Italian advance while the three companies of the accompanying Rifle Brigade advanced and dug into the hard ground. The new quick-firing 25-pounder gun-howitzers of the RHA took up positions to the rear. The tanks placed themselves behind sand dunes with only a fraction of their turrets showed above the undulations of the ground.

Meanwhile, the armoured cars of the 11th Hussars hurried off to the west to make contact with the enemy. They did not have long to wait, the incredulous reconnaissance troop spotting the dust cloud that marked the Italian advance preceded by a neat row of carefully distanced motorcyclists, as if on parade. The unseen Hussars allowed the overconfident Italians to drive within 250 yards of their position. 'The first thin chatter of their machine guns,' observed Joly, three miles away, 'told us that the battle had begun.' Six Italian vehicles were left burning on the desert floor, their erstwhile occupants crumpled bloodily beside them, while the remainder scattered in panic. After some time watching and waiting, the Italians pushed hesitatingly forward with about twenty tanks, but their courage returned when they realized that they were facing mere armoured cars. The British squadron turned on its heels and withdrew, but as the Italian pursuit gathered speed it drove straight into the ambush. Joly gave his first fire order:

'Holton, traverse right. Take the outside tank. Seven hundred. Fire.'

As I watched the tracer of the shot flying towards the enemy tank I saw out of the corner of my eye the flash of Sergeant Wharton's gun and beyond him those of [Lieutenant] Ryan's troop.

As yet the Italians had not fired. They were handicapped by having to shoot uphill, and moreover had the sun in their eyes.

Ryan was the first to get a kill. He hit an enemy tank which was turning on the slope before him fairly and squarely in the engine, shattering the petrol tanks and starting a fire which spread rapidly. Mixed with flame, clouds of billowing smoke rolled across the desert, blocking my view of the enemy entirely. With a dull roar the ammunition then exploded, throwing a mass of debris into the air. A moment later we were horrified to see a figure with face blackened and clothes alight stumbling through the smoke. He staggered for some yards, then fell and in a frenzy of agony rolled frantically in the hard sand in a desperate effort to put out the flames. But to no avail. Gradually his flailing arms and legs moved more slowly, until at last, with a convulsive heave of his body, he lay still.

During the one-sided destruction that followed the Italian column seemed rooted to the spot and became the target of the eager British 25-pounders. For three hours they stood under a withering fire, attempting no riposte. Leaving a small force where it was to hold the Italians' attention to their front, the British commander then slowly withdrew the remainder of his tanks – so as not to create the clouds of dust and sand that would give the game away – and moved twelve miles to a new position to the rear of the stationary Italian column. The order was given to advance. Surprise was total:

Moving at about 15 miles an hour, with plumes of dust billowing out behind us and the sun glinting on the barrels of the guns, we pitched and rolled over the rough desert. The unsuspecting Italians were lounging round the lorries on this hitherto undisturbed flank. We closed to within 200 yards of the vehicles on the edge of the main mass, turned west and, moving in line ahead, ran down the whole length of the Italian column, machine-gunning any and every target that crossed our sights.

Here and there a man, braver or more alert than the rest, raised his rifle to fire hopelessly against our armour until he was caught in the hail of fire and fell dead or wounded; some lorries, filled with petrol or oil, caught fire; some, filled with ammunition, burned for a few moments and then exploded; others being driven frantically away from the attack had their tyres riddled with bullets and came to a lurching halt or overturned.

Some thirty trucks were destroyed. The Cairo correspondent for the American magazine *Time*, reporting on this skirmish, noted:

The British broke up this effort with a flanking attack, and the survivors took refuge in the deserted adobe Fort Capuzzo. There they still were after a thirsty week, sucking stones to eke out their water supply, which the British cut off by removing many sections of the pipeline down from Bardia. British artillery, pounding their defences, drove them into trenches. British shells and a detachment of light tanks broke up an Italian column of 20 trucks sent to relieve the beleaguered expedition.

O'Connor's raids were accompanied by RAF attacks against strategic targets in eastern Cyrenaica. The airfield at El Adem, a few miles south of Tobruk, had been attacked within hours of the outbreak of war and eighteen aircraft destroyed for the loss of three Blenheims. Two days later the veteran Italian cruiser *San Giorgio* was attacked and sunk at her moorings, although the shallowness of Tobruk harbour meant its anti-aircraft guns remained active for several months and a hazard to flyers. The Royal Navy also played its part. Bardia was bombarded from the sea and on 6 July Fleet Air Arm Swordfish –

'String Bags' – raided Tobruk harbour, sinking a destroyer and three merchant vessels. The flying-boat base at Bomba near Derna was hit on 15 August with the destruction of twelve Italian seaplanes.

*

These raids resulted in considerable psychological dominance for the British. Italian tactics tended to be defensive. Some Italians thought British tactics cowardly, one officer writing home to criticize the gutless 'English who flee from even our lightest shelling and smallest patrols'. But the response gradually improved, with the Regia Aeron-autica striking back against Sidi Barrani and Mersa Matruh. Sergeant Alec Lewis recalled watching a flight of aircraft high above Mersa Matruh:

> Someone remarked, 'Pretty, they look just like silver birds,' when the birds laid their eggs! Len Bell was standing in his unlaced boots, shorts unbuttoned, scraping the lather off his face, when the first stick exploded 400 yards away. We all got a shock. Len went straight up, out of his boots and shorts, and hit the slit trench in his birthday suit.

But when intercepted by the RAF the Italians invariably came off worse. On 31 October, when a force of Italian bombers struck at one of 4th Indian Division's forward camps screening Sidi Barrani, they were attacked by a flight of Gladiators. 'A highly spectacular and satisfactory dogfight ensued,' recalled Lieutenant Colonel Stevens. 'The troops went mad with excitement ... Two British planes in the heat of manoeuvre rammed each other, the pilots parachuting to safety. Nine Italian machines were shot down for the loss of two Gladiators.' Alec Lewis also watched the aerial battles: 'At times, when our Gloster Gladiator biplanes were overhead, perhaps chasing a Savoia bomber or a CR42 fighter, the officers would be watching with a keen interest and shouting "Tally-ho" and other hunting terms.'

However, there was a vast difference between the behaviour of Italian bombers and fighters. The former flew high and dropped their bombs inaccurately as a result, but the latter were an ever-present threat to British armoured cars and tanks operating in the desert, which were often given away by the tell-tale plumes of dust thrown into the air by their tracks. The CR42 fighters were, for Private Harry Buckledee of the 11th Hussars, the greatest hazard, vehicle commanders anxiously and endlessly scanning the sky for the small black dots that would within minutes dive out of the sun with a deep angry buzz onto the defenceless vehicles, spitting 0.5-inch armour-piercing bullets, which easily penetrated the thin armour plating. Their pilots impressed Private A.S. Prosser, a fellow Cherrypicker, by the elan with which they pressed home their attacks, scoring 'some successes in the early days, concentrating on the troop leaders'.

One type of bomb dropped by the Italians proved a particularly dangerous nuisance to the British. The Italians had perfected the disguising of small anti-personnel devices as shaving sticks, fountain pens and Thermos flasks, as Private Tom Barker of the Argyll and Sutherland Highlanders discovered at Mersa Matruh following a bombing raid. A soldier had his hands blown off by a fountain pen he found lying on the sand, and shortly afterwards a young lieutenant tried to open a Thermos flask, which 'detonated with a roar and a cloud of sand and dust. The officer's head, shoulder and one arm were gone; the sergeant was dead; two blokes lay moaning in the hole the flask bomb had made. Four men were lost to one Thermos flask bomb.'

The British problem was how to husband their tiny land and air resources, and not dissipate them too rapidly in operations before reinforcements could arrive via the long Cape passage from Britain, or over the new air reinforcement route that crossed the width of central Africa; the Gibraltar–Malta–Cairo route had been made impassable by Italy's entry into the war. Every loss in the air, every aircraft grounded for maintenance, made a dramatic difference to the forces available for the defence of Egypt. Land operations took a fearful toll on tracks and vehicles but taught the British much about the capabilities of their equipment over the terrain. Accordingly, at the end of July the British armour was withdrawn to Mersa Matruh, the frontier becoming the responsibility of Strafer Gott's support group, together with the 11th Hussars and a squadron of A9 cruisers from 1st RTR. Large-scale offensive operations were curtailed in favour of a strong forward screen along the border and intelligence-gathering patrols into Libya designed to allow prior warning of an Italian advance. The first of these patrols by the Long Range Desert Group under the command of Major R.A. Bagnold (desert explorer and inventor of the Bagnold compass) began in September. In the air Collishaw was ordered to preserve precious aircraft and pilots and during the second half of August 1940 only two sorties were made against enemy field targets.

*

Beneath the vanity of Mussolini's aggressive ambitions most senior Italian military figures recognized the difficulties of any offensive against the British in Egypt in June 1940, even if the French in Tunisia were now a broken reed. Balbo now asked for a thousand more trucks and a hundred water tankers, together with more of the scarce M11 and the newer M13 medium tanks and also anti-tank guns. It was equipment that Italy's near-empty arsenal would struggle to provide, but Balbo knew that without transport any advance into Egypt would have to be at the speed of his marching infantry. His plan was to launch five divisions – 80,000 men – into Egypt on 15 July, but on 28 June 1940 overenthusiastic anti-aircraft gunners protecting Tobruk from the constant British air raids mistook the plane Balbo was piloting for a British aircraft, shooting it down in flames. Balbo had been an international aviator of considerable repute, and Air Commodore Collishaw arranged for a lone British Blenheim to drop a wreath over Tobruk as a mark of respect on the day of his funeral.

Mussolini's replacement was the fifty-eight-year-old Marshal Rodolfo Graziani. Both Graziani and Marshal Pietro Badoglio were men with considerable Libyan experience. Badoglio had featured as a young officer in the expulsion of the Ottoman Turks in 1912, returning as governor between 1929 and 1933. A dedicated professional soldier rather than a political general, Badoglio was responsible for the eventual capture of Addis Ababa in 1936. He was an experienced counter-insurgency campaigner. So too was Graziani, who had collected his nickname the 'Butcher of Ethiopia' (a sobriquet only used behind his back) from his time as governor there in 1936–7. He had also conducted a ruthless pacification operation in Libya a decade before in which perhaps 100,000 civilians had been taken from their homes in the lush Jebel Akhdar and forced into concentration camps deep in the desert. Tens of thousands had died of starvation and disease. Expert at quelling Senussi opposition in Cyrenaica and putting down Ethiopian resistance in the Horn of Africa, Badoglio had been less persuaded about going to war against Great Britain and France. Barefoot spear-wielding natives were one thing; fighting highly industrialized democracies with professional armies and powerful navies was quite another. Although Graziani and Badoglio hated each other, they wholeheartedly agreed on this point. Knowing full well that the Italian army was more a figment of fascist propaganda than a modern fighting machine, both men attempted to deflect Mussolini from his grand design.

Graziani also had considerable respect for the British army and despite his initial support for Mussolini's declaration of war, now began to back-pedal when confronted by the Duce's demand that he invade Egypt. Count Galeazzo Ciano, Italy's foreign minister and Mussolini's brother-in-law (which did not prevent the Duce having him shot by firing squad in 1943) observed on 3 August 1940, 'Graziani, after having emptied Italy in order to supply Libya, does not feel that he is prepared to attack Egypt, mainly because of the heat. He intends to postpone the operation until spring. I do not yet know the reactions of the Duce, but I predict that they will be violent.' Ironically, only months earlier Ciano had described Graziani as having 'more ambition than brains, yet he is influencing the Duce in the dangerous direction of intervention'.

If numbers alone were what counted, Graziani's advantage was overwhelming. He had two armies in Libya, the 5th in Tripolitania facing the French in Tunisia and the 10th in Cyrenaica, under General Mario Berti, who enjoyed the nickname 'Sly Murderer', with a total strength of some 250,000 men together with 400 artillery pieces and 300 tanks – only seventy of which, however, were the relatively modern M11. But these vast figures disguised deficiencies in military training, preparation and culture that were not apparent even to most Italians, and certainly not to Mussolini. Graziani's forces were largely unmechanized, with transport available for only four infantry battalions. Even those divisions that possessed trucks did not have enough to do much more than carry the quartermaster's store; everything else

– weapons, ammunition, rations – had to be carried on the soldiers' backs. These deficiencies were compounded by inadequate training in mobile armoured warfare and derisory desert familiarization. Furthermore, two of his six divisions comprised locally recruited Libyans, who whilst physically hardy were untrained in modern tactics. A further two were made up of strutting blackshirt bully-boys who had no training in or taste for battle. What armour Graziani possessed was formed into an ad hoc armoured unit commanded by General Maletti.

Because of these deficiencies and his claim that the heat made a summer offensive impossible, Graziani now deliberately limited his plans. Accusing Badoglio of not meeting his promise to provide the necessary supplies, tanks and transport – despite his loud and bloodthirsty rhetoric – he proposed merely to cross the Egyptian frontier to seize the escarpment above Sollum. If successful his troops would then make their way over the Halfaya Pass and on to the little fishing village of Sidi Barrani, forty miles further along the coast. Promising this limited offensive on 4 August, as the date grew closer nervousness got the better of him and Graziani decided to call it off.

Mussolini was furious, and the general was ordered home to explain himself. Three days later Graziani met Ciano. 'He talks about the attack on Egypt as a very serious undertaking,' confided Ciano in his diary, 'and says that our present preparation is far from perfect.' According to Graziani, 'The water supply is entirely insufficient. We move toward a defeat which, in the desert, inevitably becomes a rapid and total disaster . . . [I] would rather not attack at all, or, at any rate, not for two or three months.' Mussolini observed sarcastically in Ciano's hearing, 'One should not give jobs to people who aren't looking for at least one promotion. Graziani has too many to lose.' Mussolini sent Graziani unequivocal orders on 10 August to attack, his grand plan of seizing the Nile now reduced to a plea merely to make a military gesture:

> The invasion of Great Britain has been decided, its preparations are in the course of completion. Concerning the date, it could be within a week or a month, but the day on which the first German platoon touches British territory you will attack. Once again I repeat that there are no territorial objectives. It is not a question of aiming for

Alexandria, nor even for Sollum. I am only asking you to attack the British forces facing you.

According to Graziani, Badoglio had promised him 1,000 medium tanks, although this number of vehicles did not then exist in the Italian armoury and may well have included 700 captured French tanks that the Italians had requested from the Germans. The Germans refused. Badoglio sent every tank he had – seventy-four M11s and M13s – but Graziani still did not attack. Unmoved by Mussolini's pleading and undaunted by threats that he would be removed from his command if he failed to attack, on 20 August Graziani dispatched a further report to Mussolini, indicating that all his generals were opposed to the offensive into Egypt. The Duce failed to understand Graziani's hesitation; he had never grasped the essentials of modern warfare. He needed an offensive to buy a place at the peace table. 'I assure you the war will be over by September,' Mussolini declared to Badoglio, adding coldly, 'I need a few thousand dead so as to be able to attend the peace conference as a belligerent.'

But Graziani and his fellow commanders were right. Despite the posturing Italy was hopelessly prepared for war. Unlike Germany, it had not spent the previous six years preparing its population and economy. Italy's relatively small population was poor, unindustrialized and unable to sustain a large army. Its armed forces had suffered grievous losses in both manpower and equipment during the Spanish Civil War. Of the 78,500 men dispatched to Spain 20 per cent had been lost and all the equipment – 3,400 machine guns, 1,400 mortars, 1,800 artillery pieces, 6,800 vehicles, 160 tanks and 760 aircraft – left behind. The whole adventure had consumed 20 per cent of Italy's annual defence expenditure and had proved a significant obstacle to Mussolini's ambition to rearm, so much so that in government circles it was widely recognized that the nation would not be in a position to engage in a wider European war until 1943. Departure from Spain had been followed by the invasion of Albania in April 1939. Despite Mussolini's claim on Radio Rome and in front of the crowds at the Piazza Venezia that the nation could muster eight million bayonets, the army could in fact only field about 200,000 trained men and was badly stretched trying to police the rickety Italian empire.

The Italians also had problems in the air. The Regia Aeronautica was a tool of fascist propaganda rather than a serious organ of war. Its leaders were flamboyant record-breakers like Italo Balbo, more interested in feats of aeronautical endurance than creating an effective fighting organization. Instead of the 3,000 aircraft listed in its inventory, only 900 in fact were flyable. In Libya Balbo had 84 modern bombers and 114 fighters, together with another 113 largely obsolete aircraft. The most advanced fighter was the Fiat CR42 biplane, which although about evenly matched with the Gladiator was no match for the sleek new monoplanes being fielded by the British (Hurricanes and Spitfires), French (Moranes) and Germans (Messerschmidt 109s). Italy's aircraft were underpowered and obsolete, while tactics and training were significantly poorer than in other European countries. Outmatched and ill-equipped, the Italians were forced to buy German Ju 87 Stuka dive-bombers in August 1940.

On the ground the Italians were short of anti-tank and anti-aircraft guns, mines, ammunition and radio sets. Their artillery was light and ancient, though Italian gunners were to demonstrate a determination to fight to the death. Along the border with Egypt Graziani's men were forced to defuse and reuse British mines for lack of their own. The M11 eleven-ton medium tank was underpowered (it had a maximum speed of 9 miles per hour) and thinly armoured, and the turret was fixed: its 37-millimetre gun could only fire in the direction the tank was facing. The heavier and newer M13 was a better tank all round, but was slow and in very short supply in mid-1940.

*

The most decisive advantage enjoyed by the British was that they knew how to operate in the desert. The Western Desert is a hard place in which to live and survive, but the 7th Armoured Division had worked to master its challenges, learning to fight despite the flies, extremes of temperature, diarrhoea, lack of water, the difficulty of navigation and hugely demanding terrain. The importance of making oneself comfortable quickly became apparent, especially given uniforms and equipment made for entirely different climes. The officers of the 7th Armoured Division developed an informal outfit in the desert – silk neckerchief, light cord trousers, suede desert boots and in the cold weather a goatskin coat from Afghanistan or Persia – with home-knitted balaclavas de rigueur for all ranks in the cold early mornings.

The sandstorms – khamsins – were serious affairs which had to be treated with respect. Private Tom Barker of the 1st Battalion the Argyll and Sutherland Highlanders was shocked by their power when he first experienced one after arriving in the desert as part of the 16th Infantry Brigade. He had often seen a small willy-willy skipping along the surface of the sand. Like a twisting piece of rope made of fine sand particles, it would dance over the dunes then race away across the desert. But one day it seemed hotter and more still than usual, and then one of the Jocks shouted, 'Wit the fook's that?'

He was pointing to the distance where what looked like a brown mountain of cocoa powder was silently edging our way. It appeared to reach to the underside of some low clouds and it looked like it was boiling. It stretched right across the horizon:

Suddenly one became aware that the whisper of cooling breeze that had been blowing was gone and an eerie silence had taken its place. One bloke who had been cleaning his gun hurriedly put it all back together and others who had been chatting suddenly grabbed trench spades and shovelled at the sand like gophers desperate to get away from a predator. Once they had a hollow dug that would accommodate their body they dug into their pack and got out their cardigans to act as a air filter, then pulling a groundsheet over themselves they hunkered down to wait for the sandstorm.

'Take cover,' someone shouted, as bits of twigs and other debris began to drift by driven by a now gusting hot wind. The hot wind gradually increased and was no longer gusting, it was now a steady very powerful blast of very hot air and the moaning also had changed: it sounded like a huge choir but instead of singing it was like a screaming banshee. Some used a groundsheet, others a blanket, anything to cover the body as protection against the stinging sand particles. I had never experienced anything like this before and did not know what to expect. As I looked out from under my groundsheet I could see others doing likewise with a quizzical look on their faces as they wondered, same as myself, what was about to happen. Then it hit.

Where before we had been quietly minding our own business in the silence of the desert, small stones began to move on their own as if an invisible finger were pushing them. It was eerie. Sand began to lift into the air as if there was no more gravity. Then it was as if someone had reached up and switched off the sun because it suddenly got dark and there was hot grey dust as fine as flour swirling around us. Then a howling blast of burning hot air carrying dust and debris hit us. It was as if the gates of hell could no longer contain the fury of Satan and had burst asunder. The searing wind tried to drag my groundsheet away but since I was lying on part of it and in a depression there was no way it could be carried off. The hot wind shrieked and buffeted and the burning sand stung and was so abrasive it rubbed any exposed skin off. After a while one had to move because the sand began to pile on top of the blanket and it was hot. So it was a case of move or be barbecued in the hot sand.

Wet through now with perspiration I grabbed a flapping loose corner and held on to it. We lay there a long time patiently waiting for it to pass. After what seemed like hours it began to slacken . . . We were issued extra water and salt tablets after the sandstorm was gone. Everyone was wet through with perspiration and the warm water that we drank didn't help the situation very much. The side of the Bren gun carrier and our truck that had been facing the sandstorm was stripped of paint as efficiently as a sand blaster in a factory.

The lack of water placed severe physical and mental pressures on untrained troops, and little natural water was available in the desert. The bitter brackish liquid found in the few desert wells – *birs* – was insufficient to support large numbers of men and vehicles. In 1941 Lieutenant Colonel John Combe, commanding officer (CO) of the 11th Hussars, the most experienced of the British units in the desert, was 'horrified to find the men becoming really frightened of their continual thirst under the piercing heat . . . He said he saw a hunted look on their faces as the khamsin went on blowing until the armoured cars became too hot to touch.' The water ration of four pints per man per day at the start of offensive operations in June 1940, Private Harry Buckledee of the 11th Hussars recalled, was not very much when 'you consider the heat and that vehicle radiators had to be topped up out of the ration . . . The order was given, no washing or shaving, so we all grew beards and were filthy. However, after four or five weeks supplies of water improved and we were soon ordered to get ourselves cleaned up. We learned to shave and have a wash down in a pint of water.'

Training and constant practice hardened men to the environment. For Private A.S. Prosser, a vehicle mechanic on the 11th Hussars' vintage Rolls-Royce armoured cars, the pre-war months and years had been a constant round of desert familiarization:

> Before the war started and in the time before the Italian advance we carried out extensive training, scouting patrols and map reading. We also carried out night exercises using a compass and the stars . . . We also did a lot of target practice, moving vehicles against moving targets. Our main recreation was sport on makeshift football pitches, and swimming.

In the desert nothing was wasted. The British four-gallon petrol cans were a disgrace. Cheaply produced, the stamped metal containers leaked badly, losing up to half of their contents. But they proved excellent stoves and kettles. Cyril Joly described how the troops used the 'flimsies' to brew up:

> We cut in half one of the thin sheet-metal four-gallon petrol tins used at that time, punched it with holes and filled it with sand and gravel. We then poured on a generous splash of petrol and set it alight. The tea we brewed in the other half of the tin. When the water was boiling, tea, sugar and milk were all added and the whole potion was vigorously stirred. The resulting brew was strong and sweet, like no other tea that I had tasted before.

Troops practised how to move and conceal themselves in the desert, how to drive dispersed to reduce the effects of air attack; how to maintain, repair and recover vehicles that had broken down far from base. Training included learning the art of desert navigation – using the compass by day and the stars by night like seafarers – although the desert was steadily being mapped. Lieutenant Michael Carver of 1st RTR recalled spending three months forward at Mersa Matruh and becoming fully orientated to the desert, travelling across desert tracks as far south as the Siwa oasis: 'There were tracks of every kind, eventually marked with numbered barrels – rather like buoys at sea – so that you usually had some idea of where you were when you came upon one.'

The naval allegory was often commented upon. The Australian journalist Alan Moorehead, working in Egypt in 1940 for the *Daily Express*, described the desert in seafaring terms. Each truck and tank, he noted, was

> as individual as a destroyer, and each squadron of tanks or guns made great sweeps across the desert as a battle-squadron at sea will vanish over the horizon ... When you made contact with the enemy you manoeuvred about him for a place to strike much as two fleets will steam into position for action ... There was no front line ... Always the essential governing principle was that desert forces must be mobile ... We hunted men, not land, as a warship will hunt another warship, and care nothing for the sea on which the action is fought.

The importance of desert navigation was not restricted to the combat arms. It was equally vital to men of the Royal Army Service Corps, who had to travel long distances, often at night, across the vast desert wastelands without signposts, to resupply forward combat units.

In the field, either on exercise or on operations, the British prided themselves on their hardiness. They had few if any creature comforts, all ranks sharing the privations of living and fighting in an unforgiving desert environment that could reach 50 degrees Celsius during the day and drop below freezing at night. Bully beef and hard-tack biscuits were standard fare, washed down by frequent brew-ups of tea. Food was never a problem for Private Harry Buckledee of the 11th Hussars:

I cannot speak too highly of the organization in the regiment for getting supplies up to us in difficult conditions and over long distances. We were also well equipped with cooking utensils: every vehicle had a frying pan, kettle and dixie [large cooking pot] ... Our mainstay was corned beef and biscuits, with potatoes, onions and an Oxo cube for flavouring. We survived mainly on bully stew, with tinned bacon, sausages, soya bean sausages, tinned fruit and always enough tea, sugar and good old Carnation milk to make a brew whenever we wanted one or when we could make one. Sometimes we had boiled rice with sugar or jam and milk. There was flour available on the ration wagon if needed. When we had the time, which wasn't often, we made pastry with the flour and margarine, using a map board for rolling it out on and a beer bottle for a rolling pin. Small pastries were filled with apricot jam and fried in deep margarine. So we didn't starve, although there were many days when we had little time to eat. It was essential to get a brew made on our Primus stove inside our armoured car before it got light because it might be night before we got another chance.

By the time the 4th Armoured Brigade was replaced on the frontier by the 7th Armoured Brigade in early July 1940 the Italians had been shocked into action by the embarrassing British raids. They began to coordinate anti-tank guns, machine guns, tanks and aircraft to counter the British hit-and-run attacks from the desert, and were enjoying an increasing measure of success. The easy victories of June retreated into history. Sergeant Major Smith recalled one close shave when his armoured cars came under fire from a much stronger group of Italian M11 medium tanks:

During a desert patrol we were out looking for tank movement somewhere south of the coast road when suddenly we ran slap into about twenty Italian tanks. We were only about three armoured cars, so we had no option but to get out of there quickly. They started firing at us like mad and we got hit in the engine compartment. The shot blew out the petrol tank and there were flashes but no hazardous fire to make us bail out. The car still ran for three or four miles, enough to get us out of danger.

Later in July the 11th Hussars lost half a squadron in an attack on the road between Bardia and Tobruk, the cavalrymen caught by air attack and handled roughly by Italian M11 medium tanks. The Italians later chivalrously dropped a list of prisoners, dead and wounded on the headquarters of 7th Armoured Division at Mersa Matruh. On 5 August the 8th Hussars engaged thirty M11 tanks inconclusively and still later Alan Moorehead recalled observing a British tank attack against Capuzzo. To his surprise, it failed:

> Then the tanks attacked. They had half a mile to go, and each tank, shooting as it went, attacked one of the Italian guns spaced around Capuzzo's walls. The enemy guns waited perhaps two minutes. Then they spouted out a deafening salvo that enveloped the whole fort in smoke. Smoke rose everywhere. A full expanding cloud of blown dust split by gun-flashes rolled across the desert towards us, and one after another the British tanks dived into it and disappeared. In a moment the battle lost all shape . . .
>
> The Italians had driven our tanks off. The British colonel in command was wounded. One or two of our tanks were wrecked, others for the moment missing. As we ate bully stew in the mess, ambulances lumbered back over the rocky track.

*

In the event of an Italian attack on Egypt, Wavell's plan was not to fight on the frontier but to withdraw all but a light defensive screen deep into the country, allowing the Italian advance to run itself into the sands of western Egypt while preserving his forces for counter-attack. Accordingly, General O'Connor prepared defensive positions to the east of Mersa Matruh with the aim of stopping the Italian advance on the coast and decisively counter-attacking with his tanks from the desert flank.

The three-month War of the Flea (a 'peculiar flea', remarked Mussolini, when it was suggested that the war in North Africa was a fight between the Italian flea and the British elephant, when the flea 'between Sidi el Barrani, Bardia and Tobruk had at its disposal more than a thousand guns') came to a dramatic end on 13 September 1940.

Early in the month patrols from the 11th Hussars had reported that things appeared to be heating up, with greatly increased Italian activity along the coast road and at Fort Capuzzo. Aerial reconnaissance by the RAF on 9 September indicated that Graziani's long-awaited offensive was about to begin, although much of the dust raised was in fact the confused desert meanderings of the Maletti Armoured Group, which had lost its way near Sidi Omar on 10 September, delaying the attack, with many of its vehicles running out of water and overheating.

No one thought to tell Radio Rome that the advance was delayed and ludicrously the offensive was announced to the world a day before the forward screen of the 11th Hussars saw anything untoward on their front, but at dawn on 13 September the first of a long column that would eventually number 85,000 men began to disgorge itself from Capuzzo in the direction of the Egyptian frontier, aiming to cross the wire at Sollum. To the British troops watching high on the Halfaya escarpment above Sollum, and bemused RAF pilots in the air above, the advance was strangely unreal. It was as if the Italians were advancing in review order on a parade ground. They followed the road to Sollum, preceded by a ferocious artillery bombardment, and then headed east over Halfaya Pass, disdaining to utilize the open desert flank. Newly arrived M13 medium tanks proceeded one after another in single file, behind marching blackshirts itching for the glory of seizing Egypt, followed by squadrons of Lancia trucks carrying mortar troops, machine-gunners and engineers, and towing artillery pieces. Some of the Lancias carried marble milestones designed to mark the progress of Italy's newly expanding empire. In the rear marched the men of three infantry regiments.

Any element of surprise had long been lost. The concentrated Italian artillery fire on Sollum on 13 September fell on empty British positions – the single platoon from the 3rd Battalion Coldstream Guards having withdrawn according to orders after blowing up the roads and bridges and mining the roads.

Graziani had considered a thrust through the desert but elected to follow the coast instead and build a strong supply line back to Tobruk, Derna and Benghazi. The British withdrawal made Graziani believe that he had them on the run, and gave an entirely false picture of the strength of the forces opposing him. In fact the withdrawing force consisted of the ancient armoured cars of the 11th Hussars, two infantry battalions (2nd Rifle Brigade and 3rd Coldstream Guards), a squadron of 1st RTR with A9 cruisers, and two regiments of 25-pounders (3rd and 4th RHA). Every day they pulled back with the Italian advance, harrying the invaders each step of the way but avoiding pitched battles where they could. Their predictable route made the Italians easy to ambush, the British waiting to strike the flanks of the advance and withdrawing before the enemy artillery and aircraft could retaliate. Then the whole process would begin again. At night British tanks and guns would fire into the leaguers that the Italians exposed to attack because of their habit of nervously shining searchlights into the desert. Foreign Minister Ciano immediately recognized the British tactics for what they were. 'At the moment the British are withdrawing without fighting,' he wrote on 14 September. 'They wish to draw us away from our base, stretching our lines of communication.'

But to the chagrin of the Western Desert Force, dug in and waiting for the Italian 10th Army at Mersa Matruh, Graziani halted his exhausted columns sixty-five miles inside Egypt at the fishing village of Sidi Barrani on 16 September. Italian casualties were 120 dead and 410 wounded. The British had lost a mere forty men. During the entire period since war had been declared Graziani's casualties numbered 3,500 to 150 British. The Italian commander had done precisely what Mussolini had ordered him to do, and he was certainly not going to commit to any further adventures until his supply lines had been consolidated. Graziani's apparent triumph – he little appreciated that the British had decided not to fight but to withdraw to better positions – made Mussolini, according to Ciano, 'radiant with joy. He has taken complete responsibility for the offensive on his shoulders, and is proud that he was right.' Two weeks later Mussolini still remained 'in a good mood and very happy that Italy could score 'a success in Egypt which gives her the glory she has sought in vain for three centuries'.

But the Duce's jubilation did not last. He believed Graziani's success needed to be exploited by further advances towards Mersa Matruh, where, it was believed, the British were prepared to fight. When the subject was broached both Badoglio and Graziani informed their leader that the earliest possible date for further offensive action was November. Graziani demanded more vehicles – and 600 mules – if he were to continue towards Mersa Matruh. Mussolini was furious at the inability of his generals to secure what he regarded as his rightful glory. Ciano recorded on 18 October 1940 that Mussolini was 'in a very bad mood on account of Graziani'. A week later Mussolini raged at his Libyan commander-in-chief, 'Forty days after the capture of Sidi Barrani I ask myself the question, to whom has this long halt been any use – to us or the enemy? I do not hesitate to answer, it has been of use, indeed, more to the enemy . . . It is time to ask whether you feel you wish to continue in command.'

Graziani wired back to say he would resume the offensive between 15 and 18 December. In the meantime he expended the energy of his army on building a series of self-contained defensive positions running from Maktila, ten miles further on from Sidi Barrani, in a forty-mile arc across the desert to the south. The camps, designed to protect Sidi Barrani, mirrored the idea of the desert fort (like Capuzzo), with all-round defence provided by anti-tank mines and barbed wire, and stone sangars (breastworks) built at each compass point for sentries and machine guns. Most camps had some tanks and artillery. As bases from which aggressive patrols could be mounted against the British the camps made some sense, at least as a temporary measure while a further offensive into Egypt was prepared and the rearward lines of communication established. However, as the weeks passed it became clear that Graziani had no immediate offensive intentions, and the encampments dwindled from being a threat to the British into targets, each filled to the brim with thousands of troops in their sweltering tented acres, vast truck parks and huge quantities of supplies. Italian passivity had handed the initiative directly to O'Connor.

Graziani's decision to halt and consolidate his positions gave the British time to reinforce. On 24 September 1940 three additional armoured regiments arrived at Port Said, adding 152 new tanks (including forty-eight of the heavily armoured Matilda II infantry tanks) to O'Connor's armoury, along with forty-eight anti-tank guns, forty-eight 25-pounders and 500 Bren guns. The Matilda had been named after a cartoon of the period featuring an overweight duck, and was slow, with a maximum road speed of 16 miles per hour. But though it could only crawl over rocky desert at between 4 and 6 miles per hour the Matilda was immensely well protected, the thirty-ton hull cast in a single slab of metal that was three inches thick and able to withstand anything the Italians could throw at it. Its only real adversary in 1941 and 1942 proved to be the German 88-millimetre anti-aircraft gun depressed for use in the anti-tank role. The Matilda's 40-millimetre cannon fired a 2-pound solid shot a distance of 1,000 yards, which could slice though the welded armour plate of the heaviest Italian tank.

The 2nd RTR with cruiser tanks (mainly A13, but with some A9 and A10s) joined the 4th Armoured Brigade; the 3rd Hussars with Mark VI light tanks joined 7th Armoured Brigade; and 7th RTR acted as an independent armoured force attached to the 4th Indian Division. The situation for the RAF was also slowly improving, and by the end of the year two squadrons of Wellington bombers and one of Hurricanes had arrived from England to offset the five squadrons dispatched from Egypt to Greece; three squadrons of Blenheims had also been redirected from elsewhere in the Middle East for Egypt's defence.

While plans for a limited British offensive against the Italian invaders progressed, the Western Desert Force did not remain idle, and a series of operations was mounted from the British defensive area around Mersa Matruh to retain the initiative and keep the Italians on the back foot. One such resulted in the young Second Lieutenant Peter Cochrane, an 'emergency commissioned officer' (the previous course to his at the Royal Military Academy Sandhurst had contained 'gentlemen cadets'), being awarded a Military Cross leading 15 Platoon, C Company, 2nd Battalion Queens Own Cameron Highlanders in a confused but adrenalin-fuelled night skirmish against the Libyan defenders of Maktila. Cochrane had arrived in a dusty wadi along the coast a few miles south-east of Mersa Matruh on 28 August 1940 after a five-month 18,000-mile journey from Inverness to take command of Sergeant Horbury, four other NCOs and seventeen men.

The 2nd Camerons formed part of the 4th Indian Division (for reasons dating back to the Mutiny of 1857 Indian brigades each contained two Indian and one British battalion), which had now arrived to partner the 7th Armoured Division, doubling the size of O'Connor's Western Desert Force. Cochrane's platoon positions in the desert – little more than stone sangars behind rolls of barbed wire – were the front line. The battalion attack on the night of 22 October 1940 proved the perfect lesson for those who had not until then experienced the chaos and confusion of fighting at night. Crossing the start line after midnight, Peter Cochrane observed:

> Our arrival was scarcely a surprise, since the gunners had shelled the camp for three hours, and D Company bumped a post almost at once, going in with the bayonet. The shouting and firing led the major to swing us round to support them; it died down and we got back on our original line ... Changing direction in the dark, when ground hasn't been reconnoitred in daylight, is a muddling affair, and we were just getting sorted out when we were seen, or heard, and everything opened up. We dived on our bellies, and lay watching an aurora borealis of tracer whistling over us – red, white and blue.

When it was realized that the Italian machine gun was firing on a fixed line and too high, the advance continued. Cochrane's platoon got stuck into a line of enemy transport, wrecking what they could and withdrawing with a Libyan prisoner, who was forced to drive one of the captured trucks back to the British lines. 'The result was pretty meagre – eight lorries destroyed and one prisoner taken, with two enemy killed, and four killed on our side; and I doubt whether the prisoner imparted any useful information ... However it was an exceptionally good field exercise for us; fortunate is the unit whose first bloodletting is exciting and relatively painless, and which can learn the correct lessons.'

Operations by O'Connor's troops were not the only worry for Graziani, whose forces never ventured far from their own barbed wire. Mussolini had invaded Greece in late October 1940, diverting troops and resources away from North Africa to a military adventure mounted solely for reasons of propaganda and braggadocio. The consequences of the ignominious rout of the ill-prepared outnumbered Italians by the Greeks were the continued exposure of Italian weakness, fewer resources for North Africa, collapsing morale across the Italian armed forces and an emboldened enemy. The fiasco in Greece also opened the door to the humiliation of German intervention in what had been hitherto exclusively Italian military affairs. The Germans had already tentatively enquired about assisting the Italian advance into Egypt, Major General von Thoma visiting Cyrenaica briefly in September to advise on the feasibility of sending a panzer division to Libya. Von Thoma reported back to Berlin that the Italians were too scared of the British to engage them robustly, and feared that the arrival of German troops might heat up the war uncomfortably. Mussolini was strongly opposed to getting the Germans involved, advising Badoglio to refuse any German offer, arguing, 'If they get a footing in the country, we shall never be rid of them.' He was soon to have no choice.

A British attack on Cyrenaica far more substantial than the pin-prick raids to date appeared attractive to Churchill and Wavell even before Graziani resumed his offensive on 13 September. The following day Wavell ordered O'Connor to plan for an offensive into Libya. Wavell's initial idea was to conduct a five-day raid, looping deep into the desert around the Italians' southern flank to attack their positions from the rear and cut communications back to Sollum and Bardia. British Foreign Secretary Anthony Eden, visiting Cairo in October 1940 on a tour of Middle East Command, was quickly persuaded that Wavell's plan was infinitely preferable to Churchill's alternative idea of dispatching troops to Greece and recommended it to the prime minister. On 1 November Eden telegrammed, 'We cannot, from Middle East resources, send sufficient air or land reinforcements to have any decisive influence upon course of fighting in Greece . . . [although] we should presently be in a position to undertake certain offensive oper-ations which, if successful, may have far-reaching effect on course of war as a whole.' Hearing of Wavell's plans (Operation Compass) from Eden on his return from Cairo on 8 November, Churchill was enthusi-astic. In his memoirs Churchill recalled that on learning its details he 'purred like six cats'.

Marshal Graziani's passivity allowed General O'Connor the oppor-tunity to prepare thoroughly for a counter-stroke to remove the head of the invading 10th Army from its long, ponderous tail, even to the extent of providing time to re-equip all his field artillery regiments with the new 25-pounders. The Italian invasion of Greece at the end of October weakened the resources available to O'Connor, but he nevertheless judged that he had sufficient forces to conduct his offensive.

A further Italian error became apparent to O'Connor when the British commander considered his options for the offensive. A twenty-mile gap had been allowed to develop in the Italians' defensive encampments between the right flank at Sofafi and their next camp at Nibeiwa near Bir Enba, a fact identified by careful British reconnaissance. Too widely dispersed to be able to support each other, the Italian positions lay open to piecemeal attack. Ten miles to the north of Nibeiwa lay Tummar West and Tummar East, occupied by the 2nd Libyan Division, and to the north-east of these lay the enemy's most advanced camp near the coast at Maktila, occupied by the 1st Libyan Division, the object of the Camerons' raid on 22 October. In addition, although the Italians had further fortifications round Sidi Barrani there did not otherwise seem to be any organized second line of defence.

O'Connor was instructed to be prepared to exploit beyond the defences when he had broken through, but the expectation of both Wavell and Wilson was that he would limit his offensive to a four- or five-day raid. It was assumed that anything longer would exhaust O'Connor's own supply lines, and the plan was to use the gap at Bir Enba to push his troops through, before turning on the Italian camps from the rear. While this attack was under way the flanks on the coast and at Sofafi would be contained by other troops.

A final boost to Wavell's plans was the devastating blow struck against Italy's Regia Marina on 11 November 1940, when Royal Navy Swordfish torpedo bombers attacked the Italian fleet lying at anchor in Taranto harbour, sinking the battleship *Littorio* and severely damaging two more. Wavell was about to seize the opportunity that the humbling of Italy's naval pretensions in the Mediterranean and Graziani's somnolence at Sidi Barrani offered.

2 » WAVELL'S RIPOSTE

By December Graziani had about 85,000 men dug into fortified encampments sweeping in a wide arc from Maktila on the coast, a few miles east of Sidi Barrani, deep into the desert at Rabia and Sofafi. Two of Graziani's six divisions were of locally recruited Libyans, two were blackshirt divisions of fascist volunteers and two were 'metropolitan' divisions of the regular Italian army.

The plan for Operation Compass involved the 4th Indian Division accompanied by the forty-eight Matildas of 7th RTR and supported by the newly arrived 16th Infantry Brigade, including a battalion of Free French marines under Commandant Folliot, breaking through the Enba Gap and attacking the vast fortified encampment at Nibeiwa from the rear, before moving north-east to attack the two camps at Tummar. Over a mile wide and a mile and a half deep, surrounded by anti-tank mines and stone sangars, Nibeiwa contained the Maletti Armoured Group, Graziani's only tank force, commanded by the stout, bearded General Pietro Maletti, with thirty-five medium M11 and thirty-five light L3 tanks, together with 2,500 Libyan soldiers. It would be a tough nut to crack.

To prevent the Italians counter-attacking from the south while the raid was under way, the 7th Armoured Division was tasked with protecting the left (western) flank of 4th Armoured Division's attack on the camps, and securing the critical Enba Gap itself. Once the Italian camps had fallen, 7th Armoured, with its 175 Mark VIs and 73 cruisers, would drive north-north-west to the coast road at Buq Buq, about fifteen miles to the west of Sidi Barrani, to cut off Sollum. Meanwhile a force from the Mersa Matruh garrison under Brigadier Selby (Selby Force) would attack along the coast, hitting the Italian camp at Maktila, defended by the 1st Libyan Division. Then, with Nibeiwa and the two Tummar camps gone, the southern camps masked and the road to Sollum blocked, Sidi Barrani would be attacked in a pincer movement from south and east.

In order to preserve secrecy none of the troops involved in the operation were told that this was anything but a major exercise. As it was notoriously difficult to keep anything secret in Cairo this precaution was a wise one. Extreme measures were taken to keep Compass under wraps. Practically nothing whatever was put on paper, and no more than a dozen senior commanders and staff officers knew of the plan until shortly before its execution. On 25 and 26 November a training exercise was held near Matruh, which was in fact a rehearsal for the proposed operation. It duped everyone, including, most importantly, the Italians.

When the 31,000 men and 5,000 vehicles moved out during the morning of 6 December, crawling slowly south across the desert from Mersa Matruh so as to minimize the dust clouds that would give away their presence, only a handful of the Allied troops were aware that they were going into battle. Windscreens had been removed from the trucks to prevent reflections from the sun providing early warning to any watching Italian reconnaissance screen, while secret dumps of ammunition, rations and fuel had been placed in underground cisterns across the desert during previous patrols. Captain Pat Hobart of 2nd RTR was struck by the sight of 'the tanks ahead with their hulls hidden in drifting clouds of dust, but with each turret standing out clear and black against the fading western sky, each with muffled heads emerging and two pennants fluttering above from the wireless aerial'. When the columns reached a point some thirty miles south-west of Mersa Matruh the 4th Indian Division stopped and dispersed into all-round defence as dusk descended.

During that first night of 6/7 December the troops lay up deep in the desert. It was bitterly cold, Lieutenant Peter Cochrane for one bemoaning the decision that had led to their greatcoats being left behind in Cairo with the regiment's kilts and heavy baggage. The following day, safe from prying eyes and ears, the soldiers were told of their real purpose. Private Tom Barker of the Argyll and Sutherland

Highlanders guessed something was up even before one of the company officers came over to speak to the men:

> 'You men have trained hard in this desert and now we are about to see if it will pay off. I have no doubt in my mind that you are the cream of the British army and as such this is going to be a doddle. We are going to take Sidi Barrani from the Italians and we are going to hold it.'

With heads bowed, the officer then recited the Lord's Prayer. The Medical Officer stepped forward: 'OK, now anyone wanting to go to the toilet I suggest you go now, because if you get hit you stand a better chance with empty bowels.'

'Bloody charming,' I heard someone mutter. 'This is for real.' Someone else muttered, 'Prayin' ain't goin' ti 'elp. On'y bugger that's goin' tae cum oot o' this is 'im wi' biggest guns.'

On hearing the news, Second Lieutenant Roy Farran of the 3rd Hussars began asking himself endless questions such as Will I be killed? Will I do well? Am I a coward? but observed that his soldiers displayed great sangfroid and 'did not seem in the least bit excited'. During that day in Cairo General Wavell ostentatiously visited the races at Gezira and held a highly public party at the Turf Club in the evening to which all the local notables had been invited in a ploy designed to persuade interested observers that everything was normal. The US military attaché in Cairo, Colonel Bonner Fellers, was invited by Wavell to attend the 'manoeuvres' in the Western Desert the following day.

The plan was bold. A single enemy aircraft could have given the game away, but after months of desert skirmishes the British were relying on the assumption that the Italians would not suddenly change over to offensive patrolling. After spending the whole of Saturday 7 December waiting quietly in the desert, eyes constantly scanning the skies for the specks on the horizon that would threaten discovery, the whole force moved slowly forward to their forming-up positions fifteen miles south-west of Nibeiwa, reaching them without mishap by mid-afternoon on Sunday 8th. 'As far as the eye could see there were vehicles,' recalled Roy Farran. 'Just before dark I caught a glimpse of the Indian troop carriers and the heavy Matildas away on the right. Through glasses I could see grim-looking Sikhs, with turbans wound round their beards as a protection against the dust, sitting rigidly in their trucks.'

Still no Italian aircraft seemed to have spotted the force, remarkable given the volume of vehicles involved in the advance, although O'Connor's movements had in fact been spotted from the air by Lieutenant Colonel Vittorio Revetra, who signalled to Graziani's headquarters 300 miles back at Cyrene that he had seen 'an impressive number of armoured vehicles' moving west from Mersa Matruh. To his amazement Graziani replied, 'Let me have that in writing.' It appears that Italian airmen had often cried wolf regarding an imminent British attack, and Graziani decided to take no action. It seems likely that he believed the advance to be merely one of the regular training exercises to which Italian intelligence had become accustomed. Returning to Sidi Barrani Revetra was told 'to put more water in his wine next time'.

When it was dark the tanks of 7th RTR, the four artillery regiments and the infantry of 11th Brigade were led quietly forward to their start lines prior to the attack at dawn the following morning. This final journey was undertaken by Peter Cochrane and his platoon in three-ton Indian Army trucks, moving cautiously on sidelights, the long column snaking forward bumpily under the clear night sky. The routes to be taken by the columns were marked by hurricane lamps placed in old petrol tins cut out with the open side facing away from the enemy. Four miles from the camp the start lines were reached some two hours before dawn on 9 December, the noise of the tanks and trucks being masked by the sound of an ancient Bombay bomber, latterly used for towing practice targets for Gladiator biplanes, droning overhead on its way to and from an apparent mission. The sounds were also covered by a noisy diversionary attack by the 4th Rajputs on the south-west wall of Nibeiwa at 3 a.m. designed to make the defenders believe this was just another British nuisance raid. Two hours later, the cold desert now much quieter, the 5,000 men of the attacking force shivered under the dew and ate cold canned bacon washed down with tepid tea fortified with rum brought up from the rear. As the day dawned the smells of the Italians' breakfast – hot rolls and strong coffee – wafted across the desert.

The plan for the dawn attack on Nibeiwa demanded absolute silence. There was to be no preliminary bombardment to alert the defenders; rather, the guns would fire and the tanks advance at precisely the same moment. This required immediate accuracy from the gunners, as no pre-targeting could be arranged. At precisely 7 a.m. the seventy-two guns of the divisional artillery opened up on the camp, masking the noise of the 7th RTR Matildas as they started their final approach. Twenty-three M11 tanks were parked outside the perimeter to the rear of the camp. In the space of ten minutes they were all turned into burning heaps of scrap metal. The Matildas then advanced through a mine-free route to the north-west of the camp identified by aerial reconnaissance, before fanning out in the early-morning gloom into the camp at a charge, shooting and driving over everything in their path.

Surprise was total. The Matildas drove through the vast encamp-ment firing at will, the action described as akin to 'iron rods probing a wasps' nest'. As they penetrated the camp dazed and startled Italians leapt from their trenches or tents to fall to the waiting machine guns of the Matildas. In the confusion some tried to surrender; others attempted to resist. General Maletti was killed running from his dugout firing a sub-machine gun, his son falling wounded beside him. Italian artillery desperately attempted to engage the British tanks, but the Matilda's three inches of armour proved impervious to penetra-tion. The gallant Italian gun crews died at their posts.

Fifteen minutes after the tanks had entered the camp, which was resounding to the constant *whump, whump* of incoming artillery fire, the sharp boom of the Matildas' 2-pounders and the steady drumrolls of the tanks' machine guns, the order came over the radio to Peter Cochrane and his waiting men of the lead battalion, the 2nd Cameron Highlanders: 'Camerons, go!' They moved forward in their trucks to within 500 yards of the perimeter, where they debussed. Blowing steadily, the company pipers began to play as the Camerons fixed their seventeen-inch bayonets to their rifles, thrust them forward and entered the chaos of the blazing camp at a canter. It was the last time that the pipes played his platoon into battle, Peter Cochrane recalled, 'because it was the only one on flat enough ground to leave a piper sufficient breath to fill his bag'.

The camp was now a confused and blazing melee, with the flash and crump of point-blank artillery and tank fire, the zip and whine of bullets and the confused shouts and cries of the defenders as some officers attempted to rally their men and others tried to escape the affliction that had descended so suddenly upon them. 'I had two sections abreast, either side of me,' Cochrane recalled, 'with Horbury and the third section following, and can remember shouting like a madman to encourage myself as we jumped and scrambled over the wire. There was some shooting as we rushed three or four posts, Patterson bayoneting a machine-gunner. Another machine gun opened up rather too close to be pleasant, but one of the [Bren] carriers dashed up and fixed it.' The Italian reaction in places was fierce but too slow, and the consequence for Cochrane's frontal assault was only one man wounded, Private Francis receiving a bullet in the shoulder. The neighbouring platoon was not so fortunate. Second Lieutenant 'Robbie' Robertson, commander of 14 Platoon, was killed along with Corporal MacKintosh, and Sergeant Cairns wounded.

The skirl of the Cameron pipes provided an eerie soundtrack to the scene. For many men on both sides it was their first experience of battle. Private Jimmy Mearns of the 2nd Camerons, a printer's apprentice from Edinburgh, dropped to one knee and fired at a ferocious-looking African about to fire a machine gun, the man jerking back in a wild convulsion, clutching his throat. A few minutes later, after charging in with the bayonet, Mearns stood over the black soldier – his eyes rolling white in terror of death, blood pulsing in a red-black fountain from the hole in his throat – and felt the shock of taking his first life. He retched helplessly. Many Italians and Libyans fought desperately while others huddled disconsolately in clumps seeking escape or to await capture. Cochrane observed, 'The Italians were often very well led, but couldn't hold together if their commander were killed.'

By 8.30 a.m. the battle was largely over. More than 2,000 Italians and 35 tanks had been captured for the loss of fifty-six officers and men. Major Henry Rew, commanding one of the Matilda squadrons, reported over the radio, 'I am surrounded by at least 500 Italians all with their hands in the air. Can you please send somebody to collect them, because they are hindering my progress and are a considerable embarrassment to me.'

Cochrane and his men were astonished at what they found inside the camp. Sitting inside an anti-aircraft position on the edge of the encampment, the men of 15 Platoon were soon tucking into Italian tinned fruit, with Cochrane worrying about how to prevent them taking advantage of the bottles of wine and brandy lying scattered among the living quarters. From his watching place on a small knoll to the north-west of Nibeiwa the commander of the 4th Indian Division, the cheroot-chomping Major General Noel Beresford-Peirse, was sufficiently pleased with the outcome after an hour and a half of fighting to order the assault on the two Tummar camps by the second of his two brigades, the 5th. The morning had gone dramatically better than expected. The twenty-two remaining serviceable tanks of 7th RTR withdrew themselves as best they could from the fighting but almost immediately seven shed tracks in a minefield as they did so, leaving only fifteen tanks from the forty-eight that had set out from Mersa Matruh three days before.

Alerted to the calamity at Nibeiwa the Regia Aeronautica hit the 5th Brigade as it moved north to get behind the Tummar positions, but came off worse in the encounter, losing several planes as they attempted to dive-bomb the tanks and trucks moving through the desert. Watching the battle from his Mark VI at a position overlooking the Tummars Roy Farran could see 'Italian dive-bombers getting amongst our transport . . . Wicked little single-engined bombers were diving low between the bursts of ack-ack to drop their cargo slap-bang amongst the lorries.' At 1.30 p.m. the artillery concentration on the Tummar camps began and twenty minutes later the Matildas – many now chalked with instructions in Italian to surrender – entered Tummar West, garrisoned by 2nd Libyan Division, from the north. The leading infantry battalion, the 1st Royal Regiment of Fusiliers, following in trucks driven by New Zealand drivers twenty minutes later, debussed within 500 yards of the camp in a repeat of the tactics employed by the Camerons in the morning. Leaping out onto the desert floor the Fusiliers trotted forward with fixed bayonets following the swirling dust trails of the tanks. One group went in kicking a football, until it was unsportingly punctured by an Italian bullet. Not willing to be left out, the Kiwis abandoned their vehicles and, clutching whatever weapons they could grab, charged in with the Fusiliers shouting, 'Come on, you Pommy bastards.'

However, the attack was an unexpectedly bloody hand-to-hand affair, the Fusiliers losing a number of officers at the head of their men. After slicing through the first camp the tanks went on immediately to attack the second, leaving the infantry behind without any support. Libyan resistance did not cease until 4 p.m. Some Italian troops rallied bravely but foolhardily. Just as 7th RTR began the advance against Tummar East a counter-attack with light tanks and trucked infantry was repulsed by machine-gun fire from the Vickers medium machine guns of the Northumberland Fusiliers. In ten minutes 400 Libyans had been mown down, their broken bodies littering the ground in dark clumps between their smashed and burning trucks. By nightfall Tummar West and most of Tummar East was in British hands and 4,000 prisoners taken. Of the 7th RTR Matildas only twelve now remained serviceable. O'Connor, however, desperate to ensure that the Italians were given no opportunity to recover, ordered that the troops press on to Sidi Barrani that night in preparation for an assault on the heart of Graziani's defences the following morning.

Meanwhile, Selby Force, which had been observing Maktila camp on the coast since the evening of 8 December, moved forward to prevent the escape west of the 1st Libyan Division. The CO of the 1st Battalion Durham Light Infantry, Lieutenant Colonel Eustace Arderne, had barely heard two bursts of gunfire before one of his officers shouted, 'There's a white flag, sir!' 'Nonsense!' Arderne snapped. But it was true. Inside the fort a brigadier and his 500 men stood rigidly to attention. 'Monsieur,' the brigadier greeted Arderne in diplomatic French. Standing beside a pile of unspent ammunition he declared, 'Nous avons tiré la dernière cartouche.' Owing to the comparative weakness of Selby Force (1,750 troops with a few Mark VI light tanks and guns) and the difficult going, it was unable to prevent the withdrawal of the enemy towards Sidi Barrani, but the formation pursued them with all possible speed on 10 December.

At the same time the 7th Armoured Division had successfully

fulfilled its role of protecting the left flank of the attack through Enba and against the camps, and by 10 a.m. on the first day of the attack the cruiser and light tanks, together with the Hussars' veteran armoured cars, had driven north-west to straddle the Sidi Barrani–Buq Buq road. As they advanced through the Enba Gap they could see and hear the battles for the camps as the struggle for Nibeiwa and the Tummars raged. 'We could clearly see the Indian soldiers in extended order moving across the desert towards the low stone walls of the camp,' recalled Captain Rea Leakey of 1st RTR:

> Our passage through the gap was uneventful and we advanced some twelve miles before making contact with the enemy. As we came over a small ridge we saw about twenty Italian tanks cutting across our front to the north. They were M13s, which were about the same size as our cruisers and mounted a similar gun. Over the air I gave orders to my squadron: 'Enemy tanks ahead, form battle line on me and stand by to engage.'
>
> My eight cruiser tanks raced forward to their battle positions, while the light tanks, who were in the lead, moved across to either flank of the cruisers. They could do no good in this battle.

Leakey's tank gunner was Private Milligan, who despite strict instructions against smoking in armoured vehicles, fired best with a cigarette dangling from his bottom lip. Closely confined in his hot tin coffin it was his way of coping with the stress of battle. Leakey barked out his orders: 'Gunner, AP [armour-piercing] action. Traverse right, traverse right, steady. On. Enemy tanks 800, and here's your cigarette. Now, for goodness sake, shoot straight.'

He did so. A quick engagement left eight burning Italian tanks, the standard of their gunnery not up to that of Milligan, his cigarette and his colleagues. Sending back the prisoners escorted by some Mark VIs, Leakey's squadron then burst onto the coast road at the village of Buq Buq. Winston Churchill recalled being struck by the radio message sent by a young tank commander who, looking at his map, reported his position: 'Have arrived at the second B in Buq Buq.' Their arrival came as an unexpected shock to the Italians streaming in both directions between Sollum in the west and Sidi Barrani in the east:

As we approached the coast we saw before us a mass of men, lorries, guns and a few tanks, and we were on them before they knew what had hit them. There were so many targets I hardly knew which to engage first. Milligan was having the time of his life, and even the young sub-turret gunners with their machine guns were getting rid of belts of ammunition at an alarming rate. For a while the Italians fought back, but then white handkerchiefs and scarves began to appear in all directions. We stopped firing and closed in on them.

That night the leaguered squadron was reached by its resupply vehicles and provisioned with fuel, rations and ammunition. Victory was in the air. The Camerons at Nibeiwa were guarding 7,000 prisoners. Many hundred enemy soldiers lay dead; over 1,000 wounded had been collected for treatment; forty tanks had been destroyed; and more than a hundred guns and several hundred vehicles had been captured. Surprise, deception and training – combined with a bold plan – had resulted in the destruction of two Italian divisions for the loss of twenty-two dead and fifty-two wounded. Given the size of the Italian positions O'Connor had decided beforehand that he would withdraw his forces if he suffered 50 per cent casualties. At the end of the first day, he had reason to be pleased.

But Sidi Barrani was still untouched, and remained the greatest prize of the raid. During the night of 9 December the 16th Infantry Brigade, led by the Argyll and Sutherland Highlanders, marched through the night towards the town, their empty three-ton trucks following slowly behind. After a while orders came back to the men of Private Tom Barker's platoon: 'The Italian positions are only half a mile away so keep the noise down.' They trudged on in the African night until at last a halt was called and whispered commands issued.

It was 2 a.m. Each man quietly and quickly dug a shallow pit in the ground. The order was whispered from mouth to ear: 'No smoking, no talking, lie down in your pit and wait for daylight and the whistle.' Tom Barker lay alert, willing himself not to sleep because of the fear of having his throat cut by an Italian patrol. He need not have worried as the Italians did not emerge from their bunkers. After what seemed an eternity the sky lightened and finally a thin bright-red strip appeared on the horizon. The strip grew wider and wider and shadows began to form. Now he could see some of his mates standing up in the early-morning light to stretch and shake out their blankets. It was a mistake. They were in sight of the enemy, and the Italians were alert:

Suddenly the silence was shattered by a sound like a heavy truck travelling at high speed with flat tyres. The noise came rushing through the air and then [there was] an enormous explosion and the bloke with the blanket was gone. Where he had been there was just a huge cloud of dust swirling and rising in the air, and a ringing in the ears and a blast of hot air and sand and an acrid smell. A bloke was on the ground and writhing in agony while another was walking in circles as though drunk until someone jumped up and pulled him to the ground and held him down. Everyone who had been standing for a brief second stood like statues then as if by magic they disappeared into the ground as more whistling noises and explosions were heard.

Now when I looked out all I could see was dust and fine sand hanging in the air. Then all hell let loose as shell after shell hit the ground. The ground was now shuddering as explosion after explosion made the sand and dust into a blanket it was impossible to see through. I could feel grit in my mouth; my eyes were watering, even though I was wearing eye shields made of thin clear plastic the dust still got in.

Barker attempted to chamber a round in his rifle, but found that the bolt was sluggish and difficult to operate. It was clogged with dust. The man next to him had managed to get his bolt out and was licking the dust and sand off and spitting it out onto the ground. 'There were snapping noises like someone slapping a wet leather belt on a tabletop and I suddenly realized they were bullets going by, so close . . .' Nearby trucks were targeted by the Italian artillery and burst into flame, men dying in and around the vehicles as they were caught in the maelstrom of fire which had engulfed the battalion:

Someone in the fog of sand and dust was screaming, 'Fix bayonets!' As I drew my bayonet I saw Ginger Craig next to me. He grinned at me and slammed down on his bayonet to fix it to his rifle. We moved forward away from the now useless truck as another shell exploded and suddenly there were noises like angry hornets as bits of shrapnel whizzed by. Ginger Craig sank to the ground like a balloon losing air.

His friend had been struck in the chest by a piece of shrapnel. Barker rushed to wrap a first field dressing on the mortally wounded man and tried to make him comfortable. Then someone hit Barker on the shoulder and screamed in his ear, 'Leave him, you can't help him.'

Elsewhere on the Argylls' line, Captain Cyril Joly's troop of A9 cruiser tanks also found itself caught up in the maelstrom. The 2nd RTR cruisers were lined up across the desert facing the Italian guns, tasked with ensuring that no Italians managed to break out of the encircled town. The rest of the regiment was moving to take up positions to the left. The cruisers were too light to take on the guns, ruling out a fast frontal assault, and Joly and his tank crews were forced to await the arrival of the heavier Matildas of 7th RTR to lead the advance. In the meantime the scattered infantry was taking a terrible beating from the Italian artillery:

From the safety of the firmly closed down turret of my tank, I watched through the periscopes with awe and horror the scene of destruction and suffering which surrounded us. Some of the shells fell wide of their mark, leaving behind them only a cloud of dust and black smoke which drifted slowly across the battlefield, carried by the little breeze there was in the sudden calm. Others fell near the tanks, and we could hear the dull metallic clang as the shell splinters hit the armour plate. Others fell among the small groups of infantry, leaving behind the twisted, mangled and distorted bodies of the dead and wounded.

Joly saw a shell hit a platoon headquarters consisting of an officer and three men:

For a split second all that I could see was the dull red flash of the explosion. Then in the swirling dust and smoke I saw with shocked dismay what was left of the three men. One was dead; there was no doubt about that, since all that remained of his face was a dull red mass of flesh and bone . . . Another was staggering with hesitant, tottering steps away from the scene, clutching with both hands where his stomach had been and where now, through the gaps in his outspread fingers, a red mass of straggling entrails was hanging out.

The third man was apparently untouched, staring in stupefaction at the scene around him and standing over the officer, who was lying on the ground, a bloody stump of raw flesh and bone where his right leg had been. Joly immediately threw open the turret cupola and climbed out of his tank:

'Anything I can do?' I enquired. 'Have you got a shell dressing? We must put on a tourniquet at once.'

Still dazed, the officer slowly turned an uncomprehending gaze on me and said, 'I don't feel anything. My foot's gone and it doesn't hurt. I can't understand it. All I can think of is that I shall be lame for the rest of my life. Oh, God, I can't bear the thought!'

But he soon pulled himself together and with surprising calm said, 'Call for a doctor, can you? I can't feel anything yet, but when the nerves wake up it'll be bloody hell. Besides, this poor chap here will need some pretty careful attention. For God's sake get one along soon.'

Under the continuing deafening blast and shock of incoming shell-fire Joly did what he could with the tank's first aid kit, wrapping a first field dressing around the bloody stump of the officer's leg and injecting morphia into both wounded men. Despite these attentions, the man with the stomach wound died minutes later in agony. It was some relief when, some moments later, the ten remaining 7th RTR Matildas swept through the 2nd RTR position and made for the Italian gun line in the distance. Joly had no further time for reflection, as he left his wounded charges and led his troop of tanks into battle behind the Matildas.

*

Captain Walter Drysdale's anti-tank company of the 16th Brigade moved forward behind the Argylls when the first shells began to fall at 5.55 a.m. He could see the enemy guns plainly on a low ridge about one mile ahead, puffs of white smoke marking each discharge. There was no sign of British artillery and the exposed brigade quickly suffered considerable casualties. In hospital some weeks later Drysdale noted down the course of events that led to the death or wounding of virtually every man in his company:

07.00. Brigadier [Tony Lomax] returned & wirelessed Divisional HQ to ask for artillery urgently. While wirelessing one operator was killed beside him.

07.05. Machine-gun company came into action at the double. Cannot see the effect of their fire. Shell burst plumb on two ammunition carriers ten yards from me and blew them to bits.

07.15. One of my trucks hit . . . Shelling is heavy and there is enemy machine-gun fire in our direction – luckily not lower than head high. Was kneeling in front of the radiator and had just bent down when shrapnel simply plastered the radiator. Looked up and saw Jock rolling on the ground. Ran to him and found he had a nasty wound in the right shoulder . . . shell burst just by it and blew off the head of Clark, my batman. Poor sod, but it was a quick death.

07.50. Received orders to take my guns into action.

08.00. Led guns into action. Chose as target a knoll to right of Argyll and Sutherland Highlanders forward company from where fire seemed to be holding them up. One gun going into action was hit and burst into flames. Got remaining guns into action & directed fire onto knoll. Shooting was accurate but armour-piercing shells cannot have very much effect. Enemy artillery fairly plastering my guns; our own troops moving forward slowly.

08.20. Only one gun left in action.

08.25. Shell burst wounded two of the crew.

08.30. Direct shell burst on my gun. Fell flat on my side and passed out for half a minute. Came to and saw my left arm jerking up and down. Thought at first it had been blown off. Heard someone say 'Gawd, the Captain's been killed' so managed to sit up and say 'No, you bugger, fire the gun.' Realized blood was spurting out of a wound just above the heart. Corporal Bishop came to me and tried to bind it [and] told me the gun was wrecked and all gun crew wounded. Tried to get up but couldn't and fainted. Came to later and crawled over to No.1 of the gun who was obviously in pain. Reached him.

In the absence of artillery and with the destruction of Drysdale's anti-tank company the attack against Sidi Barrani now depended entirely on the courage of the remaining infantry. Reluctantly leaving Ginger Craig to his fate, Private Tom Barker climbed to his feet and followed the rest of his platoon, who were moving towards the Italian guns in a skirmish line, the Argylls advancing about four yards apart. His earlier apprehension disappeared. 'I was so full of hate all I wanted to do now was get to the enemy lines and kill as many as I could.' The battalion advance continued, the men running forward as the Italian guns reloaded and dropping to the ground when they fired. The piper would stop playing each time the whistle blew and blow again each time they rose and advanced again. Barker could not but admire the regimental sergeant major, a picture of nonchalant calm, smoking his pipe and 'swinging his stick with one hand and a .38 Smith and Webley revolver in the other and the pipe going full blast in his mouth as if he were having a Sunday afternoon stroll'. But without artillery cover the advance over open ground to the Italian trenches was a bloody affair:

One bloke was advancing; the next minute his head was gone and twin spurts of red came from his neck as he collapsed to the sand. Another was trying to keep pace with us while holding his intestines in. He had dropped his rifle and was hugging his middle with both arms while staggering forward. The whistle blew and we all got down, but he kept staggering, hoping to catch up, then he jerked as though hit by a big fist and sank to the sand and remained still.

It was now past midday. Suddenly, the long nightmare was over as the Argyll skirmish line hit the forward Italian trenches:

I was face to face with an Italian who was desperately trying to reload his rifle; he never succeeded ... We were now upon the dugouts where the Italians were hunkering down. Some jumped out and ran away into the desert, some stayed to fight and were butchered. 'Anywhere to get away from that advancing line of bayonets,' one Italian said.

There were Italian bodies lying in all kinds of postures: one had a bayonet still in his body and I thought the Jock it belonged to had either not fixed it properly and it came off his rifle as he withdrew, or he had used it like a sword and maybe had been too busy fending off another Italian and just forgot about it. Either way it did not matter now because it was over.

One hundred and thirty-five Argylls fell, killed or wounded, in the attack. Following this assault they were ordered to launch a bayonet attack on some small knolls to their front. To his chagrin Pipe Major Hill was unable to get a note from his pipes, as the drones had filled with sand. The 2nd Camerons were brought up to assist. As they were rushed forward the orders Peter Cochrane received were succinct: 'The Camerons will take Sidi Barrani; the tanks may be on our left and the Queen's on our right. The Argylls got heavy casualties this morning attacking it and the Leicesters were badly cut up. A Company leads, C follows.' Without further ado the Camerons went in with the bayonet, tracing the source of enemy fire to locate positions to attack:

15 Platoon rushed three little hillocks from which fire was coming [recalled Cochrane] and then stumbled into a maze of dugouts or camouflaged emplacements. I fell through the roof of one as far as my armpits just as [Sergeant] Horbury pitched a grenade into its entrance. It is amazing how athletic acute fear can make one; I came out of that roof like a champagne cork, and just in time.

Private Jimmy Mearns was bowled over but a heavy blow to his foot, to discover that an Italian bullet had taken off the heel of his boot.

The only support for the hard-pressed infantry – apart from the Matildas on a portion of the line – was the 15-inch shells fired from out at sea by the Royal Navy monitor HMS *Ladybird*. But the pressure from all points of the compass, now including the sea, was too much for the defenders, and they began to surrender. Barker and his fellow Jocks were disgusted and gave no quarter:

> Upon seeing some of our blokes writhing in pain and some not moving I felt the terrible rage building up inside again. Also one or two Italians were now standing up and raising their arms, but some were still frantically shooting at us. All I wanted to do now was get at these bastards who had been firing at us since dawn . . . Now we had got this close did they expect to put their hands up and surrender just like that, because now there was a chance of their lives being in danger? . . . We ploughed into them.

In the late afternoon to the west of Sidi Barrani the 3rd Hussars joined in a mass tank assault on the town, the pennants of their little tanks fluttering against the setting sun as the vehicles churned over Italian trenches cutting down Italians as they fought or ran:

> Two bursts of Vickers [at one position, described Roy Farran] produced a horde of shouting, pleading and gesticulating prisoners, hands aloft, waving white handkerchiefs. Firing a few rounds at their heels with a pistol, I set them off towards battalion head-quarters at the double. One Breda gunner in the centre fired his weapon to the last, killing the squadron leader of the second wave of cruisers. He was eventually silenced by Sergeant Roper, who ran his light tank over the position.

At nightfall, after a bloody and exhausting day, the Italians surren-dered, and Sidi Barrani was in British hands. Farran was astonished to be confronted near the old white-walled fort by one Italian prisoner with an unusual accent: 'OK, Bud. I'm an honest-to-goodness Ameri-can citizen. Pittsburgh, yeah. I'm no goddamned wop. Yeah, and I fought right alongside the British in 1918. Yeah, and if I could get my hands on that goddamned bastard Mussolini, I'd kill him right now.

Duce! Duce! Who the hell does he think he is with this goddammed Duce?'

Tom Barker sat on the ground and ran the blade of his bayonet through the sand to clean it of Italian blood, his hearing temporarily gone because of the noise of battle. His anger suddenly dissipated and left in its place only feelings of sadness and emptiness. 'What had happened here today was beyond tears. The quiet was unreal except for a ringing in the ears.' Peter Cochrane, likewise, was shocked by his first real experience of battle:

> I was never to get used to the terrible lack of dignity in nearly all the bodies; it seemed in a muddled way that if one had to be killed, one had the right to die decently and not to be left lying about in a posture that too often could only be described as ludicrous. The pathetic was easier to bear – the young man, for instance, doubled back over a gun barrel, letters and snapshots of his girl spilling from an unbuttoned pocket. Ludicrous or pathetic, hideously mutilated or clean killed, they were our fellows though in an unfamiliar uniform, and they had to be buried. But I drew the line at extracting the charred remains of men from burnt-out tanks. That was a sight that led to nightmares.

*

The entirely unexpected success of O'Connor's raid prompted him to ask permission to pursue the enemy out of Egypt. Wavell immediately agreed, but that night the British tanks, doing what they had trained to do during peacetime, went into a leaguer in order to replenish and refuel. This incurred O'Connor's wrath and the pursuit did not resume until the next morning – 11 December – by which time many Italians had escaped into the coastal fortresses of Bardia and Tobruk.

The loss of Sidi Barrani led to the withdrawal of Graziani's shattered forces from Egypt, but the Italian retreat was not always a rout. In the desert far to the south British reconnaissance showed that the Italians had abandoned Rabia and Sofafi camps without a fight but west of Buq Buq the 64th Catanzaro Division, under General Armico, strongly dug into the dunes and cunningly sited behind some salt flats, decided to resist O'Connor's seemingly relentless advance. Armico had thirty-five artillery pieces and anti-tank guns covering the route to the east and another twenty-five guns guarding the south. A hastily assembled force of cruiser and light tanks under the command of Lieutenant Colonel John Combe of the 11th Hussars was sent in to attack the position. To their consternation the British were stopped by a combination of excellent Italian gunnery, poor reconnaissance and the dangerous enthusiasm of British cavalry for the charge. Many of the light tanks of the 3rd Hussars were caught in the salt flats and, once immobilized, destroyed by the Italian guns, their hapless crews incinerated in their vehicles or scythed down by Italian machine-gun fire as they attempted to flee. The position was finally broken following a flank attack by cruisers of the 8th Hussars along the Italians' seaward flank, and O'Connor's advance continued.

On the fourth night of the advance Captain Leakey was told to cut the road to the north that linked Fort Capuzzo with Sidi Azeiz and Bardia. Creeping forward without lights in the pitch darkness, with Leakey walking in front to lead the way, the British force soon spotted the road, which was busy with heavy trucks full of troops and supplies.

I ordered the tanks to form line on either side of my tank, and warned them about the closeness of the enemy. When all reported that they were in position and had identified their targets, I gave the order to open fire. In a second the darkness was cut by line after line of tracer bullets, and each line found its mark in an Italian lorry. The poor devils never stood a chance; as each lorry burst into flames the survivors could be seen clambering over the back and disappearing into the darkness. Not a shot came back at us, and within a minute all guns were silent. Only the groans of wounded Italians and the crackle of fires disturbed the stillness of the night.

Not everything went as planned, however. Next day a somewhat foolish attempt to rush the gates of Bardia was repulsed by Italian artillery fire and anti-tank weapons as Leakey's squadron (1st RTR) indulged in an ill-considered charge. Recognizing that in this instance discretion was more sensible than valour, Leakey ordered his tanks to turn around and retire. It was very nearly his last command:

> As my tank turned off the road, a shell exploded beneath one of the tracks and we were immobilized. As Doyle [his driver] and the two sub-turret gunners were now serving no useful purpose by staying in the tank, I told them to bail out. Through the dust and smoke I could see two tanks inside the barrier shooting at us. I got Milligan on to them, and he fired one shell, and that was all.
>
> At that moment Adams shouted, 'She's on fire,' and I saw the flames spreading across the bottom of the turret. We were out before the ammunition exploded and I dashed round to the front of the tank to check that the other three had got away. One sub-turret was half open, and a glance was enough to convince me that this young soldier was dead. An anti-tank shell had pierced the armour and hit him square in the face. He was not a pretty sight.
>
> A ditch alongside the side of the road saved our lives, and fifteen minutes later we were back with the rest of the squadron.

*

The news took time to filter back to Britain. The situation on 11 December remained unclear in London. Having fully supported Wavell's plan in the face of Churchill's determination to send troops from Egypt to Greece, Foreign Secretary Anthony Eden waited anxiously for news:

> As I was reading a later telegram which showed us still closer to Sidi Barrani but situation still obscure, Haining [vice chief of the Imperial General Staff] came in with a brief but triumphant message that Sidi Barrani had been captured with large numbers of prisoners. 7th Australian [sic] Brigade and support group manoeuvring to cut off enemy in Sofafi area. Three generals captured. Rang Winston, who congratulated me warmly on a great victory. Spoke to Jack Dill [Chief of the Imperial General Staff

(CIGS)] later, who was delighted. Sent a joint telegram to Wavell. It all seemed too good to be true.

At the same time the news also reached Rome, and came, Ciano recorded, like a thunderbolt. When the news broke on 10 December, Ciano at first thought that the situation was not serious, 'but subsequent cables from Graziani confirm that we have taken a beating'. The following day the news got worse:

> Things are really going badly in Libya. Four divisions can be considered destroyed, and Graziani, who reports on the spirit and decision of the enemy, says nothing about what he can do to parry the blow. Mussolini still hopes that Graziani can and will stop the English advance. If it can be stopped at the old boundary, he thinks the situation will not be serious; if the English should reach Tobruk, then he thinks 'the situation would become tragic'.
>
> During the evening news arrives that the Catanzaro division [at Buq Buq] did not hold against the English push but was itself torn to pieces. Something is the matter with our army if five divisions let themselves be pulverized in two days.

Five days later Ciano received the Marchesa Graziani, who tearfully waved her husband's latest letter, enclosing his will, in which he had written that 'one cannot break steel armour with fingernails alone'. Ciano concluded that the marshal – to say nothing of his wife – had 'lost his self-control'.

The British success at Sidi Barrani electrified the world, constituting the first large-scale defeat of Axis forces – albeit Italian and Libyan – in the war. Colonel Bonner Fellers returned from the desert full of admiration for how the British operation had been kept secret. 'General Wavell told me they were going to do manoeuvres, so up I went as an observer, and – God damn it – it was the works,' he effused to whosoever would listen. Sirry, the Egyptian prime minister, was especially surprised that his own otherwise impeccable intelligence sources had failed to predict the British offensive. The victory had a profound effect on the United States, and did much to garner support for plucky Britain standing alone against the bully-boy tactics of the fascists. It also attracted many foreign journalists – especially American – to Cairo, with the result that the campaign, as it developed over the following days and weeks, was well covered in the world press. 'The Old Country is in there pitching,' exulted the famous American columnist Walter Winchell from Cairo, reflecting the excited sentiments of many.

Shocked by the ferocity and magnitude of the British land, sea and air attack, the Italian army was now in full retreat. In the days that followed the forts at Capuzzo and Sidi Omar, ten miles to the south, were cut off by the encircling tentacles of 7th Armoured Division's advance. On 16 December 2nd RTR led an assault with the 3rd and 7th Hussars on Sidi Omar, approaching the fort from the west – opposite the expected direction of attack – in what Roy Farran described as a 'glorious charge, in the old cavalry style, with the pennants flying in the wind, the commanders cheering and waving their hats, and the Vickers chattering away like rattles at a fair'. With two batteries of 25-pounders from the RHA in support, the fort surrendered in a mere ten minutes, with nearly 1,000 soldiers going into the bag. Captain Pat Hobart, commanding C Squadron 2nd RTR, led the charge:

> The enemy must have suffered pretty severely from the attentions of the RHA, for in we went unscathed, with every gun and machine gun firing. My orders to the squadron were to drive straight through the perimeter, doing as much destruction as possible, out the other side, and then to rally back on the near side. I was in the centre of the squadron line, and in an excess of zeal and enthusiasm charged the fort itself.

Unfortunately for Hobart his Matilda struck part of the wall of the fort and became wedged. The driver of the next tank, Sergeant Bermingham, recalled that, looking through his visor, he 'could see Captain Hobart, with steel helmet on, shooting away over the top of his cupola with a pistol. The sight of a second tank inside the fort must have been too much for the Italians and very soon they were appearing from nooks and crannies everywhere to give themselves up.' Entering the fort, Cyril Joly was staggered at 'the fabulous nature of the loot which fell into our hands.'

> In the captured camps and stores we found pistols and automatics to delight the eyes of all; cameras, brilliant dress uniforms, gorgeously jewelled swords, silver and gilt belts and emblazoned leather equipment. Some found huge quantities of Italian money. Most important to anyone living on the barest rations, as we in the Western Desert Force were compelled to do, were the stocks of food which we captured: rich red and white wines, cases of matured brandy and liqueurs, bottled fruits, frozen hams and anchovies, tins of beef, sacks of macaroni, potatoes, onions and carrots, minestrone soup.

Not all Italian soldiers enjoyed these luxuries. The vast gap between the comforts enjoyed by the officers and those available to the other ranks astonished the British and Australians and presumably contributed considerably to the unwillingness of the Italian rank and file to sacrifice their lives in battle with the willingness that their officers demanded. While Italian officers slept in beds with sheets, the soldiers had a far rougher time, suffering poor food and spartan conditions.

By 15 December all enemy troops had been driven out of Egypt, and the 4th and 7th Armoured and the 16th Infantry Brigades now set their sights on Bardia, to where many of the retreating Italians had fled, believing themselves safe within its miles of concrete defences, guns, mines and barbed wire. After the success at Sidi Barrani an exuberant Churchill had signalled Wavell, 'Naturally pursuit will hold the first place in your thoughts . . . It looks as if these people were ripe corn for the sickle.' Four days later he signalled again: 'Your first objective now must be to maul the Italian Army and rip them off the African shore to the utmost possible extent.' The day following, delighted to hear Wavell confirm the pursuit to Bardia, he telegrammed, 'St. Matthew, chapter 7, verse 7. "Ask, and it shall be given to you; seek, and ye shall find; knock and it shall be opened unto you."' Not to be outdone, Wavell replied, 'St. James, chapter 1, verse 17. "Every good and perfect gift is from above, and cometh down from the Father of lights, with whom is no variableness, neither shadow of turning."'

Six days after the first attacks had begun on Nibeiwa camp, over 38,000 prisoners, 400 guns, more than seventy tanks and much other war material had now fallen into British hands. British casualties amounted to a mere 133 killed, 387 wounded and 8 missing. It was an entirely unexpected victory for the exhausted British, who at best had expected a five-day raid to unsettle Graziani. 'You know, I never thought it would go like this,' Wavell admitted to his naval opposite number, Admiral Andrew Cunningham, C-in-C Mediterranean Fleet. On 6 December Wavell had sent a telegram to General Dill, CIGS in London, warning against excessive expectations about what the raid would achieve. 'We are greatly outnumbered on the ground and in [the] air,' he wrote, 'have to move over 75 miles of desert and attack enemy who has fortified himself for three months. Please do not encourage optimism.'

The outcome of O'Connor's offensive was equally unexpected to the Italians, whose collapse shocked Mussolini into speechlessness. On Christmas Eve he returned to a recurring theme in his discussions with Ciano: the weakness of the Italian race. The Italians had failed in North Africa because as a people they were pathetic. Observing the snow falling outside he remarked, 'This snow and cold are very good. This is how our good-for-nothing men and this mediocre race will be improved.' Of Graziani, Ciano had noted on 12 December that he had suffered grievously 'from the blow he has suffered, and besides it seems that his nerves are quite shaken ... In Libya he has a shelter built in a Roman tomb at Cyrene, sixty or seventy feet deep. Now he is upset and cannot make decisions. He pins his hopes on the possible exhaustion of the adversary, and not on his own strength, which is a bad sign.' It got worse. The following day, it was clear that 'Graziani has lost his self-control'. 'A catastrophic cable from Graziani has arrived, a mixture of excitement, rhetoric and concern. He is thinking of withdrawing to Tripoli, "in order to keep the flag flying on that fortress at least", but he is inclined to accuse Rome, meaning Mussolini, of having forced him to wage a war "of the flea against the elephant".'

Observing the pessimistic signals emanating from Graziani's

Cyrene tomb, Mussolini could only observe wearily, 'Here is another man with whom I cannot get angry, because I despise him.' Nine days later Ciano was shocked to hear Mussolini openly talking about possible German military help in Libya, wondering whether they might consider sending two armoured divisions.

As Christmas approached, O'Connor's forces isolated Bardia from the road to Tobruk and prepared to assault the formidable fortress-port. Wavell had decided to send the 4th Indian Division to fight the Italians in Eritrea, and to replace them in the Western Desert Force with the Australian 6th Infantry Division, which had been training in the Nile Delta since arriving from Palestine in September. The decision was a blow to O'Connor, as the 4th Indian Division had demonstrated considerable skill in the fighting. He was loath to lose it, facing the prospect of clearing Bardia with a depleted armoured division (now reduced to 108 light and 59 cruiser tanks, while the 7th RTR had only 26 Matildas left) and the blooded but dwindling British 16th Infantry Brigade and its contingent of Free French marines. Clearing the desert of Italian forces, bringing up the untried Australians – who were not expected outside Bardia until 27 December at the earliest – and resupplying his corps took time, and a coordinated attack against Bardia could not be planned before the New Year.

The fortified port of Bardia would be a tough proposition, an entirely more worrisome prospect than the camps. It was defended on its landward side by an eighteen-mile concrete perimeter complete with barbed wire and an anti-tank ditch and garrisoned by an estimated 25,000 troops, together with over 400 artillery pieces and 12 medium and 100 light tanks. The garrison was commanded by Lieutenant General Annibale Bergonzoli, known to both Italians and Britons as *Barba-Electrica* (Electric Whiskers) on account of his carefully groomed forked beard. Despite his somewhat theatrical appearance he possessed a formidable reputation as a soldier. 'In Bardia we are, and here we stay,' he replied dramatically to Mussolini's exhortation to defend the fortress whatever the cost. To make things worse for the Allies the weather turnéd over Christmas, heavy rain, icy winds and sleet bringing the daytime temperatures down, making life in the desert for the ill-clad infantry truly miserable. 'Defences of Bardia are strong . . .' warned Wavell in a message to London on 19 December.

'Hunt is still going but first racing burst over, hounds brought to their noses, huntsmen must cast and second horses badly wanted. It may be necessary to dig out this fox.'

Such references to hunting were frequent in British cavalry and yeomanry (Territorial Army cavalry) regiments, and all Sandhurst cadets were expected to follow the beagles in order to develop an eye for ground. For Gunner Leonard Tutt of 414 Battery, Essex Yeomanry, equipped with 25-pounders, his CO's exhortations before the attack on Bardia 'were so peppered with tally-hos and talk of flushing out the fox and making a good kill that in the end we were not sure whether to put on our tin hats or our hunting pinks. I think, had we raised a fox in the course of the battle, we would have lost half the battery after it.'

Despite the weather British morale remained very high, and when combined with the green enthusiasm of the 6th Australian Division and the shattering reverse suffered by the Italians, O'Connor judged that the advantage remained with him. In addition he enjoyed naval support: the Royal Navy monitors HMS *Terror* and HMS *Aphis*, which could lob 6-inch high-explosive [HE] shells into the confined fortress, together with the guns of the battleships *Warspite*, *Valiant* and *Barham*. He also had Wellington bombers flying in from Malta, and Blenheims from Egypt.

The attack began before dawn on Tuesday 3 January 1941 with an artillery assault by every one of O'Connor's available 120 guns, following a night of heavy bombardment from the air and sea. Combat engineers had crept forward under cover of the barrage to clear mines and create a path through the anti-tank obstacles for the infantry to break through. In little under an hour this task was completed, after which the infantrymen of two Australian brigades forced their way through the defences. Wrapped against the biting cold in thick sleeveless sheepskin jerkins, the Diggers (as Australian soldiers were universally called) secured a path into the fortress for the 7th RTR Matildas, and the much vaunted defences began to crumble. But although the outer perimeter was breached relatively quickly and some defenders rapidly surrendered, fierce independent actions and the vast extent of the fortress meant that the fighting continued until the late afternoon of Saturday 7 December.

The report filed by the British journalist Jan Yindrich for the Australian Associated Press on 6 January 1941 was headlined SMASH WAY THROUGH MODERN HINDENBURG LINE: FEW CASUALTIES IN CAPTURING 25,000 PRISONERS. Yindrich had made his way to the front and was in a position to report back what he had seen at first hand. He marvelled at the courage and ability of the raw Australian troops: 'To bring about the capture of Bardia ... the Australian infantry, supported by British tanks, broke though a fortified line, comparable in strength with the Hindenburg Line of the Great War. It was manned by an Italian force which outnumbered by over 5 to 1 the troops who actually made the assault and carried it through to Bardia itself.'

'The attack, when it came,' reported an Australian sergeant to Jan Yindrich, 'was a sight a man will never forget':

With the engineers in the ditch the infantry advanced across the open, firing Bren guns from the hips, shouting 'Bardia or bust' and singing 'Roll out the Barrel'. They were on top of the Italian posts before the Italians knew they were there, and pushed onwards to the next line of posts. Twenty minutes later the tanks went through.

Here and there a handful of men were left to clean up the posts. At one post two young infantrymen took a whole garrison of over seventy officers and men who occupied a labyrinth of deep concrete trenches, equipped with four heavy machine guns.

'We went over with such a rush,' said a weary major afterwards, 'that the Italians just threw up their hands.' Although fighting continued throughout the day and was fierce in places, tanks and infantry making repeated counter-attacks, it rarely took much to induce the surrender of an Italian post. Corporal Rawson of 2/3rd Battalion (Australian infantry) advanced into the assault but struggled to make his way through Italians crowding out, trying to surrender. Most Italian posts surrendered after a few well-aimed grenades. One machine-gun post resisted for a while, and the Australians prepared to launch a bayonet attack against it. 'The section leader gave an order to charge, but before we got very far a row of white flags went up as if by signal. The gunner in the centre had apparently been shot in the head and when he was killed the others surrendered.' Yindrich mused:

The Australians probably bayoneted very few Italians, because their zeal in mopping up terrified them into surrender. One private took thirty prisoners with a mere whirl of the bayonet. After the Australian commander hauled down the Italian flag, hundreds of Italians, with resignation stamped on their bearded and haggard faces, voluntarily submitted. Five hundred were rounded up in the town itself, many more in the surrounding gulches, and innumerable of them in the caves. A single Australian officer, with eight men and a Bren gun, captured 2,000 in one cave, and marched them off without further assistance. The prisoners were then marshalled into batches of 500, usually with a single guard, and none tried to escape.

For Gunner Leonard Tutt, however, the striking thing about the defence of Bardia was that inside the defences the Italian gunners had remained with their guns, and died at them. 'Their bodies were scattered close to their firing positions and they must have remained in action until our infantry tanks and the Australians had overrun their gun sites.' The ease with which many Italians surrendered hid the reality that a large number fought ferociously. However, the Australians convincingly demonstrated that their valour and the hard training in Palestine and Egypt in recent months were more than adequate to bring them through the trials of battle. In the course of the fighting 130 Australians were killed and a further 326 wounded.

While the Australians were attacking from the south-east Captain Rea Leakey and his squadron were ordered to provide a diversionary attack in the north-east. The aim was to distract the Italian gunners and so give the assaulting Australians a chance to get through the defences. A number of rushes against the perimeter with all guns blazing were successfully undertaken. But then things went wrong:

In the last run that we made one of the light tanks got a little too close to an anti-tank gun and received several direct hits which penetrated the armour. Of the crew of three the driver was killed by the first shot, and the commander, our newest young officer, had one of his hands shattered. The driver's foot still rested on the accelerator and the tank continued to motor in towards the enemy. All this the young commander told us over the air, and we were powerless to help him.

He was still talking on the wireless when suddenly he yelled, 'The tank's on fire.' He must have then dropped his microphone, but the wireless was switched to Send, and it broadcast to the rest of the squadron the happenings inside that turret. The tank was closed down, and before the two in the turret could bail out they had to open up the hatches. We heard the gunner yelling to his officer to help him because by this time he had evidently been wounded, while the commander shouted that both hatches were stuck fast. Then we all heard the most terrible screams of agony; they were being burnt alive while their tomb of fire still drove on towards the enemy.

The heavy naval and aerial bombardment of Bardia had significantly demoralized the defenders. On New Year's Day 1941 the British dropped 20,000 pounds of bombs before lunch from RAF Wellingtons and ancient Bombay bombers, as well as from Fleet Air Arm Swordfish; the following day forty-four sorties were flown over the fortress and on the evening of 2 January a further 30,000 pounds of bombs were dropped. One of the two Italian generals captured said that the garrison was so harassed by British air attacks that by the time the final assault came, with shelling from all sides, including the sea, and continuous bombing and machine-gunning from the air, the defenders had been reduced to utter helplessness. He admitted that he had only escaped the attentions of the RAF by hiding beneath some desert scrub. Of the two captains with him, one was killed outright and the other died of heart failure.

The scale of the British and Australian victory only began to emerge gradually, but it was soon clear that Yindrich's estimate of 25,000 prisoners was a serious miscalculation. When the counting was over 45,000 prisoners and 462 guns, 117 light and 12 medium tanks and 700 trucks had fallen into Commonwealth hands. Many of the Italians (presumably those quickest to surrender) were evacuees from Sidi Barrani. In Rome news of this further disaster shook public confidence to the core. The reasons for such a massive defeat eluded Ciano. On 5 January he wrote desperately in his diary, 'Ever since 4 p.m. yesterday Bardia radio has been silent. We know what is happening only from the British communiqués. The resistance of our troops was brief – a matter of hours. And yet there was no lack of weapons. The guns alone numbered 430. Why didn't the fight last longer?' For Mussolini the reason was glaringly simple: the unwarlike temperament of his troops. 'Five generals are prisoners and one is dead,' he moaned. 'This is the percentage of Italians who have military characteristics and those who have none.' London was staggered at the scale of the victory, prompting the prime minister to ponder what might come of Italy's humiliation. 'Time is short,' warned Churchill presciently on 6 January. 'I cannot believe that Hitler will not intervene soon . . .'

Surgeon-Commander Sorley, principal medical officer on HMS *Barham*, wrote to his wife in England on news that Bardia had fallen:

The war is going fairly well for us at the moment. The Italians are beginning to wish they had never heard of Mussolini. The Western Desert campaign has almost culminated in the capture of Bardia by the Australians. Just imagine the Aussies up against the Italians. They'll go through them like a knife through butter, and won't stand on ceremony. I like a story I saw in the paper today. Graziani sent a message to Mussolini by telegram: 'What do you know about these Australians, Musso?' Musso said, 'Well, I don't know much about them,' and Graziani replied, 'Well, somebody told me that eleven of them beat all England – and there are thousands coming at me now.'

A few days after its fall, Padre J.C. Salter, chaplain to the 4th Australian General Hospital, moving through Bardia after being rescued from shipwreck, was amused to see how his countrymen had already placed their stamp on the once proud Italian frontier town. 'Rue de Mussolini, for example, by which name the main street was designated,' he noted, 'had its name plate almost obliterated, and Rue de Ned Kelly substituted.' Like Cyril Joly at Sidi Omar, the Australians were astonished at the luxury in which the Italian troops – especially officers – lived in the field. Moorehead described

> Officers' beds laid out with clean sheets, chests of drawers filled with linen and an abundance of fine clothing of every kind. Uniforms heavy with gold lace and decked with the medals and colours of the parade ground ... Pale blue sashes and belts finished with great tassels and feathered and embroidered hats and caps ... great blue cavalry cloaks that swathed a man to the ankles, and dressing tables ... strewn with scents and silver-mounted brushes.

Twenty-one-year-old Gunner John Kelly of 51st Heavy Anti-Aircraft Regiment was also staggered at the amount of kit left by the Italians. Vehicles, weapons and ammunition of all descriptions littered the place: trucks, cars, motorcycles, bicycles, tanks, Breda guns, rifles, thousands of rounds of ammunition and red 'money box' hand grenades by the thousand. He was shocked by the comparative luxury in which the Italian soldier lived: electric lights, beds, cognac, wine and even women. He picked up a small Italian Beretta automatic pistol and enough rounds to prosecute a small war of his own, as well as a pair of comfortable boots, tins of food, a cask of cognac and a motorbike! Likewise, Rea Leakey found himself examining hastily vacated Italian accommodation: 'I was amazed at the comfort in which these Italians lived, but even more so by the quantity of scent, hair grease and other effeminate toilet articles that were to be found in every man's room; they must have spent much of their day beautifying themselves for the benefit of the ladies of the brothel which occupied the best buildings in the place.'

*

The momentum gained by the fall of Bardia persuaded O'Connor that Tobruk should also be seized, even though this formed no part of the original plan. Wavell immediately agreed. Lying some eighty miles further west, the town boasted a shallow harbour like a lagoon – the only natural anchorage between Sfaz in Tunisia and Alexandria in Egypt – and was surrounded on three sides by hills that sloped gently to the water's edge. During the 1930s the Italians had spent a small fortune here creating a military base from which they could govern the coast. The massive defensive works included thirty-five miles of extensive concrete fortifications spreading protectively in a half-moon shape through the desert to surround the small town and its harbour, which formed the apex of the defences. The 127 concreted emplacements on the perimeter were flush with the surface of the desert. The perimeter was defended by an anti-tank ditch – which was however at many points not deep enough to be effective – as well as extensive barbed-wire, minefield and anti-aircraft defences. The *San Giorgio*, its shattered hull sitting on the harbour bottom, nevertheless still employed her anti-aircraft guns effectively.

To Mussolini's anguish Tobruk fell in only two days. The 7th Armoured Division had cut off the town from Derna in the west by 6 January, and forced the Italians to withdraw into the fortress to join those who, like General Bergonzoli, had managed to escape from Bardia. The attack was a repeat of the successful assault on Bardia. The Australian 16th Brigade broke into Tobruk on the south-east perimeter in an assault that began at first light on 21 January through a point in the defences where aerial reconnaissance and extensive patrolling had indicated that the anti-tank ditch was passable. Following a heavy artillery bombardment, the eighteen remaining Matildas of 7th RTR punched a hole deep in the defences, from which the Australian infantry fanned out. Roy Farran, commanding his troop of Mark VIs, was impressed by the sight of the attack. 'The great tanks lumbered forward, spitting death from their guns, while hordes of Australians swaggered along behind, the sun glistening on their bayonets as they moved along with the same steady, loping gait.' A naval and aerial bombardment also preceded the attack, RAF Wellingtons and Blenheims dropping twenty tons of bombs during the two preceding nights. The first target for the assaulting troops was the crossroads at Sidi Mahmoud, soon to be known to Briton and Australian alike as King's Cross. The *Melbourne Age* exulted:

> British sappers were first in the field gashing the heavy barbed-wire entanglements which were protecting strong points, although

under heavy fire. Tanks crashed their way through with steel-helmeted British and Australian troops close behind. They quickly subdued the two nearest strong points, and then the bulk of the troops poured through the gap. The Italians, after the fan-like movement was carried out, found themselves sandwiched by attackers, and surrendered after a brief struggle. The British consolidated their advanced position throughout the night, and dawn found them ready for the final drive.

The 17th Brigade followed through the hole that the 16th had punched in the perimeter, and the 19th Brigade arrived with the third wave to secure the town. Hard initial fighting was often quickly followed by the mass surrender of hundreds of Italian soldiers unwilling to die for the Duce's ambitions: groups of 300, 600, 1,000 men were not unusual. When a group of Australians began attacking a complex of tunnels built into the side of the lower escarpment in the area of Fort Solaro, they were approached by an Italian officer and told that the commander of the Tobruk garrison was inside but would surrender only to an officer. Lieutenant Copland was sent into the complex and led to an Italian officer who appeared, old, dignified and tired. '*Officier?*' enquired the Italian. '*Oui, officier,*' replied Copland. They saluted each other and seventy-two-year-old General Petassi Manella handed the young Australian his pistol. '*C'est la guerre,*' said Copeland, in an attempt to commiserate with the dejected Italian general. '*Oui, c'est la guerre,*' replied Manella. By the end of the day it was clear that the end was nigh. As triumphant though exhausted Australians gazed towards the oily smoke pouring skywards from the stricken harbour some 8,000 bedraggled Italians made their way to the large POW cage at King's Cross, built to house their expected British and Australian prisoners.

That evening and through the night the crump of explosions in Tobruk town and port were testimony to the efforts of the defenders to sabotage what they could before surrendering. The next morning the Australian 19th Brigade advanced into the town, descending through the final escarpment led by two Bren gun carriers commanded by Lieutenant Hennessy of the 6th Division's cavalry regiment. No opposition was put up, and even when stopped by a barrier across the road two Italian soldiers ran out to help remove it. After firing some warning shots at Italians who appeared to have hostile intentions the force proceeded cautiously into the town, where they were met by an Italian naval officer who took them to receive the surrender of Admiral Massimiliano Vietina, who offered Hennessy his sword. Very lights were fired into the air to signal the surrender, and in the absence of a flag a Digger ran a distinctive Australian slouch hat up a flagpole, and thousands of Italian naval personnel began to assemble themselves in an orderly fashion to march into captivity. The Australian journalist Chester Wilmot came across a party of Italian POWs escorted into captivity by a Digger decked out in the uniform and badges of an Italian captain. When enquiry was made as to the provenance of the uniform the Digger replied, 'I swapped 'em – for a coupla fags; for 'alf a bloody packet I coulda been a blasted general.' In the days that followed the most accurate count indicated that about 27,000 Italians had been taken prisoner, together with 208 guns, 237 tanks, 200 vehicles and enough supplies of food and bottled water to keep the Italians going for two months, although once again General Bergonzoli managed to evade his pursuers. After walking the eighty miles from Bardia, he had been flown out of Tobruk before the attack began. Australian casualties were less serious than at Bardia, with 49 killed and 306 wounded.

Despite the destruction in the harbour a number of jetties remained usable, as were the two water plants which converted seawater into fresh. Wavell wasted no time, sending convoys into the port within days to resupply O'Connor's heavily stretched troops. Doctor Theodore Stephanides, medical officer to a Cypriot labour battalion supporting the British advance, observed acutely the shambolic after-effects of defeat on the morning of the Italian surrender:

> We soon passed the barbed wire and concertina wire and the tank traps of the Tobruk perimeter and the usual litter of a rout began to appear. Burst-open suitcases . . . accoutrements, weapons, a few steel helmets, scraps of uniforms and an occasional dead body (usually Italian) which had not yet been cleared up . . .
>
> At first glance – when seen from a distance – Tobruk made a beautiful picture with its flat-roofed, dazzling white houses

crowded together on the flank of a low slope overlooking a small landlocked and brilliantly blue bay. What struck me most was the immense amount of Italian shipping sunk in the harbour, masts stuck up everywhere out of the water like pins in a pin cushion.

The headline in the *Melbourne Age* on 24 January read BRILLIANT ATTACK WINS TOBRUK. Headlines of a different sort would have dominated the Italian newspapers had the fascist regime allowed freedom of the press. 'Tobruk has fallen,' lamented Ciano to his diary on 22 January. He could not believe the news.

There has been a little more fighting but only a little. The Duce is allowing himself to be lulled by his illusions. I thought it necessary to speak to him with brusque frankness. 'At Sidi Barrani,' I said, 'they spoke of surprise. Then you counted upon Bardia, where there was Bergonzoli, the heroic Bergonzoli. Bardia yielded after two hours. Then you placed your hopes in Tobruk because Pitassi Mannella, the king of artillerymen, was there. Tobruk has been easily wrested from us. Now you speak with great faith of the escarpment of Derna. I beg to differ with your dangerous illusions. The trouble is serious, mysterious, and deep.'

Private John Parish of the Kings Royal Rifle Corps arrived in Tobruk on the day it surrendered and was set to work to make the port usable. He had Italian POWs to assist in clearing up the debris, many of whom were only too willing to help. The port had been heavily sabotaged and much plant and equipment destroyed or damaged. The job involved rebuilding demolished quays, clearing wreckage. As time went by, the Italians on these duties were allowed to travel daily between the POW cage at King's Cross and the harbour without guards. On one occasion an Italian POW wearing British khaki drill paraded with his new colleagues for an inspection by a new senior officer who had clearly, by his white knees, only recently arrived from the UK. Moving along the line of soldiers the officer enquired of the man where he came from. 'Italy, sir,' was the answer. 'Excellent,' replied the officer. 'We need more chaps like you.' Lieutenant Commander Lamb, harbourmaster at Tobruk, commented that everybody employed Italian prisoners. 'They rarely turned out to be cooks,' he commented, 'but invariably made admirable, if rather effusive, waiters.'

Cyrenaica now lay open to O'Connor but for Graziani's remaining forces, which were entrenched on the coast at Derna and at the desert fort of Mechili, where his armour was concentrated under General Babini. O'Connor attacked the former with the Australians of the 19th Infantry Brigade, while the 7th Armoured Division struck at Mechili.

The first tank-on-tank battle of the campaign took place at Mechili on the evening of 23 January, the seventy tanks of Babini's armoured brigade fighting with unusual tenacity. By the end of the battle Cyril Joly's 2nd RTR had knocked out nine Italian M13s for the loss of one cruiser and six light tanks of the 7th Hussars, one of which was Second Lieutenant Roy Farran's. At Derna extremely strong defences to the east of the town in Wadi Derna held up the Australians for four days, with Italian shellfire being particularly effective. But by the end of the month resistance was visibly diminishing, the remaining armoured forces from Mechili escaping into the Jebel Akhdar by 27 January and the defenders of Derna beginning to withdraw on the 30th.

By early February it was clear to O'Connor that Graziani was not merely pulling back in the east, but was preparing to withdraw his forces from Cyrenaica entirely. This assessment offered O'Connor a brand new opportunity: despite the exhaustion of his troops, the heavy wear on his tanks and vehicles and the bitter cold of the wet desert winter, an audacious move now might enable him to destroy Graziani entirely. As the crow flew, the distance between Mechili and the coast south of Benghazi on the Gulf of Sirte was a mere 150 miles, cutting across the desert south of the Jebel Akhdar. The route, however, was unmapped and unreconnoitred but known to be rough, waterless desert. While the Australian 6th Division pushed hard against the Italians in the north along the coast, O'Connor determined, with Wavell's blessing, to send what was left of the 7th Armoured Division by this route to cut the road south of Benghazi and destroy the remainder of General Tellera's 10th Army as it attempted to flee into Tripolitania.

O'Connor had hoped that he might be given two weeks to resupply his exhausted 13th Corps (the Western Desert Force had changed its name on 1 January) before continuing his advance. The 7th Armoured Division was by now reduced to about forty cruisers and eighty light tanks, all of which were in a poor state of repair. It was clear by Monday 3 February, however, when the Australians discovered the ancient Greek and Roman town of Cyrene (latterly Graziani's Cyrenaican headquarters) evacuated, and Barce further to the west also abandoned, that Graziani was beginning a full-scale withdrawal from Cyrenaica. This forced O'Connor to act immediately with what he had to hand. Accordingly, he ordered an immediate reconfiguring of his forces. His desert thrust comprised a group of some 2,000 men based around the newly reinforced 4th Armoured Brigade (3rd and 7th Hussars and 2nd RTR) with two squadrons of the 11th Hussars and a squadron of armoured cars from the newly arrived King's Dragoon Guards; the infantrymen of the 2nd Rifle Brigade in trucks; the 25-pounders of the 4th RHA and a battery of 2-pounder anti-tank guns of 106th RHA. Each tank was loaded with two days' worth of rations and water, and topped up with ammunition and fuel.

The advance across the uncharted desert from Mechili began at dawn on 4 February. The terrain was littered with rocks and large boulders, and the tanks had to pick their way carefully to avoid throwing tracks or otherwise damaging the vehicles. Ordinarily the armour would have stopped at last light to leaguer but on this occasion, as speed was imperative, the advance continued in the moonlight. 'It was bitterly cold,' Cyril Joly recalled, 'so that my face soon became frozen and raw and was painful to touch.'

> Occasionally I glanced down into the turret to reassure myself that I was not dreaming the whole situation. In the eerie light cast by the single red warning bulb of the wireless set I could see, beyond the glinting metal of the gun breech, the huddled figure of Tilden. At my feet, crouched forward peering through the gun telescope – his only view of the outside world – sat Holten, on the alert ... Beyond, and further down and forward, I could see Syke's head and shoulders silhouetted against the panel and instrument lights on the forward armoured bulkhead.

Stopping in the dark cold at about 1 a.m. some distance short of Msus, the division was ready to depart again at first light on Tuesday 5 February. Because of the slowness of the tanks and the urgency of getting to the coast road before the retreating Italians it was decided to divide the force into two groups. The faster, under Lieutenant Colonel John Combe of the 11th Hussars, set off with all haste. Combeforce comprised two squadrons of the 11th Hussars, the 2nd Rifle Brigade in Bren gun carriers and trucks, and two batteries of 25-pounders. Behind, advancing more slowly, came the remainder of the 4th Armoured Brigade, with the understrength 7th Armoured Brigade and the rest of the support group bringing up the rear. Broken-down trucks and tanks littered the route. 'My God,' O'Connor said nervously on seeing yet another abandoned vehicle as he followed. 'Do you think it's going to be all right?'

It was. On their last drops of petrol Combeforce struck the coast road near Sidi Saleh about noon ten miles south of Beda Fomm, the road dominated by a rise to the north – nicknamed the 'Pimple' by the troops – and a white mosque to the east. The 2nd Rifle Brigade immediately deployed in a thin screen of rifles, machine guns and 2-pounder anti-tank guns between the road and the sea, dug in among the undulations of the sand and rock, behind which, nearly half a mile to the rear, were placed the guns of 4th RHA. The old armoured cars of the 11th Hussars and Kings Dragoon Guards found fire positions as best they could. The few anti-tank mines they had were placed on and astride the road. Almost immediately battle was joined. At 2.30 p.m. the front end of a vast convoy of retreating Italians stretching as far as the eye could see encountered the block. The road erupted in sheets of flame and billowing smoke as the first shells found their mark, and the Rifle Brigade's machine guns began to chatter.

The British force was a rude shock to the Italians, many hundreds of whom were base and support staff and civilians being escorted to safety away from the rapidly approaching Australian threat to the north. Graziani had known that the British were attempting to strike through the desert but had no notion that the threat was of a scale sufficient to take on the remainder of the entire 10th Army. For the rest of the afternoon the Italians fought desperately to find a way through, but despite the rapidly diminishing British stocks of ammu-

1. British troops and tanks make their way through the Western Desert, January 1941.

2. A British 40mm Bofors anti-aircraft gun overlooking the harbour soon after the capture of Tobruk from the Italians in January 1941. These were soon dug in, and operated in defence of the water distillery.

3. The Queen of the Battlefield. The British 'I' (Infantry) tank, commonly known as a Matilda, was largely invulnerable on the battlefield, until the Germans began using new 50mm anti-tank guns, and the 88mm anti-aircraft gun in the ground role. In this photograph a Matilda can be seen entering Tobruk on 24 January 1941, carrying an Italian flag to indicate the cessation of fighting.

4. The Italian cruiser *San Giorgio* on fire following a British attack on 21 January 1941.

5. Tobruk harbour on the day it was captured from the Italians on 24 January 1941. The tanks in the foreground are Italian M13s, painted with a distinctive white kangaroo by their new owners.

6. Major General Leslie Morshead, GOC of the Australian 9th Division that successfully defended Tobruk between April and October 1941. Australian infantry, manning the perimeter defences, were supported by British artillery, anti-aircraft artillery and tanks.

7. Lieutenant General Manfred Rommel in his staff car in the desert outside Tobruk, 1942.

8. Australian 'Diggers' guard a group of German and Italian prisoners captured on 14 April 1941.

9. One of the Panzer Mark IVs destroyed during the April battles.

10. German field artillery in action against Tobruk.

11. British 25-pounders of the Royal Horse Artillery during the fighting on 1 May 1941.

12. A British 25-pounder gun/howitzer in action inside Tobruk on 8 May 1941.

13. The scourge of the defenders: a JU87 Stuka dive bomber. These were flown by both Italian and German air forces. In this photograph aircraft are attacking the Wadi Auda with its water supply, and close to two British anti-aircraft sites.

14. Stukas over Tobruk, 1942.

15. A cleverly camouflaged Messerschmitt Bf 109E in the desert skies near Tobruk.

16. A Marmon Harington armed with a captured Italian 20mm Breda anti-tank gun taken inside Tobruk on 8 May 1941. This South African-built British armoured car was widely employed in the desert in 1941.

17. Diggers occupying makeshift positions pose for a photograph on the Tobruk perimeter on 13 August 1941.

18. The remains of Tobruk town, 13 August 1941.

19. The escarpment at Tobruk is riddled with caves, which during the siege
provided sanctuary for the defenders.

nition, could find no way to do so. In the late afternoon the three armoured regiments of 4th Armoured Brigade, which had been picking their way slowly forward through rocks and Italian Thermos bombs, finally arrived in the sand dunes on the eastern flank of the road some miles to the north. The eager tanks of the 7th Hussars hurtled into the masses of Italian transport lining the road, driving at speed along the flanks of the stricken column while, with turrets traversed, their guns spewed fire.

No Italian tanks were yet on the scene as dusk settled over the battlefield, and a quiet of sorts allowed the British positions to be reinforced and resupplied, while broken-down and redundant vehicles were drained of their fuel for the tanks. British Bren gun carrier patrols worked the Italian flanks through the night, during which the first muted sounds of arriving Italian armour could be heard. The British plan for the continued defence of the block on 6 February was to allow the 4th Armoured Brigade to eat into the Italian flank while awaiting the arrival to the north later that day of the 7th Armoured Brigade and the support group.

The plan worked perfectly, but the day was not without its worrying moments, as Italian pressure remained heavy and the British supply situation became precarious, with fuel just about exhausted and ammunition rapidly dwindling.

As dawn on 6 February allowed the first struggling rays of light onto the wet and windy battlefield, gradually bringing to view the smoky hulks from the previous day's fighting, 2nd RTR arrived short of the Pimple in the vicinity of the white mosque after spending the night leaguered in the desert. Captain Cyril Joly was not prepared for what he would find:

> As my tank came to the top of a ridge about two miles east of the road I was staggered by the amazing scene before me. South, to my left, I could see the puffs of the shell-bursts on the brilliant white dunes which marked the positions of the blocking force. From there, and directly in front of me and to my right, stretching as far as the eye could see, the main road and the flat ground on each side of it were packed tight with every conceivable type of enemy vehicle and equipment.

The 2nd RTR tanks moved quietly into hull-down positions 2,000 yards from the road, unseen by the enemy. After hurried orders, the regiment, with only nineteen operational tanks, attacked, Cyril Joly's troop stationary and hull down in the middle acting as a pivot to the remainder. The cruisers advanced against the huddled mass of Italians, firing as they went. The enemy responded immediately and aggressively: 'Twenty Italian tanks which had been moving down the east side of the road to join the vanguard attacking the blocking position wheeled left at once and engaged. The first sounds of machine-gun fire and the crack of the high-velocity tank guns turned the attention of the Italian gunners to this new menace. In a matter of moments they too had switched to engage the new targets.'

Despite their efforts the Italian tanks could not break through. Instead of attacking en masse, they went forward in groups of two and three, which were relatively easily dealt with by the hull-down cruisers of 2nd RTR. Later in the morning, as cold heavy rain began to fall over the battlefield, three desperate attacks were made against the Combeforce block by units of Italian *bersaglieri* supported by light tanks, but were beaten off by the anti-tank guns. Despite the capture already of thousands of prisoners, many Italian units remained full of fight, although their efforts were now increasingly tinged with desperation. At the Pimple the light tanks of the 3rd and 7th Hussars harassed the extended flanks of the column and engaged much of the Italian artillery, breaking up the groups of tanks making their way towards the cruisers of 2nd RTR.

At noon on 6 February, with 2nd RTR and the 7th Hussars down to ten operational tanks between them, 1st RTR from the 7th Armoured Brigade arrived in the nick of time and smashed into the Italian flank at the Pimple, firing everything they had into the packed Italian columns. 'There were endless targets,' recalled Rea Leakey, 'and on the first day of this battle my tank ran out of ammunition twice.' As the afternoon wore on, despite continued heavy fighting it was clear that the Italians were losing heart. Vehicles and men were attempting to flee to the north-west, but the British trap held: the Hussars harassing the Italian column from the rear, 1st RTR flaying its flanks and 2nd RTR resisting any attempt at the block to break through.

With total viable British tank strength reduced to thirty-nine 'runners' the Italians mounted a series of fierce night attacks against the 2nd Rifle Brigade's positions at Sidi Saleh. Although the first attack penetrated the Rifle Brigade's defences the onslaught was held, the combination of mines, anti-tank fire and the 25-pounders of the RHA proving too strong even for the gallant *bersaglieri*. The attacks continued, accompanied by heavy Italian shellfire, on the morning of 7 February, and once again the Rifle Brigade positions were penetrated, this time by M13 tanks, one of which was only halted outside battalion headquarters. The cruisers of 2nd RTR had withdrawn during the night south from Beda Fomm to support the heavily pressed Combeforce block, and helped push back the Italian tank attack that morning.

To the relief of the exhausted British this was the final Italian effort. Gradually the noise died down and Joly became aware of a startling change on the landscape in front of his tanks' positions at Sidi Saleh: 'First one and then another white flag appeared in the host of vehicles. More and more became visible, until the whole column was a forest of waving white banners.' The Italian 10th Army was surrendering. 'Italians of all shapes and sizes, all ranks, all regiments and all services swarmed out to be taken prisoner.' They included some women. Joly's gun loader shouted:

> 'Look, sir, there's a couple of bints there coming toward us. Can I go an' grab 'em, sir? I could do with some home comforts.' We took the two girls captive, installed them in a vehicle of their own and kept them for a few days to do our cooking and washing. I refrained from asking what other duties were required of the women, but noted that they remained contented and cheerful.

The battle for Libya was over. Strewn across the battlefield was the detritus of a defeated army – broken and abandoned equipment, tattered uniforms, piles of empty shell and cartridge cases. The ground was littered with paper, rifles and bedding. Here and there small groups of Italians tended their wounded. Others were collecting and burying the dead. Still others, less eager to surrender than the majority, stood or lay waiting to be captured. Some equipment was still burning furiously, more was smouldering. Many oil and petrol fires emitted clouds of black smoke. 'We were well content,' Joly remarked, as calm returned to the scene and he was able to enjoy the luxury of reflection. 'Except for the Matildas, our equipment had not been greatly superior and we had at no time superiority in numbers. Speed of manoeuvre and preparation, determination and the confidence born of a great and growing moral ascendancy were the weapons which had brought the final victory.'

At 11 a.m. General Virginio, chief of staff of the 10th Italian Army, arrived at the headquarters of Blood Caunter's 4th Armoured Brigade to report that his commander, General Tellera, had been killed in a bayonet charge, and he was authorized to seek the surrender of the army. Generals Babini of the tanks, Bignani of the *bersaglieri*, Negroni of the engineers, Cona, Bardini and Giuliano, along with many other senior officers of the Italian garrisons as well as the 10th Army, were taken prisoner, the greatest prize being Electric Whiskers himself, General Bergonzoli, who had managed to escape British clutches at both Bardia and Tobruk was captured by Lieutenant James 'Nobby' Clark of the 11th Hussars. Clark had caught Bergonzoli outside Benghazi. 'When I stuck my tommy gun through the window of his Fiat, he said to me, "You got here a bit too quick today." He looked tired.' Clark was awarded the Military Cross for his feat. 'I haven't seen so many Italians since the 1911 durbar,' quipped O'Connor.

Over 25,000 prisoners, 100 tanks, 216 guns and 1,500 other vehicles were captured along the road between Sidi Saleh and Beda Fomm. The cost to the British was nine men killed and fifteen wounded. 'I'm sorry you are so uncomfortable,' General O'Connor apologized to his senior officer prisoners after the battle in their temporary POW cage at Solluch. 'We haven't had much time to make proper arrangements.' 'Thank you very much,' General Cona replied politely. 'We do realize you came here in a very great hurry.' Sending a message back to Cairo to alert Wavell to the scale of the 13th Corps achievement, O'Connor described the situation in the language both men knew and understood: 'Fox killed in the open.'

While the 7th Armoured Division was making its epic dash across the desert to Sidi Saleh and Beda Fomm, the Italians in the north of Cyrenaica were being pressed back along the coast by the Australians: cannibalizing vehicles, siphoning fuel to enable the runners to continue round the clock and recycling sixteen Italian M11 and M13 tanks. The divisional cavalry regiment was delighted to acquire armour at long last; Bren gun carriers did not have the cachet or usefulness of even abandoned Italian tanks. To prevent errors in identification, large white kangaroos were painted on each side of the hull and turret and on the frontal armour of the tanks. When the 2/8th Battalion reached the outskirts of Benghazi on the evening of 6 February the brigade intelligence officer, Lieutenant Knox, drove into the town leading a patrol of Bren gun carriers. The inhabitants were waiting for them and somewhat disconcertingly almost the entire population of Greeks, Jews, Italians and Arabs turned out to wave and cheer the conquering Australians. At the town hall the mayor, bishop, police chief and other officials greeted the weary and dust-covered Diggers with protestations that the Australians were 'our brave allies'. The following morning, when the men of the 2/4th Battalion marched into the town square, they were met by thousands of inhabitants clapping and waving in an atmosphere of cordiality. Before long the troops were sitting in cafes drinking Chianti and strong black coffee, to the amazement of the natives, who had feared the conquerers would loot and pillage.

It took three days for news of the scale of the triumph to reach Cairo, the Countess of Ranfurly excitedly noting in her diary entry for 10 February 1941, 'The Seventh Armoured Division has made a brilliant spurt and cut off retreating Italians about sixty miles south of Benghazi and captured an immense quantity of prisoners and equipment.' Back in London following his visit to the Middle East Anthony Eden joked in a note to the prime minister, 'Never before has so much been surrendered by so many to so few.' During an offensive of two months O'Connor's tiny force had advanced 500 miles and destroyed the entire Italian 10th Army, captured 130,000 prisoners, 400 tanks and 1,290 guns, besides vast quantities of other war material. Commonwealth casualties had been 500 killed, 1,373 wounded, and 55 missing.

The humbling of Italian arms had a worrying consequence for Britain, however. Mussolini's musing before Christmas 1940 about the possibility of German help quickly became a dangerous reality. The Luftwaffe's *Fliegerkorps* X (10th Air Corps) began to land in Sicily in late December 1940. On 9 January 1941 it numbered 61 dive-bombers,

77 long-range bombers, 12 long-range reconnaissance aircraft and 20 twin-engined fighters. Hitler also agreed to provide a specially constituted force of one armoured and one mechanized division, to be sent to Tripoli to help defend that part of Libya which remained in Italian hands. Even more dangerous for the Allies in North Africa was the fact that, immediately after achieving their victory in Cyrenaica, the vast bulk of O'Connor's troops were sent back to Egypt to refit and then transported by ship and aircraft to Greece. Nothing except for a thin reconnaissance screen of armoured cars was left in western Cyrenaica to keep watch on any renascent Italian ambitions.

3 » THE BENGHAZI HANDICAP

Back in Tobruk reinforcements were being shipped directly into the port from Alexandria. On a cold, wet, wintry day in late January 1941 Major John Devine, a surgeon with the Royal Australian Army Medical Corps, found himself on an ancient Greek freighter bound for Tobruk. The 900-ton vessel bristled with anti-aircraft guns but boasted, to his consternation, no lifeboats. The cargo was an assortment of British and Australian troops destined for the front line, which at that time was advancing rapidly beyond Derna in the direction of Benghazi. On the quayside the Britons, quiet and thoughtful, provided an interesting contrast to the noisy bunch of Aussies 'sprawled all over the road, shouting and singing, thinking neither of the past nor the future'. On board, crammed into quarters for twenty officers that measured no more than twenty feet by fourteen, Devine came across British army officers, veterans of the desert battles against the Italians, who 'wore velveteen trousers and dusty-coloured sweaters, and spoke of "wadis" and "sides" and "trigs" with great authority'. It was a language that Devine was quickly to learn. Unable to sleep in the fetid air below decks, he braved the cold, spray and patches of oil on the freighter's crowded deck, to find disrupted sleep among a jumble of other huddled bodies. After an uncomfortable night on hard steel, Devine had his first view of the coast through the slowly lifting darkness of the morning. 'We saw the tiny V punched out of the land that is Tobruk harbour. The country seemed indescribably beautiful and peaceful in the sunlight, a golden brown in colour, with fading distances of almost as bright a blue as the Mediterranean upon which we rode.'

The wrecks of the fire-ravaged and beached Italian liner *Marco Polo* and the half-sunk cruiser *San Giorgio*, her impotent guns pointing drunkenly to the sky, together with a score of other semi-submerged vessels contrasted bizarrely with the gaily striped bathing boxes occupying the sandy beach at the furthest extremity of the harbour. The detritus of broken vessels and the slowly swirling rainbows of oil leaking from sunken ships marred what had previously been a picturesque, peaceful haven for Italian garrison troops. The town was scattered around the harbour in clumps of neat whitewashed concrete buildings constructed during the interwar years by Italian colonists. Set against the azure of the Mediterranean, the lighter blue of the cloudless sky and the light orange of the desert landscape, it presented a picture of considerable beauty, even of tranquillity. If one ignored the mess of the harbour, it was only when confronted at close quarters with the town itself that the evidence of war became apparent. Shell pockmarks marred the whiteness of virtually every building, and shrapnel debris littered the streets. Bomb craters had gouged out great holes in the landscape, sometimes in patches of empty space and sometimes creating new spaces in rows of buildings, the shattered masonry where the shell or bomb had struck destroying the otherwise perfect symmetry of the street. The town's workshops were a tangle of burnt, twisted steel and corrugated iron, evidence of an accurate RAF bombing raid.

Devine was struck by the desolation of the town, camel-thorn blowing through its devastated streets in a North African parody of the Wild West. Shops and cafes lay gutted; discarded vehicles littered the streets; stores were piled high in abandoned disarray. Sweat-stained clothes still hung in the hastily vacated dwellings. 'The sight of this used clothing hanging so intimately in its cupboards affected me strongly. It was as if the lid had been raised from the saucepan of people's lives and, on looking in, one saw the private imprints of their existence.'

The sense of unreality in the hiatus between the chaos and confusion of battle and the yet-to-arrive orderliness of military administration struck him forcefully. Libyan soldiers roamed about, exploiting the dangerous freedom that existed between being regarded as enemy combatants and becoming registered as prisoners of war. Disconsolate Italian POWs did likewise, but in the subdued melancholy of defeat rather than the childlike exuberance of the Senussi, who pillaged the litter-strewn town. Evidence of looting lay everywhere, the temptation of war booty challenging the discipline of even the most ordered troops. The Australian journalist Chester Wilmot, who arrived in the town on the heels of the leading troops the day after the battle, spoke of 'thoughtless damaging of property' and widespread plundering in Tobruk in the days after its capture by irresponsible rear-echelon soldiers of the AIF, drunk on the exhilaration of victory but heedless of the fact that the properties would soon be needed by the victors. 'Scrounging', as Devine called it, got so bad that men started stealing from each other. When 'one of the dispatch riders left his motorbike outside headquarters, the magneto was removed before he arrived back, and soon after took its place in another bike whose magneto had been damaged':

> It was amazing how much scrounging had been going on. We had cases of the most excellent Italian milk, *sterilizato*, cases of beautiful cherry jam and cases of not so good Italian bully beef. We were using Italian sterilizers for our medical equipment, Italian dressings and many Italian instruments. Everyone seemed to have his own Italian car . . . Our men were wearing Italian khaki military shirts, and in many cases Italian trousers and boots, and we were all sheltered by Italian groundsheets.

Running above the town was a dusty escarpment, upon which the Italian anti-aircraft defences had been sited. Some guns had been destroyed by their erstwhile owners before they fled, but many others had not, neat piles of ammunition lying ready for their next engagement. They were to prove extremely useful to their new owners, and many would shortly be shipped to Greece.

*

On 14 February 1941 a new and more aggressive enemy appeared in the skies above Libya, the first twin-engined Messerschmidt Bf 110C heavy fighters of the *Fliegerkorps X* startling the thin-skinned armoured cars of the King's Dragoon Guards on reconnaissance forward of

El Agheila. In fact German aircraft had been operating in Libya since January, but their numbers grew dramatically during the first two months of the year. The persistence of the Luftwaffe pilots in pressing home their attacks came as something of a shock for the British accustomed to the Regia Aeronautica. Private Harry Buckledee recorded the effect of a German air attack on British Marmon Harrington armoured cars:

> One afternoon . . . I saw three [Me] 110s attack one of our troops, and in about two or three minutes they had destroyed all three cars. Our troop was sent to their assistance. I was anxious as I knew my mate, Lance Corporal Bob Ramshaw, from West Stanley, Durham, who had joined up the same day as me, was in that troop. All but two of the crews were dead or wounded. Bob was badly wounded but recovered from his wounds, although he had a leg amputated.

By late February near-daily Luftwaffe attacks had made Benghazi unusable as a port, forcing 13th Corps to rely for its supplies on the long road back to Tobruk and thence via sea or land to Egypt. HMS *Dainty*, bringing in stores to Tobruk, was sunk by Stukas on 24 February. These unwelcome events heralded the arrival of a small German land force – part of Operation *Sonnenblume* (Sunflower) – designed to insert backbone into the Italian defence of Tripolitania. The commander of this force, the newly promoted Lieutenant General Erwin Rommel, arrived in Tripoli by the ubiquitous Junkers Ju 52 transport plane – distinctive as much for its three motors as for its square, corrugated sides – from Rome via Catania in Sicily at midday on 12 February 1941. Flying at low level across the Mediterranean, Rommel noted a constant stream of Junkers crossing in the opposite direction, the aircraft having deposited supplies for the *Fliegerkorps* X build-up in Tripoli.

On 11 January, much against his will and following the disasters at Sidi Barrani and Bardia, a humbled Duce was forced to accept the offer of a German light (motorized) division to support the reinforcements that the Italians were even then shipping to Libya. These included the 132nd Ariete ('Ram') Armoured Division, with its complement of 6,949 men, 163 tanks (only 70 of which were the M13, the remainder the puny L3), 36 field guns and 61 anti-tank guns.

The original plan of the German armed forces high command, the OKW (*Oberkommando der Wehrmacht*), was for Rommel's single light division to act as a *Sperrverband* (blocking formation) to prevent any further British advance towards Tripoli. But the 5th Division was in fact much more powerful than its British equivalent. It consisted of the 5th Panzer Regiment (three panzer battalions each with forty Mark III and Mark IV tanks) together with the 3rd Reconnaissance Battalion with armoured cars, a machine-gun regiment (again with three battalions), a battalion of the 75th Artillery Regiment and an anti-tank (*Panzerjäger*) regiment equipped with a mixture of mobile 20-millimetre cannons and the powerful 88-millimetre anti-aircraft/ tank gun. The 5th Light Division was, with 9,300 men, 130 tanks, 111 guns and 2,000 vehicles, a powerful formation, all the more so when led by a determined and capable commander. Hitler had insisted that Italian mechanized forces also come under Rommel's command, although Rommel himself was nominally subordinate to the Italian commander-in-chief in North Africa.

Erwin Rommel's orders were to stabilize the front and prevent the British from humiliating Mussolini any more than they had already done, by ensuring that Tripoli did not fall. He had received his orders a mere six days before his arrival in Libya from the Führer and Field Marshal von Brauchitsch, the *Wehrmacht* commander-in-chief, in Berlin. Hitler showed Rommel British illustrated magazines describing Wavell's humbling of the 10th Italian Army in Cyrenaica. Sidi Barrani, Capuzzo, Bardia, Tobruk, Derna and Barce had fallen, and now Benghazi was threatened. The Italians were in no mental state to resist the British. Panic had set in among the troops in their haste to escape the British advance, and Tripoli was full of staff officers with packed suitcases seeking a quick exit back to Italy.

Rommel was an extraordinarily good choice for this command. 'I picked him,' remarked Hitler, 'because he knows how to inspire his troops.' This was true, although to a man his subordinate commanders and staff officers hated him, in part because of the demands he placed on them, and also because of his refusal to accept any attitude or behaviour on the battlefield that did not display the same thrusting aggression as his own. Not yet fifty years old, he was fit, highly motivated and experienced, having successfully commanded the 7th Panzer Division only months before during the invasion of France and prior to that in Poland. He was imbued with a personal dynamism and driving energy that set him apart from most of his peers. His three tactical principles, which he had learned in the First World War, developed through intensive study during the interwar period (including assiduous examination of the works of British commentators on mobile armoured warfare) and honed through experience in Poland and France, were: shock action, preferably against the enemy's weakest point, in which massive and overwhelming firepower against ill-prepared opponents would shatter their will to resist; surprise, by which the enemy would be thrown off balance by an unexpected move; and speed, in which the sheer pace of his operations left the enemy unable to react quickly enough to changes on the battlefield. In all operations of war he sought to do the unexpected, to deceive, surprise and bluff. 'His magic word is speed,' wrote a fellow officer of Rommel's tactics in France, 'boldness is his stock in trade. He shocks the enemy, takes them unawares, overhauls them, suddenly appears far in their rear, attacks them, outflanks them, encircles them . . .' The Germans even had a word for it: an enemy overwhelmed by these tactics was *Gerommelt* (Rommeled).

The First World War had taught Rommel that the psychological dimension to fighting was often more important in securing battlefield success than any other factor. If, by bold and decisive moves accompanied by overwhelming and concentrated firepower at the decisive point, he could persuade his enemy that all was lost, the battle would almost certainly go his way regardless of the true state of his forces. His personal courage in the face of the enemy was legendary, an inspiration to his men, and while his driving energy was often cursed, it also brought with it undoubted success, and it was success that soldiers – his own and his enemy's – respected more than anything else. He was undoubtedly an unusual man, and like all men of action was not cut out for the certainties or forms of peacetime soldiering. His intensity made him more suited to the battlefield, particularly where full rein could be given to his creativity. As Private Frank Harrison of the Royal Signals was to observe with not uncritical awe,

'One man does not make an army, but not since Napoleon had a military commander been such a symbol of leadership and battlefield victory over superior forces as Erwin Rommel.'

On arrival at the Castel Benito airfield outside Tripoli in the stifling heat of the Libyan noon Rommel knew very little of the Allied strength in North Africa. All he had to go on was what the headlines in the British newspapers were telling him: Wavell had launched a brilliant overwhelming attack on Italian forces in eastern Libya, and nothing now stood between the forward British units on the Gulf of Sirte and Tripoli. For all he knew, a further advance was being prepared to seize Tripoli. On landing, therefore, he immediately deluged Graziani's successor, General Garibaldi (to whom he was, on paper at least, subordinate), with a flood of ideas to form a defensive line in the desert anchored on the Gulf of Sirte to block the route of a British advance on Tripoli and to allow space for the Luftwaffe to build up its strength around the capital. Garibaldi, who had only been in post for a day, dismissed the impetuosity of the German with the advice: 'Go and see for yourself.'

Rommel did so. That very afternoon he and a small number of his staff flew by Heinkel 111 over the Gulf of Sirte, noting the Via Balbia, the metalled road hugging the coast from Tripoli to Bardia, built on the instructions of the late Italo Balbo, stretching out like a long black thread into the treeless distance. The flight confirmed Rommel in his determination to create a defence line at Sirte, 300 miles to the east of Tripoli and 160 miles west of the forward British positions at El Agheila. This would at least give him the ability to resist a British attack along the coast while collecting what armour he could muster to launch a counter-attack.

The vanguard of the 5th Light Division (Major General Johannes Streich), the 3rd Reconnaissance Battalion commanded by Major Baron Irnfrief von Wechmar, together with the 39th Anti-Tank Battalion (Major Jansa) arrived in Tripoli on board the *Saarfeld* on 14 February, although the division would not be complete until mid-April. After disembarking his battalion from the 6,000-ton freighter during the night, von Wechmar was briefed by Rommel and was at Sirte by the 16th. Then, less than a week after his arrival, Hitler agreed to double the size of Rommel's force by adding to it the 15th Panzer Division, naming the combined force the *Deutsches Afrikakorps* (more usually rendered in English as Afrika Korps). At the same time, Mussolini having instructed his forces to fall in with Rommel's plans, the 10th Italian Corps – comprising the Brescia and Pavia Infantry Divisions, together with the newly arrived Ariete Armoured Division – began also to move forward. As the troops trickled into Tripoli over the coming six weeks, Rommel rushed them forward. On 5 March he wrote to his wife, Lucie:

Dearest Lu,

Just back from a two-day journey – or rather flight – to the front, which is now 450 miles away to the east. Everything going fine.

A lot to do. Can't leave here for the moment as I couldn't be answerable for my absence. Too much depends on my own person and my driving power . . .

My troops are on their way. Speed is the one thing that matters here.

*

For the troops of the Afrika Korps the journey by sea to Tripoli was short but dangerous. For Sergeants Krügel and Wolff of the 15th Motorized Infantry Battalion the crossing from Italy in early March had been made in the *Alicante*, an old tramp steamer running the Royal Navy gauntlet in the Mediterranean. Both men had been horribly ill, and attempted to take their minds off their seasickness by standing in the bows of the old tub looking out for mines and submarines. Lieutenant Joachim Schorm, commander of the 6th Company of one of the three panzer battalions arriving on the *Marburg* in the same convoy, entered the relative safety of Tripoli harbour on 10 March with considerable relief:

We enter the harbour at Tripoli. We have done it! Fifteen miles from us . . . an Italian merchant ship and two tankers were sunk by submarines. The scene in the docks is indescribably pictur-esque. Rommel and German officers in field grey, the Luftwaffe in khaki trousers, breeches, shorts, the Italians in every conceivable uniform . . .

Schorm had reason to be jubilant at his survival as in early 1941 the Mediterranean remained a British lake. On 16 April Royal Navy destroyers sank an entire convoy off Sfax, Tunisia, carrying elements of the 15th Panzer Division: the 115th Regiment (Lieutenant Colonel Schutz) and the 33rd Artillery Regiment. Three hundred and fifty men were killed and 300 vehicles together with 3,500 tons of stores lost. Despite these risks by the end of March 1941 some 25,000 men, 8,500 vehicles and 26,000 tons of stores had arrived safely in Tripoli in 15 convoys, with a loss of 9 German ships sunk and 9 damaged. Nevertheless, between January and May 1941 the Germans and Italians lost 31 ships attempting to supply the Afrika Korps in North Africa.

A month later, while their tanks and other vehicles attempted the journey by sea, a vast Luftwaffe fleet of Ju 52 transport aircraft – 208 in total – brought together for the forthcoming airborne invasion of Crete, flew 3,500 soldiers of the 15th Panzer Division from Sicily directly to desert airfields outside Tripoli. It was a dangerous journey. Flying in groups of three less than a hundred feet above the choppy waves and at a steady 150 knots the German aircraft were easy prey for British fighters flying out of Malta. For Private Rolf-Werner Völker it was his first ever flight and a daunting prospect. The only safety devices were uninflated rubber life jackets the eighteen soldiers in each plane were instructed to place over their necks and tie around their waists. They were to inflate them manually only if they found themselves in the sea. The Ju 52 had no seats, the troops making themselves as comfortable as they could for the 180-mile flight on the floor of the aircraft among their kitbags and weapons.

Völker's worst fears were realized far out over the Mediterranean long after their Messerschmidt Bf 110 escorts had returned to Sicily. Suddenly, above the noise of their engines they heard the hammering of machine-gun fire. They were being attacked by British fighters. The pilot took evasive action, sharply twisting the plane from side to side, which threw men and equipment around the inside of the aircraft. Clinging on grimly for their lives they could see the British aircraft fleetingly through the windows in the fuselage, and sought a means to fight back. Taking a Spandau MG-42 machine gun from its packing they broke one of the windows and, feeding belt ammunition into the weapon, blazed away at the swooping enemy aircraft. As he did so, watching the tracer bullets from his weapon streaming into the sky, Völker realized that other men in other aircraft were doing the same thing: 'I don't know whether we hit any of them but it was good for morale to be able to shoot back and they seemed to be backing off. Then our pilot suddenly banked and before I could stop firing I had put several holes in our own wing. Luckily, I didn't hit an engine or anything important.'

*

From the moment he set foot on African soil Rommel sought opportunities for offensive action. Berlin wanted him merely to contain the British threat in Libya; Hitler did not want his secret preparations for the invasion of Russia in June – four months hence – to be jeopardized by an unplanned war in North Africa. But Rommel was not a man to be restrained. Although he had a relatively small army, he deduced the weakness of his British opponents and recognized the potential of an attack on the very fulcrum of the British empire – Egypt and the Nile. A hint of his offensive intentions could be seen in his demand during his stopover in Sicily that Benghazi be bombed. General Geissler, commander of *Fliegerkorps X* in Sicily, demurred, observing – to Rommel's astonishment – that 'many Italian officers and civil officials owned houses there'. Rommel immediately complained to Berlin, and within hours Geissler's bombers were lifting off from Sicily in their first strikes against the town.

Rommel made no secret of his aspirations. On 12 March he told his startled new ADC, Lieutenant Heinz Schmidt, 'We shall reach the Nile, make a right turn and win back everything.' That same afternoon Rommel briefed the assembled officers of the 5th Panzer Regiment, which had hurriedly been disembarking its 120 tanks since 10 March in Tripoli harbour:

> With the arrival of your panzers the situation in North Africa will be stabilized. The enemy's thrust towards Tripolitania has been

brought to a standstill. Our reconnaissance units under Lieutenant Colonel von Wechmar have reached the Italians' advanced positions on the Gulf of Sirte at El Agheila, and have morally and materially strengthened the front. It is our task to restore the confidence of the Italian people in their arms, and to bolster up the fighting spirit of our allies.

We *must* save Tripolitania from the attack of the British army. We *will* hold them.

Because of his initial numerical weakness in Libya Rommel engaged in subterfuge to mislead the British about the strength of his forces. To deceive the RAF aircraft that made occasional forays over the city he had his men mock up a large number of wood and canvas tanks built over Volkswagen chassis. In addition, after reviewing his troops following disembarkation he ordered the tanks to make a number of tours of the streets of Tripoli before they travelled east towards Sirte to exaggerate the size of his force to any watching British spies. 'At 1800 hours,' recalled Schorm, 'the panzers rumble through the port along the Via Balbia towards the east. All night long we are greeted by soldiers, settlers and natives.'

Rommel need not have bothered with the charades. Though Wavell had no sources of intelligence this far west in Libya the British had cracked the German military Enigma coding system, and at Bletchley Park deep in rural Buckinghamshire a programme codenamed Ultra delivered deciphered enemy messages to London, which in turn sent them to Wavell's headquarters in Cairo. London had a good idea therefore of the size and scale of the forces being shipped into Tripoli. But what Ultra could not provide was accurate interpretation of intelligence, and it was in their assessments of German intentions that the British failed. Although he knew by mid-March that the German equivalent of a British brigade had arrived in the Libyan capital, Wavell assumed, interpreting Berlin's instructions to Rommel too literally, that it would be at least two months before these troops would be in a position to undertake a serious offensive against Cyrenaica. Rommel, the impetuous risk-taker, was to wrong-foot both Cairo and Berlin in his seizure of the initiative in Libya.

Moving forward to Sirte with the 5th Panzer Regiment on 13 March

Rommel was forced by a severe sandstorm to travel by road rather than by air. He was shocked by the power of the North African elements as he confronted a khamsin for the first time:

> Now we realized what little idea we had of the tremendous force of such a storm. Immense clouds of reddish dust obscured all visibility and forced the car's speed down to a crawl. Often the wind was so strong that it was impossible to drive along the Via Balbia. Sand streamed down the windscreen like water. We gasped in breath painfully through handkerchiefs held over our faces and sweat poured off our bodies in the unbearable heat.

At this stage Rommel did not know that he would be pushing at an open door in Cyrenaica. He was ignorant of the fact that Churchill had ordered the strongest possible reinforcements to be detached from Wavell's already weak Army of the Nile for the defence of Greece. At the conclusion of the Beda Fomm battle every inclination of the British commanders in Cyrenaica had been to press on to Tripoli, in captured Italian vehicles if necessary. Brigadier Eric Dorman-Smith, whose fertile and unconventional brain had assisted O'Connor to come up with the plan to attack Nibeiwa and the Tummars from the rear, rushed back to Cairo to seek permission from Wavell for the onward advance. The journey to Tobruk took him fourteen hours, and then a further eighteen exhausting hours to complete the final 570 miles to Cairo. At Wavell's office the C-in-C's welcome was warm but, waving to the maps of Greece and the Balkans on the wall, Wavell said, 'You find me busy with my spring campaign.' There was to be no advance on Tripoli.

O'Connor's dramatic success had been entirely unplanned and unexpected, and the strategic consequences of defeating the Italians in Cyrenaica but of not occupying the whole of Libya had not been thoroughly considered. Moreover, Greece was now Wavell's priority. Later in the month it was agreed that Britain would dispatch four divisions from Egypt to Greece (two Australian, one New Zealand and one British), together with five air force squadrons. This left very little to defend Cyrenaica. In fact, the forces in Libya, the remainder of O'Connor's victorious 13th Corps (now commanded by Lieutenant General Philip Neame VC since O'Connor had been sent to Egypt for a rest and a knighthood) had by mid-March been thinned down to the 9th Australian Division (replacing 6th Division, already dispatched to Greece) and the newly arrived headquarters of the 2nd Armoured Division consisting solely of the tired and desperately understrength 3rd Armoured Brigade, its other brigade having also gone to Greece.

The 2nd Armoured Division commander, Major General Justice Tilley, an experienced Royal Tank Regiment officer, had been killed in an accident shortly after arriving in Egypt in January 1941 and replaced at short notice by Major General Michael Gambier-Parry. He was not an ideal choice for the post, being known as a conventionally minded and rather conservative soldier, but at the time Cyrenaica was not regarded as being in the front line. The tank strength of Brigadier Rex Rimington's 3rd Armoured Brigade was pitiful. Virtually all the British tanks that had fought through Operation Compass required major overhaul. Lieutenant Colonel Henry Drew's 5th RTR had only twenty-three worn-out cruisers while the 6th RTR (only one squadron of which was available) and 3rd Hussars had been forced to equip themselves with captured Italian M13s salvaged directly from the battlefield at Beda Fomm. Second Lieutenant Roy Farran found himself part of this underequipped force dependent on scavenged armour. It was with considerable horror that he realized 'however much we painted the insides of the tanks, we could not remove the awful bloodstains round the turrets'.

A regiment of Marmon Harrington armoured cars (the King's Dragoon Guards) and the 2nd Armoured Division's support group completed the force. Brave and resourceful, the support group consisted of the Territorial Army soldiers of 1st Battalion Tower Hamlet Rifles, the 104th RHA (25-pounders), the 3rd RHA (2-pounder anti-tank guns), and Y Company of the Royal Northumberland Fusiliers (Vickers machine guns). Commandant Folliot's battalion of Free French marines was also attached. The 9th Australian Division, commanded by the newly promoted Major General Leslie Morshead, was understrength though well trained and eager for action. At the end of March Morshead had only four battalions (three battalions of Brigadier John Murray's 20th Brigade and one battalion of the 26th) defending the escarpment east of Benghazi at Regima, with the remaining brigade (the 24th) in Tobruk. The division was supported by a grand total of sixteen British guns, and had none of its authorized complement of Bren carriers, no reconnaissance troops and few radios. As for air force support, there remained in eastern Libya merely one Australian (No.3) and one British (No.73) squadron of Hurricanes. Although they were to do sterling work in the early days of the campaign these two dozen fighters were to be swamped by a force five times their number.

Although both Neame and Morshead had made worried representations to Cairo during March 1941 about the clear German build-up in Tripolitania, both men were assured that the matter was well understood and that the threat not as serious as they might assume. Reflecting these assurances on 30 March Neame concluded publicly that the Germans had 'so far shown no signs of contemplating a further advance' and that it was unlikely that 'the enemy intends to take the offensive on a large scale, or even that he is likely to be in a position to do so in the near future'. These conclusions were the result of the failure of both London and Cairo to understand anything of Rommel as a man. The instructions to Rommel not to launch a precipitate offensive in Libya had been explicit, and signals to this effect had been picked up by London through Ultra. Indeed, he had made a flying visit back to Berlin on 19 March, where he had been told that the OKW envisaged no immediate attack in North Africa, but that, when his second division – the 15th Panzers (Major General Heinrich von Prittwitz) – arrived in Tripoli in May he could consider an advance against Benghazi. On 3 April Berlin ordered, 'attacks . . . must not be extended . . . before the 15th Panzer Division arrives. . . . Under no circumstances should the open right flank be endangered, which would necessarily be the case in an advance to the north of Benghazi . . . Even after the arrival of the 15th Panzer Division a large-scale offensive, aimed perhaps at Tobruk, should not be launched.' Such plans, Berlin concluded, could be changed only if the bulk of the British armoured forces were withdrawn from Cyrenaica.

These intercepted messages were sent to Wavell and accepted at face value. But Rommel, to the surprise of both London and Cairo, disobeyed his orders, thus at a stroke undermining Wavell's Ultra-based assumptions. Unaware of the OKW's vast plans against the Soviet Union, Rommel was flabbergasted at what he perceived as his military superiors' lack of vision. He had argued in Berlin that it was not possible or sensible to seize Benghazi without also securing the whole of Cyrenaica but had been ignored. He was convinced that now was the time to exploit British weakness in North Africa and drive for the Nile. He had observed the British defensive activity around Mersa el Brega after the Germans'surprisingly easy recent capture of the fort at El Agheila. This served to make Rommel's next decision easier. He could either wait until the remainder of his corps arrived or attack now with everything he had, hoping to unsettle the British into a precipitate retreat. The tactic had worked in France, and he had no reason to doubt it would not work again. Unsurprisingly Rommel chose the more aggressive option.

*

Lieutenant Fred 'Dusty' Miller and his friend Lieutenant Nobby Clark of the 11th Hussars, now attached to the King's Dragoon Guards, were lying atop a sand dune east of El Agheila on the night of 31 March 1941. In the pitch black not even stars brightened the darkness. All was quiet as they looked out over the desert towards the German-held fort in the distance, which had been wrested from them by the newly arrived Afrika Korps exactly a week before. The nineteen-year-old Miller had only arrived on the front line days before, but Clark was something of a veteran, having been personally responsible for the surrender of Electric Whiskers at the conclusion of the battle of Beda Fomm. Their patrol represented the foremost reconnaissance screen of the British forces in Cyrenaica. Nothing appeared to be happening to their front, so the two men walked back to their armoured car, hidden behind another dune. Private Felton, the driver, had prepared a concoction of exotic food that even now, months after first tasting it, remained unusual fare for the young Britons: captured Italian spaghetti, tinned cherries and Parmesan cheese. Felton had filled every spare space in the armoured car with these luxuries on 7 February when Benghazi had fallen. After their meal the men fell asleep underneath their vehicle, huddled in blankets against the bitter cold of the desert night.

Some hours later they were jerked awake by the clanking of tank tracks. In an instant the entire crew were awake, straining their ears and peering into the gloom from underneath the armoured car. Suddenly, only thirty yards away, they saw German tanks. Five drove past, but the sixth spotted them and veered in their direction. 'Move off!' shouted Clark, and the crew managed to mount and start their vehicle in a fraction of the normal time and speed away to raise the alarm before the German could engage. Fortunately, it was still dark enough to use the shadows of the sand dunes. The KDG reconnaissance patrol had found itself in the midst of tanks from Lieutenant Colonel Olbrich's 5th Panzer Regiment advancing through the night against the coastal position at Mersa el Brega.

Gunner Leonard Tutt, with his 25-pounder battery of the 414 Battery Essex Yeomanry, on the coast at Mersa el Brega, saw the German tanks approaching over the dunes like warships:

Our battery position was shielded by some low hills. We saw tanks coming over them, wireless aerials with pennants atop like a field full of lancers. They assumed hull-down positions and blasted the thin screen of recovered [British] tanks which were deployed to face them. The men of the [1st Battalion] Tower Hamlets [Rifles] went forward to face them in Bren carriers and were virtually destroyed in a matter of minutes . . . Both our batteries fired a heavy concentration on the German Mark IVs and they were forced to withdraw slightly, but it was only a temporary respite as their infantry moved against the flank exposed by the withdrawal of the Free French [battalion].

German frontal attacks failed to break into the position. 'Again the British artillery blazes away,' recorded the young panzer commander Lieutenant Schorm. 'I throw myself down flat. [It is] not very comfortable, but nothing to worry about. Shells burst on every side, fifty yards away. Three troops withdraw into cover. We can't manage it yet, so I move back. We take up positions covering the south-east, fill up with petrol, then sleep.' Tutt observed with some relief the arrival of the company of Northumberland Fusiliers with their Vickers machine guns to plug the gap left by the gallant sacrifice of the Tower Hamlets. 'The Fusiliers had a most fearsome reputation. The unit was made up of hard uncompromising men of little polish; they obeyed their own officers but treated anyone else in authority with contempt . . . They were the dourest fighters we were to meet in a long day's march and we were always glad to have them about.'

But pressure on the flanks of the weak Mersa el Brega position by Major Voigtsberger's 2nd Machine-Gun Battalion supported by Stuka dive-bombers worried the British brigade commander and he ordered the defences to be evacuated and the force to retire northwards. The withdrawal had not been planned or rehearsed and proved, as Tutt observed, poorly managed:

It was dark by the time we were able to disengage from the enemy. Once we pulled out of our positions the rot seemed to set in. We dropped into action a little way down the road but had hardly surveyed the position before we were ordered to withdraw again. There seemed to be no overall direction. Too many units were on the move at the same time, a mistake which contributed to a growing panic . . .

Reconnaissance and aerial reports confirmed to Rommel the following day that the British were withdrawing rather than staying to fight. On 1 April 1941 Schorm recorded in his diary:

The Tommies have made April fools of us. Under cover of night, they withdrew unobserved. Our advanced panzers are now six kilometres beyond El Brega. I visit the squadron commander. We share the booty. One officer's mess lorry and so for the first time we have corned beef for breakfast and RAF cigarettes. Two 18-ton tractors haul a tank back to its base. A little way off prisoners are being interrogated . . . Everywhere abandoned lorries.

Worried by the sight of British trucks rushing along the coast road towards the north, Second Lieutenant Roy Farran of the 3rd Hussars (whose C Squadron was now attached to 6th RTR at Beda Fomm and still in the process of acquiring its Italian tanks) was aghast to discover the true situation only when he managed to halt some vehicles making their way at high speed in the direction of Benghazi. The Germans were advancing with tanks, he was told, and had broken through at

Mersa el Brega. There appeared to be no one in overall command, no orders or information, and a feeling of panic growing among the forward troops. With no instructions and unable even to contact brigade headquarters, the CO of 6th RTR decided to move to Antelat (north-east of Agedabia) to see what help they could render. Placing their newly acquired tanks hull down in the sand dunes in the direction of the advancing Germans the Hussars were despondent to see around them a scene of indescribable confusion: 'Trucks, carriers and tanks were jammed together in a confused huddle with many small detachments separated from their parent units. An air of panic, even of terror and of lost confidence, ran through the whole army.' But within an hour of arriving they were ordered to withdraw, not back on their supply depot at Msus, but north in the direction of Benghazi itself. 'Even the most junior subaltern,' observed Farran, 'knew that this was unwise, for an armoured regiment cannot fight without its supplies and our nearest dump was Msus.'

One of the reasons for panic was the clear superiority of German equipment, which was quickly obvious when fighting began. Lieutenant Williams of the Reconnaissance Troop, Kings Dragoon Guards, pushed out of El Agheila on 24 March, complained that all the British had to oppose the Germans were '2-pounder anti-tank guns and a lot of worn-out tanks'. The panzer Mark IIIs with their 50-millimetre guns and the Mark IVs armed with 75s were faster and better armoured than anything the British had at the time and their guns outranged the puny British 2-pounder (40-millimetre) main armament. Armoured cars were equipped with 20-millimetre cannon in contrast to British machine guns, and the eight-wheeled SdKfz 232 (Puma) had all-wheel drive and a top speed of 85 miles per hour.

Rommel was surprised at the speed of the British withdrawal. He thought it was due to the success of his bluff in Tripoli, which he assumed had misled the British as to his true strength, and he now decided to inflate the size of his force. Tanks were ordered out onto the flanks of the advancing formations with the sole purpose of raising dust. Trucks trailed chains and drove across the rocky desert line abreast, stirring up behind them clouds of sand that rose high into the sky, giving the impression of vastly greater numbers than in fact existed.

Knowing that if he could gain the initiative, the momentum of retreat could destabilize the British right across Cyrenaica, Rommel ordered an immediate attack on Agedabia. On the evening of 2 April, having pushed the British beyond Mersa el Brega, Schorm engaged the capured M13s of 5th RTR after a day of fast driving north across the sand. The Italian tanks confused the Germans, who were unaware of just how desperately short the British were of cruisers:

1800 hours. On high ground about 1,000 metres away I see vehicles. We halt for observation. No doubt about it, they are tanks. British or Italian? Squadron commander radios: 'Presume enemy tanks.'

Commanders and gunners are naturally standing or sitting on deck. Swish! That one fell ten metres from the left-hand track. Everyone disappears inside the panzer. The hatches are slammed. Straight ahead, 11 o'clock! High explosive, 1,000 metres.

Fire! Bang! A dud! The tracer shells whizz by! Driver overtake! Left steering, brake! In front, behind, to the right and left, the shells burst. High explosive, 800 metres! Same tank. Bang! Too short! But my other tanks have the direction from the impact. Soon the enemy is on fire. Now for the next. Stop. Hatch open, breech open, out with the shell. Change position, right ahead. Armour-piercing shell, 800 metres! Tank moving on right. Sighted! Carrying [enemy] commander's pennant. Fire! Bang! A hit? Already three enemy tanks are burning. Stop! Breech won't open! Radio message: 'Attack tanks on high ground. Roll up the flanks!' And the gun won't open. It must, must! Driver, one o'clock, to the high ground. Panzer 625 is out of the battle for the moment – brakes overheated. I reach the height with three panzers, past the burning British tanks and look for some more.

Crash! That came from the left. Heavens! British crews who have left their tanks come forward with their hands up. Six British tanks are burning. Well, thank God for that! Radio order: 'Squadron halt.' But I go forward 500 metres on the dune to gain a view of observation and fire . . . We have to increase speed as it is getting dark. As the sun goes down, we really do look like wild huntsmen roaring along at 30 kilometres per hour towards Agedabia. It is an incomparable experience. The enemy is smashed. Who will oppose us now? . . . With the exception of myself, all the troop commanders are missing

... With the satisfaction of having passed through my baptism in panzer combat without the loss of a man or panzer, I fall asleep.

Rommel recorded in his diary that in this engagement seven British tanks were left burning for the loss of three German. The 5th RTR suffered twenty-three dead in the encounter. By late on 2 April the British had withdrawn north of Agedabia, a jumbled-up mass of armoured cars, trucks and tanks scrambling to escape north at a speed, Farran recalled, 'which indicated that the panic of the higher command had communicated itself to the troops'. Rumours were rife. One was that the Germans had managed to infiltrate the retreating columns, until it transpired that the 'enemy' were in fact the new and unfamiliar South African-built Marmon Harrington armoured cars of the King's Dragoon Guards bringing up the rear. On the basis of his Ultra-generated intelligence Wavell believed that the threat was to Benghazi rather than to the whole of Cyrenaica, and so authorized Neame to withdraw if necessary, but to hold on to the high ground above Benghazi at Regima.

The confusion among the British falling back in front of the German advance made this a difficult task. The situation was so chaotic that the headquarters of the 2nd Armoured Division at Antelat on 2 April departed north for Benghazi during the night, forgetting to inform its attached Lysander crew and leaving the surprised RAF personnel behind in the desert. Searching for its missing parent headquarters the following morning, the aircraft flew first to the division's main supply dump at Msus, before finding the HQ thirty miles to the west. During these aerial perambulations one of the pilots spotted what he reported to be a small enemy force only five miles from Msus. The pilot insisted that the trucks were Italian and that they had opened fire on his aircraft.

This news caused consternation. If Msus fell it would not merely result in a dangerous and unanticipated threat to the British desert flank but vast stocks of stores and fuel would fall into enemy hands. That morning Wavell had authorized a change to the original plan of withdrawing all forces to the area between Benghazi and the escarpment. The remnants of 2nd Armoured Division's battered support group were to continue to retire north to make a stand on the escarpment at Regima with the 9th Australian Division, while what was left of the 3rd Armoured Brigade – a pathetic group of about twelve cruisers, twenty light tanks and twenty captured M13s – would move east across country to congregate on the escarpment on the road to Msus at Sceleidima to protect the Australians' left flank and deny the Germans access to the escarpment. The road to Benghazi would have to be left open, as there were now no resources left to cover it.

But with Msus now apparently threatened, Gambier-Parry ordered an adjustment to this plan, sending the armoured brigade, struggling to cope with its worn-out tanks (registering an average of one break-down every ten miles), a lack of radios and appalling terrain, further east to secure the division's supply dump at Msus. While this move-ment got under way the remainder of the division, now on the high ground to the east of Benghazi, watched the evacuation of the town and the demolition of key stores. Throughout the day they could see von Wechmar's vehicles heading towards the port, entering Benghazi to cheering crowds that evening.

For the remaining tanks of the desperate 3rd Armoured Brigade the journey to Msus over the night of 3/4 April was terrible. By now the original report of the threat to Msus had been so inflated that the Germans had reportedly captured the depot and set the fuel dumps on fire. More vehicles broke down and were left where they stopped, their crews setting fire to their abandoned charges and catching lifts where they could. There was no water. Farran could see dark smudges of smoke all the way south to Antelat, marking the route of the retreat. On arrival at Msus at dawn on 4 April, the tank crews found that although some of the dump had been destroyed by the withdraw-ing Free French marines, it contained no diesel. This powered all of the Italian tanks and trucks, which now made up at least half of the British strength. No one had given any thought to adding stocks of diesel to the petrol at Msus. Without it much of the motley collection of British and Italian armour that had made it from the coast road had to be abandoned, with fuel being siphoned from vehicles to provide enough for the remainder to make good their escape north.

*

As this work was under way Stukas found the British leaguer and dive-bombed the cowering troops, turning a number of trucks into smoking pyres. It was a miserable, ignominious reversal of their capture of Cyrenaica, and all felt the humiliation keenly, especially as the glories of Beda Fomm had hardly begun to fade. The period was, thought Farran bitterly, 'perhaps the most inglorious in the history of the British army', most men blaming the newcomers of the 2nd Armoured Division (whom the desert old-timers dismissively referred to as 'inglesi') for the debacle. The remnants of Rimington's brigade, shattered not so much by fighting as by order, counter-order and disorder, were ordered north through the Jebel Akhdar to Charruba to meet up with the divisional headquarters. Only a handful of tanks (eight cruisers and fourteen Mark VIs of 5th RTR, and only two M13s from 6th RTR) managed the journey by the following morning, 5 April. Unsure of what was now happening across the wider battlefield, desperate for fuel and harried by Stukas, the brigade made its way north by truck, together with its few remaining light tanks. Reaching Derna at dawn on 6 April, and thinking that being so far behind the front line they were safe, the men cooked breakfast and washed away the accumulated dirt of the past week in the surf. The survivors of 3rd Armoured Brigade (32 officers and 374 men) were ordered to fall back on Tobruk, where 6th RTR were told to expect to collect eighteen light tanks inside the perimeter and to form a vehicle-mounted mobile infantry reserve.

It was late on the afternoon of 3 April that the chaos evident in the British withdrawals confirmed in Rommel's mind what he had been playing with mentally for some days: 'The British apparently intended to avoid, in any circumstances, fighting a decisive action; so, that afternoon, I decided to stay on the heels of the retreating enemy and make a bid to seize the whole of Cyrenaica at one stroke.'

Rommel's amended plan was to continue pushing von Wechmar's 3rd Reconnaissance Battalion beyond Benghazi, followed by the infantry of the Italian Brescia Division (led by the German tropical warfare specialist Major General Kirchheim), and then to follow the coast road to Derna. The bulk of his other forces – the 5th Light and Ariete Divisions – would drive inland 280 miles across the desert to cut off the Cyrenaica 'bump' at the coast between Gazala and Tobruk.

Ponath's 8th Machine-Gun Battalion, together with Lieutenant Colonel Graf von Schwerin, commanding a small force of the Ariete and Major the Marchese Santa Anna's Italian Infantry Battalion (under the *bersaglieri* commander Lieutenant Colonel Fabris) were to advance on Mechili via the desert outpost of Ben Gania. A second thrust would take Lieutenant Colonel Olbrich and the main body of the 5th Panzer Regiment, the 2nd Machine-Gun Battalion and forty tanks of the Ariete Division to Mechili via Msus. That night Rommel wrote to Lucie:

> Dearest Lu,
>
> We've been attacking since the 31st with dazzling success. There'll be consternation among our masters in Tripoli and Rome, perhaps in Berlin too. I took the risk against all orders and instructions because the opportunity seemed favourable. No doubt it will all be pronounced good later and they'll all say they'd have done exactly the same in my place. We've already reached our first objective, which we weren't supposed to get to until the end of May. The British are falling over each other to get away. Our casualties small. Booty can't yet be estimated. You will understand that I can't sleep for happiness.

On 4 April he excitedly told Lucie that the Führer had congratulated him on his success, and that his spectacular advance was fully in accord with Hitler's own wishes. But Rommel overestimated the plaudits he would receive in Berlin. The *Wehrmacht*'s chief of staff, Colonel General Franz Halder, who considered Rommel a jumped-up self-publicist, recorded his detestation of the uncouth Swabian in his diary on 23 April: 'I have a feeling that things are in a mess ... Rommel is in no way equal to his task. He rushes about the whole day between his widely scattered units, stages reconnaissance raids and fritters away his forces.'

*

Worrying signs of catastrophe in the west were beginning to filter through to Egypt despite the confused battlefield situation and wartime censorship. In Cairo on 4 April Lady Hermione Ranfurly, who had followed her yeomanry husband to the Middle East and had stayed there in defiance of all instructions to return home, confided to her diary a worrying development in Cyrenaica: 'The enemy has attacked in the Desert. They have chosen their time well – we've sent so much of our strength to defend Greece. There is a horrid rumour that Germans have arrived in North Africa.' There was one consolation for her. 'Thank God Dan has a staff job,' she wrote.

It was now clear to Neame and Gambier-Parry that their weakness relative to the reinvigorated and reinforced enemy meant that they could not effectively defend western Cyrenaica, and that remaining where they were would invite being cut off by the sweeping thrusts of the Germans to the south and east. Morshead's eager Australians and the remains of 2nd Division's support group were ordered therefore to withdraw along the coast to Derna, while the now rather purposeless Headquarters 2nd Armoured Division traversed the Jebel Akhdar to Mechili, hopefully there to meet up with what remained of its subordinate 3rd Armoured Brigade. Communications were so poor, however, that Gambier-Parry did not know that his few remaining tanks already lay useless in the sand at Msus, and that the survivors were even then making their way north through the Jebel to join the exodus westwards along the coast road to Tobruk.

On the afternoon of 4 April the German vanguard came up against the Australians in North Africa for the first time in the war. The Australian 2/13th Battalion was perched precariously on the escarpment 400 feet above the Benghazi plain at Regima, guarding the route to the north. Unable to dig into the rock the Australians had built themselves stone sangars, and their fierce determination to live up to the standards of their fathers in the 1st AIF resulted in the German attack, by tanks, infantry and armoured cars, being halted after a day of bitter fighting, allowing the battalion to disengage and withdraw north to Barce under cover of darkness. The withdrawal was a hurried and confused affair, and although the initial intention was to stand firm at Barce, on the morning of 6 April Morshead discovered that Rommel had exploited his open desert flank and was now a mere forty-eight miles south of Derna while the bulk of his division was still one hundred miles to the west. If the Australians did not move towards Tobruk as fast as they could they would find themselves cut off by the

German advance. Desperate to prove that they could give as good as they got, the Australians made their way over the following four days via the clogged coast road first to Derna and thence to Tobruk. En route they passed the ancient Greek and Roman settlements at Cyrene and Apollonia, the former until recently the location of Graziani's headquarters, buried in the depths of one of the tombs which littered the escarpment.

Major John Devine, by now at the British casualty clearing station at Derna, found himself caught up in the rush and uncertainty of the retreat. The announcement of the withdrawal to Tobruk was received in early April, and then as each day passed the news got bleaker and bleaker. When Benghazi was evacuated on 3 April streams of exhausted troops flooded back to avoid being cut off. 'Past us continually were troops moving, cars roaring along the road,' he recalled. 'There were rumours, the sound of guns, the sound of dumps being blown up, wounded arriving, tank people passing whose tanks had run out of petrol and had to be blown up.' Traffic accidents increased dramatically on the winding coastal road. Night movements needed to be conducted without lights, and many vehicles drove over cliffs. Within days of the first news that the Germans were outflanking them across the desert in a mirror image of General O'Connor's dramatic advance only a month before, Devine could hear the guns along the coast being destroyed. Then 'We heard that we were to be on one minute's notice to move, and we were to leave our kit behind . . . We left so hurriedly that the table was set for dinner and the joint was still cooking in the oven. Many lights were left burning, and clothes and trucks were abandoned in hurried disorder.'

Rommel's crossing of the Cyrenaican desert was an extraordinarily deft achievement. Based solely on bluff it could easily have gone wrong. It was conducted by small groups of troops out of contact with each other, chasing an even more confused enemy across the desert but with a single clear goal: to capture Mechili. Rommel's personal presence in the advance was vital. Constantly chivvying, he kept his men on the move when their natural inclinations were to rest, regroup and recover. Urging them on despite the huge sandstorms that reduced transport to a crawl, demanding navigation through unmapped wilderness, relying solely on compass and stars (when visible), Rommel's few battalions managed to outflank and surprise the few British units left scattered and largely uncoordinated across Cyrenaica. Rommel flitted tirelessly from unit to unit in his Storch (sometimes flying the aircraft himself, as he was a competent pilot), landing alongside his troops in the desert, urging them on, berating them and demanding ever more speed.

Rommel's forcefulness alienated some of his more conservative commanders, forty-nine-year-old Major General Johannes Streich among them. Ordered to take his division across uncharted desert with no preparation Streich refused. Rommel instructed him to do as he was told, and to reconfigure his forces to ensure that his tanks had fuel. 'One cannot permit unique opportunities to slip for the sake of trifles,' recorded Rommel in his diary of this incident, one of an increasing number of disagreements with Streich that convinced him of the need to have his subordinate replaced. Major von Mellenthin, who joined Rommel's staff in May, recalled that during the advance '[Rommel] flew over a company which had halted for no apparent reason, and dropped a message: "Unless you get going at once I shall come down. Rommel."' The company set off immediately in the direction of the enemy. On 5 April 1941, the day after Rommel's great advance through the desert began, Lieutenant Colonel Ponath recorded in his diary, 'In the desert we meet elements of Brescia Division. Incredible track. Everything is stuck. In the dark, panzers run over nine motorcyclists. We lose our way . . . The march remains strenuous. It is very hot. Vehicles repeatedly fall out, lost in the lonesome desert . . .'

Rommel's titular commander General Garibaldi was aghast at the risks he was taking. According to Rommel's diary, the Italian berated him 'violently' on the evening of 3 April for disobeying orders. Rommel ignored the rebukes, defending his actions by the need to ensure that tactical opportunities did not 'slip by unused'. From his own subordinates Rommel brooked no excuse for delay of any kind. Lack of fuel, impossible sand, temperatures as high as 45 degrees Celsius or more, mines (British and Italian) sandstorms and enemy action: were all distractions to the primary goal, speed. Ponath's diary for the following day reads, 'Detestable march on a mine-infested track at Ben Gania . . . At 0430 hours, Rommel bellows and chases us forward, out of touch with the battalion across the stony desert. Only ten vehicles are with us. With these against the rear of the enemy at Derna.' On the same day Schorm worried that the pace Rommel was setting would be too much for his panzers:

At 0300 hours we move off. After an hour we give up. Even by day, with the sand whipped up by the panzers and wind it is wretched enough. By night, it is impossible. Every vehicle loses its way. When we reach the Via Balbia again – who will? – our panzers, or at least their engines, will be ruined. According to instructions, the engines must be changed at 2,000 kilometres. Their life is given by the firm at 2,500 kilometres. They have already done 500 in Germany. We have come 1,000 kilometres along the Via Balbia. By the time we reach Derna, every panzer will easily have passed the limit of 2,000. Six hundred kilometres will have been carried out across the desert – in dust and heat, and that counts for more than treble [normal wear and tear].

When Rommel decided to cut through Cyrenaica's southern desert flank on 3 April his objective was the British-held fort at Mechili. However, within a very short time it became clear to his staff that Tobruk presented a more strategically valuable target. With Rommel rarely at headquarters Chief of Staff Colonel von dem Borne authorized the change of objective to Tobruk after Major Ehlert, operations staff officer, explained to him the need to change the plan: 'It is my opinion . . . that the thrust should bypass Mechili and make for Tobruk before the enemy has time to consolidate there. The present orders to the 5th Light [Division] are "Thrust towards Mechili." In the absence of the general, will you authorize a change of orders and direct that the attack be launched direct against Tobruk instead of Mechili?'

It was almost impossible, however, to get the message to either Rommel or to Streich's division, scattered as it was far and wide across the desert and out of radio contact. The only chance was Rommel's Storch, which Lieutenant Schmidt was ordered to take and find Streich, instructing him to ignore Mechili and make directly for Tobruk. The young ADC rushed to find the pilot and get airborne. However, by the time Schmidt had his orders the wind had got up, and dust was swirling above the desert floor in anticipation of an imminent dust storm. In normal circumstances this was not flying weather, but Schmidt, pressed by the importance of his mission, insisted. The pilot reluctantly coaxed the light aircraft into the sky, straining to gain height by circling slowly into the sky.

But even Schmidt's enthusiasm was not enough. With the wind increasing, the fragile craft swinging violently all over the sky, and with the pilot only barely in control, the aircraft was eventually safely brought down. While the pilot hurriedly tied the plane to stakes hammered into the ground, Schmidt ran blindly into the sandstorm. Extraordinarily he came across the German war correspondent Baron von Esebeck, ploughing slowly through the swirling sand in a Volkswagen. But he too was lost. It was a full day later, after spending an uncomfortable night in the desert, that the frantic young officer was finally able to locate Streich's headquarters near Mechili and deliver his message. He was too late. Rommel had been at the headquarters only an hour before, and he had given orders to attack Mechili. So it was Mechili that felt the weight of Rommel's tanks. If Schmidt had managed to get through earlier, and Mechili had been ignored in favour of an all-out dash on Tobruk, Rommel's advance might have had a very different outcome, preventing large numbers of British and Australian stragglers swelling the Tobruk defences just in time for Rommel's first attack on the perimeter on 9 April.

Far south of the Cyrenaican coast road from Benghazi to Bardia, Mechili lay on the route that O'Connor had used for his tiny force only weeks before. Then the British had surprised the Italians with the audacity of their advance, and the whole of the mighty 10th Army had been destroyed as a result. Now Rommel was giving the British the same medicine, and they were equally unprepared. The headquarters of the British 2nd Armoured Division, the force newly arrived, untrained, slow and inexperienced in desert ways, reached Mechili on the evening of 6 April, where it met up with reinforcements sent from Egypt, the 3rd Indian Motor Brigade. This comprised three Indian cavalry regiments without any armour and equipped only with trucks and rifles. Waiting in vain for the 3rd Armoured Brigade to arrive, unaware it had been forced to abandon most of its tanks in the sand at Msus, the garrison of Mechili was doomed. Advancing on the town in three columns from the south, south-west and west, the Streich and Schwerin Combat Groups reached the outskirts that evening.

During 7 April Streich's forces slowly increased in number and boldly demanded the British surrender. It was refused. When, on the 8th, the British attempted to break out of the tightening German noose, the small number of panzers that had arrived prevented all but a few units – the 1st RHA and parts of the 18th King Edward's Own Cavalry, Indian Army with some Australian anti-tank guns – from escaping. The remainder, including their luckless commander, Major General Gambier-Parry, were captured. Even more devastating than the loss of Mechili was the interception by a German motorcycle unit, on a track below the Jebel Akhdar, of a vehicle containing both Neame and Lieutenant General Sir Richard O'Connor, who had flown back from Cairo on Wavell's instructions on 2 April to help Neame. The whole command structure of Wavell's 13th Corps in Cyrenaica had been decapitated by Rommel's bold stroke. Unknown to his anxious wife in Cairo, one of those captured was Second Lieutenant the Earl of Ranfurly, General Neame's ADC.

Five miles to the east of Mechili Captain Cyril Joly with a mixed troop of Italian A13s and battered old British A9 cruisers had deployed in all-round defence to protect Mechili's left flank after a long and difficult withdrawal from Msus. At midday on 8 April came the last message from the garrison: 'We cannot resist any longer. Some are going to try to break out and make their way back as best they can. It will be every man for himself. Make for Tobruk. Good luck.' Turning north-east Joly pointed his tanks in the direction of the coast road, and the troop drove off as fast as it could manage.

At Mechili that afternoon, to Schmidt's surprise, the Fiesler Storch in which he had been grounded the previous day dropped out of the sky, having somehow become reunited with its rightful owner, depositing a smiling Rommel in front of a despondent group of British prisoners. He seemed to get everywhere, thought Schmidt. Gambier-Parry had three large-wheeled Dorchester armoured command vehicles. Christened Mammoths by the Germans, two were immediately pressed into use, one as Rommel's HQ vehicle, the other as his caravan. Equipped with radios and writing facilities, they were ideal mobile command vehicles. 'Rommel inspected the vehicles with absorbed interest after a brief interview with the captured British generals. He watched them emptied of their British gear. Among the stuff turned out he spotted a pair of large sun-and-sand goggles. He took a fancy to them. He grinned and said, "Booty – permissible, I take it, even for a general." He adjusted the goggles over the gold braid rim of his cap peak.' Those goggles were to become the distinguishing emblem of the Desert Fox.

Meanwhile, on the coast at Derna Roy Farran and the survivors of the 3rd Hussars and 6th RTR, bathing contentedly in the surf, were startled to hear a series of loud explosions emanate from Derna, columns of smoke rising above the town. Packing up rapidly, they discovered that far from being safe, stores and equipment in Derna were being blown up prior to its evacuation. Miserably, they joined the endless bumper-to-bumper convoy of retreating vehicles winding its way slowly up the steep escarpment out of the town. After long delays getting to the far side of the Wadi Derna, a vast tear in the landscape that split Derna from the escarpment, Farran heard the sound of gunfire. A small German force of fifteen vehicles under the command of Lieutenant Colonel Ponath had managed to reach the airfield and was raking the road and the retreating convoys with tank and machine-gun fire. Most vehicles simply put on maximum speed until they reached safety. The Germans were finally driven off, Farran recalled, 'in a gallant, desperate little action by odd fighting units which emerged in turn at the top of the pass . . . Only by a narrow margin did we avoid a reversal of the Battle of Beda Fomm.'

For Major John Devine a long and frightening night followed as he sought to escape the rapidly closing German pincer in an Italian ten-ton diesel truck which had lost its exhaust silencer and deafened the passengers crammed into every available inch of space. At long last the Tobruk perimeter was sighted, just as the long-threatened khamsin came sweeping in. The final part of the journey was pure torture:

> The twelve miles took us several hours, for most of the time someone had to walk in front of the truck. Sand was in our noses, ears, mouths, in fact everywhere . . .
>
> Tired and dejected, choked and blinded by sand, with only odd portions of our kit left to us, we entered the barbed-wire perimeter

defences of Tobruk in the early morning, and at long last lay down on stretchers in the Tobruk hospital and slept, caring nothing about what might happen.

For the time being they were safe, entering the Tobruk perimeter through the posts guarded by Captain Vernon Northwood's A Company, 2/28th Battalion. Having only just arrived in Tobruk as part of the reinforcements hurried up by Wavell, the Australians were amazed: 'That was what we called the Benghazi Handicap. There didn't seem to be any organization. They were saying to us, "Better get out of Tobruk, there's trouble coming. Rommel's coming!" We said, "We don't get out of here. We're here!" Then all of a sudden the perimeter closed.'

With Mechili seized Rommel ordered Streich to strike east to the coast without delay. Speed had achieved the capture of Cyrenaica, and Rommel was insistent that the same relentless pace be carried on to complete the capture of Tobruk. While the 5th Light Division was pressing overland through Cyrenaica, the coastal advance had made rapid progress, and Derna had been captured on 8 April by Ponath supported by combat teams led by Schwerin and Olbrich rushed up from Mechili. At the same time Tripoli had seen the arrival of Heinrich von Prittwitz's 15th Panzer Division, with troops flying directly into Benghazi. Within the month they would also be flying into Derna.

Rommel recognized early on just how vital Tobruk would be to his advance into Egypt. In British hands it would prove a constant sore in his flank, as well as denying him the use of its port for supplies and reinforcements. Rommel was therefore concerned to overrun it as quickly as possible before its defences could be organized.

Late on the evening of 8 April Rommel reached the sea at Derna only hours after the retreating Australians, the 2nd Division Support Group and the tank-less remnants of the 3rd Armoured Brigade had managed to extricate themselves from the town, although large numbers of other troops and equipment fell into German hands. Ponath scribbled quickly in his diary that night:

Unit advances on Derna. No enemy. Odd POWs keep arriving. A heavy sandstorm is blowing up. A German aircraft lands and makes contact and takes the mail. Derna is clear of the enemy. Brescia Division approaches from the west. Order to move to Tobruk [arrives] at 2100 hours. Rommel is pleased with our success. Dead tired. Night march. Handing over of prisoners and captured material.

Details of the Tobruk defences were as yet unknown to the Germans. They had no maps and no idea of what they faced. But given the rapid advances his troops had already made, Rommel could not believe that he would meet anything other than mild resistance. He had seen nothing over the last few days to make him believe that Tobruk would be anything other than a walkover. On 9 April he received reports of activity in the town, including news that the British were attempting a Dunkirk-type evacuation from the harbour, and that same day the Italian Brescia Division arrived after its advance along the coast road from Benghazi. Like the dash across Cyrenaica, and entirely in keeping with Rommel's character, Rommel's first plan to take Tobruk depended on speed and surprise. He ordered an immediate assault. The Brescia would advance from the west, raising a great cloud of sand to confuse the enemy into overestimating Axis strength and intentions. At the same time Streich's 5th Light Division would sweep around the southern perimeter to attack it from the south-east, while Prittwitz would assault the town directly from the Derna Road.

Rommel had assumed that Streich would by this time have joined him on the coast, but the 5th Light Division was dismantling and repairing the turrets of its tanks, jammed shut by the sand, at Mechili. Rommel was furious with the delay and ordered Streich to Gazala by the next morning, Thursday 10 April, from which point he was to attack Tobruk. In the afternoon Rommel moved east to Tmimi, and informed Prittwitz of his plan. Given command of the 3rd Reconnaissance, 8th Machine-Gun and 605th Anti-Tank Battalions, Prittwitz was ordered on the evening of 8 April to drive on to Tobruk without delay. Having only just arrived from Benghazi, Prittwitz was staggered. 'But I've only just arrived in Africa,' he complained to Lieutenant Colonel von Schwerin. 'I don't know the first thing about the troops or the terrain.' Schwerin found him a bed, and the exhausted Prittwitz fell asleep only to be shouted awake by Rommel at dawn the next morning, 9 April. 'The British are escaping!' A confused, disorientated Prittwitz leapt into Schwerin's *Kübelwagen* and sped towards Tobruk.

On the same morning Major General Heinrich Kirchheim, in temporary command of the Brescia Division, was ordered by Rommel to find a suitable area to prepare his division to attack Tobruk. On the Derna road Kirchheim suddenly saw sand kicked up on the road ahead. 'Aircraft!' shouted his driver as three Hurricanes approached at speed just above the desert. Machine-gun fire engulfed the vehicle and Kirchheim was struck in the arm, shoulder and eye. As Kirchheim's wounds were being dressed, Prittwitz arrived on the scene. After exchanging pleasantries – Prittwitz congratulating Kirchheim on wounds that would send him home – Prittwitz drove on towards Tobruk.

Ponath's forwardmost troops had been held up eleven miles short of Tobruk on the Derna road by intense artillery fire from the guns of the British 51st Field Regiment and Australian anti-tank guns, some of them siezed Italian weapons. It was into this hail of fire that the unfortunate Prittwitz, with Schwerin's driver, drove on the morning of 10 April. At Milestone 13 a direct hit from an Australian anti-tank gun killed them both. Streich – whom Rommel had sidelined for the attack that morning in favour of Prittwitz because he believed the former slow and conventional – was furious at what he regarded as Prittwitz's unnecessary death and laid the blame squarely on Rommel's shoulders, a result of his arrogant impetuosity.

Thirty-one-year-old Captain Vernon Northwood of A Company, 2/28th Battalion watched the first German troops come unwarily into his sights. The Australians – individual toughness and raw courage making up for what they lacked in battlefield experience – saw no reason why they should be 'frightened of Jerry' and were grimly determined to hold the line come what may.

On the first day, 10 April, ten o'clock in the morning, we saw the German tanks coming over the rise. The Royal Horse Artillery were firing over open sights, but they copped an awful bashing from the tanks. We could hear men screaming. They carried them to a bit of a ditch. I was up a water tower, with a wonderful view, so I was

able to report back what I was seeing. I was cold with fury when I
saw the Germans machine-gunning an ambulance as it came up to
get these fellers. Our men just took it in their stride though. Many
of them had worked in the goldfields [of Western Australia]; they
were men who knew what rough living was all about.

Private Peter Salmon, also of the 2/28th Battalion, was surprised by
the nonchalance of the advancing Germans. They clearly believed
Tobruk would be a walkover:

I was on the Derna Road when the Germans came. I remember it
very vividly – it was a surprise to see them. They were in trucks
and they came to the perimeter and I still see them getting off
those trucks. I don't know what they expected to find, but then of
course we opened up on them with small arms and artillery – the
blokes that were using the bush artillery were quite incredible,
because they had no sights (the Italians had stripped the guns of
their sights) but they were getting some very accurate firing, and it
was amazing what they did.

The 'bush artillery' comprised Australian soldiers manning siezed
Italian artillery pieces. The stripped sights proved no impediment to
the Diggers, who were assisted in their efforts by the vast quantities
of ammunition left behind in the fortress. John Devine came across
guns and men of the bush artillery on the El Adem road only yards
short of the Red Line:

This particular lot of bush artillery was operated by a mixed crew
of batmen and cooks . . . they had their OP [observation post] fully
twenty yards in front of them at the roadside . . .

The OP would take up position, and after the shell had been
pushed into place in the spout, and the fuse had been wrenched to
the desired time setting with the aid of a spanner from the truck
[which had brought up the ammunition], there followed little bags
containing Italian cordite. These were pushed in after the shell in
no very definite quantities, and finally the breech was rammed
home. The gunners then retreated down a very long rope lanyard

... This lanyard then being pulled, fired the gun. The burst was watched, and the OP signalled the result of the shot.

A typical signal following observation of a burst would be 'Move her two telegraph poles to the right. Knock out a bloody brick.' Traverse was measured in telegraph poles along the road, and to vary the elevation bricks were pushed under the trailer.

The bush artillery did not claim to achieve much more than raise the morale of the troops, although Devine records that the amateur gunners claimed many Italian trucks and a stationary aeroplane that had been forced to land beyond the wire. Private Frank Harrison spoke with real affection about these untrained but determined Australians sighting their guns by squinting along the barrel and shouting 'Let 'er go, mate!' at the required moment.

If improvised, the defensive block was nevertheless extremely effective, and the death of Prittwitz dealt the overconfident Germans a significant blow. On the same day Rommel's party (including Schmidt) in its newly acquired Mammoth came under accurate British artillery fire from El Adem, which the British evacuated later in the day, when the 7th Armoured Division Support Group withdrew back into Egypt. Von Wechmar's 3rd Reconnaissance Battalion then moved through Acroma and across the desert tracks south of Tobruk to El Adem. At one stage Rommel noticed two vehicles following the Mammoth, one of which was clearly British. Ordering his men to stop and train an anti-tank gun on the pursuing cars, he was surprised to be confronted by a red-faced Streich, yelling at him that his actions had cost Prittwitz's life. Rommel was unmoved. 'How dare you drive after me in a British car? I was about to have the gun open fire on you.' Streich retorted, 'In that case, you would have managed to kill both your panzer division commanders in one day, *Herr General*.'

*

It was now clear to the British that Tobruk was Rommel's target. On the 7th an alarmed Churchill telegrammed Wavell, 'You should surely be able to hold Tobruk, with its permanent Italian defences, at least until or unless the enemy brings up strong artillery forces. It seems difficult to believe that he can do this for some weeks. He would run great risks in masking Tobruk and advancing on Egypt, observing that we can reinforce from the sea and would menace his communications. Tobruk, therefore, seems to be a place to be held to the death without thought of retirement.'

Wavell was not so sure, observing rather pessimistically to Churchill in reply the following day, 'Tobruk is not a good defence position. The long line of communication is to all intents and purposes unprotected and lacks the necessary installations.' In London Major General John Kennedy, director of military operations, agreed. It seemed unlikely that the force caught in Tobruk would be strong enough to break out once surrounded or to launch attacks on the German line of communications. Kennedy believed the best strategy would be to withdraw well into Egypt, to extend Rommel's supply lines back through Libya. Nevertheless, Wavell changed his mind and decided on 7 April to hold Tobruk. Churchill and Wavell were wise to reject Kennedy's advice. After all, if Rommel held Tobruk the Royal Navy would become less of a threat to Axis communications in the Mediterranean than it currently was and the port facilities in Tobruk would also dramatically reduce Rommel's logistical problems and make him a greater, rather than a lesser, threat to Egypt.

The single tarmacked coast road from Tripoli east to Alexandria in Egypt is 1,875 miles long. All fuel and supplies coming into North Africa for the Axis forces had to be moved along this road to the front. The further east Rommel advanced, the greater the drain on fuel and vehicles this tenuous line of communication became. It was essential therefore to scavenge, and Axis forces utilized food, fuel, armour, vehicles, ammunition and weapons captured from their foes whenever they could. Between them the ports of Tripoli and Benghazi provided a capacity of about 60,000 tons per month, and Tobruk 24,000. To sustain the whole of Rommel's Afrika Korps – which would grow to some seven divisions by the end of 1941 – required a monthly port capacity of 70,000 tons. The mathematics was clear: without Tobruk, Rommel did not have the port capacity he required to sustain his troops in North Africa. Tobruk was a vital element in the German offensive equation.

In any case, in April 1941 Wavell had insufficient transport available to evacuate all the troops remaining in Cyrenaica. Aside from holding Tobruk, the only other option was to allow them to fall into German hands. On the 8th Wavell flew into Tobruk with Major General Lavarack, GOC of the 7th Australian Division, appointed to replace the unfortunate Neame. Scribbling his instructions to Lavarack on a scrap of paper, Wavell told him there was nothing between him and Cairo and that reinforcements might be available in two months.

That night all remaining troops except for the support group at El Adem were ordered within the perimeter, where feverish efforts had been made to organize the defences. Having the opportunity to stand and fight was what the men of Morshead's 9th Australian Division now craved more than anything else. After more than a week of withdrawals and embarrassing confusion the Diggers wanted to strike back. As one Australian officer remarked, 'We couldn't let it be said that the 9th had lost what the 6th had won.' Evacuated into Tobruk during the first week of April, Gunner Leonard Tutt recalled, 'Once we were apprised of the decision to hold Tobruk, we were pleased to be part of it. We had found running to be very demoralizing.' Rommel was in for a fight. Churchill recognized that a siege would make heavy demands on Axis forces, and in a directive from London on 14 June insisted that Tobruk be defended so as to provide 'an invaluable bridgehead ... on the communications of the enemy. It should be reinforced as may be necessary both with infantry and by armoured fighting vehicles, to enable active and continuous raiding of the enemy's flanks and rear.' To Air Vice-Marshal Arthur Harris the prime minister mused, 'A sally port ... Yes, a sally port; that is what we want, that is the thing to do with them. The farther he advances the more you threaten, the more he has to fear. That is the answer, a sally port ...'

Forward defences – the Red Line – were hurriedly prepared. Lavarack decided that the long outer perimeter needed to be held despite the fact that he had only seven battalions to do so. A shorter line would allow the Germans to place their guns closer to the port and probably make it unusable. The ex-Italian perimeter positions, while admirably camouflaged, did not allow all the occupants to fire their personal weapons at the same time. The Australians and the Northumberland Fusiliers were forced to extend and improve these defences rapidly, to avoid a repeat of the successful breach in January. Additional minefields were laid, wire prepared, Italian emplacements and defensive positions cleaned up and repopulated with Diggers eager to show what they could do. Defence in depth was organized and mobile counter-attack forces based on the few available tanks prepared. Captured Italian weapons, especially anti-tank guns and artillery pieces, were placed at key points on the perimeter; of the garrison's 113 anti-tank guns, half were Italian. Infantry battalions were deployed with two or three companies forward and a reserve company half a mile to the rear for counter-attacks. In due course a second line was prepared – the Blue Line – two miles to the rear of the forward defences. At the three main crossroads – King's Cross, Pilastrino and Derna/Pilastrino (Fort Airente) – Lavarack placed an infantry battalion in trucks as his reserve.

Once the decision had been made to defend Tobruk and the 9th Australian Division given responsibility for its defence, Morshead brought his battalion commanders together and, reflecting their own determination to stand and fight, told them emphatically, 'There will be no Dunkirk here. If we should have to get out, we shall fight our way out. There is to be no surrender and no retreat.' Morshead was a militia officer of considerable ability who had gained experience during the First World War, commanding the 33rd Battalion at the age of twenty-six. He was widely known and respected in the AIF for being precise, meticulous and straight to the point, his men giving him the sobriquet 'Ming the Merciless' because of his strict approach to discipline. Chester Wilmot observed, 'It is popularly believed that the Australian soldier chafes under strict discipline, but Morshead has always held that without it there is nothing to bind the strong individuality of the Australian soldiers into an organized fighting force.' From the outset of the siege Morshead insisted on an offensive stance. No-man's-land was patrolled aggressively and enemy posts raided regularly. 'I determined we should make no-man's-land our land,' he insisted. Reacting to a newspaper report that 'Tobruk can take it' he retorted, 'We're not here to take it. We're here to give it!'

Unaware that he was now facing the steadfast opposition of four brigades of Australian troops desperate to 'have a crack' at the Germans and determined to show themselves worthy of their forefathers

– after all, this was why they had enlisted and travelled halfway round the world – Rommel refused to allow his advance to be halted by Tobruk. He immediately dispatched Lieutenant Colonel von Wechmar's 3rd Reconnaissance Battalion, together with the 15th Motorized Infantry Battalion (less its two artillery companies) and a company of Lieutenant Colonel Knabe's 33rd Anti-Tank Battalion equipped with a battery of 88-millimetre anti-aircraft guns deployed in the anti-tank role, to the Egyptian frontier.

*

Rommel's attempt to overrun Tobruk by rushing its porous defences had failed, so he now determined to tighten the noose. He ordered the Brescia Division, still under the command of the wounded Major General Kirchheim, who had not been sent home to recuperate after all, to move up to relieve the 5th Light Division, which in its turn was directed to move around the desert flank to close the eastern exit from Tobruk. The Ariete Division with its sixty tanks was ordered up to El Adem.

Over the next few days Rommel could be found everywhere in the Axis positions encircling Tobruk – measuring, assessing, planning. All the while British and Australian stragglers tried desperately to break through the cordon that had been thrown up around the town. After setting out for the coast on the afternoon of the 8th from east of Mechili Captain Cyril Joly and his tank troop soon noticed the dust clouds of following panzer Mark IIIs. As darkness drew nearer, so did the German tanks. Just before last light faded the faster panzers finally drew into range, firing into the thin rear plates of the British tanks. The inevitable happened and one of the A13s was struck and immobilized. 'We're hit in the engine and have a fire in the turret,' radioed the tank sergeant. 'It's no good trying to fight it out, 'cause I reckon we shall blow up soon and we'll all go with it if we don't bail out. Best of luck. Cheerio.' With that, the crew bailed out and were still running when the tank exploded, showering the desert with burning pieces of metal and rocking Joly's own tank now hundreds of yards away. Then Joly's own tank was hit and a track sheared. The six-hour chase had come to an end, but the darkness allowed the tank to slew into a small ravine and remain hidden from the pursuing, but equally exhausted, Germans.

Joly and two of his crewmen faced a hundred-mile journey on foot to Tobruk through the desert, which was now swarming with German and Italian troops. Walking at night, hiding up during the day, they reached Tmimi first, then nudged their way along the coast, avoiding the Italian encampments that had sprung up with the advance of the Brescia Division, stealing food and water where they could. Five days later, at the end of their tether, exhausted and hallucinating, they managed to crawl into the waiting arms of Australian infantrymen at the furthest extent of Wadi es Sefl on Tobruk's westernmost perimeter.

*

Captain Rea Leakey of 1st RTR felt he deserved his leave. He had enough sand in his shoes to consider himself a veteran of the desert. He had certainly spent more time in it than most and had been the first to discover a secret descent to the otherwise inaccessible Qattara Depression. This route was to be extensively used by British Long Range Desert Group patrols in 1941 and 1942. A natural, enthusiastic and incorrigible fighter, he loved his men, his tanks and the desert in that order. But on the balmy evening of 7 April 1941 he was enjoying a spot of sailing in Alexandria harbour with his friend Jimmy Noel and two pretty Scottish nursing sisters. All had made the 120-mile journey in Rea's little car from Cairo and each was attired in a bathing costume.

Leakey's fun was interrupted by the sight of an unmistakable black beret atop a soldier walking along the quayside towards an old merchant vessel. What was a soldier of the RTR doing in Alexandria? Intrigued, he manoeuvred the dinghy closer and to his surprise recognized a man of his own squadron. He should by Leakey's reckoning have been at least 120 miles away in Cairo. Asked why he was in Alexandria, the soldier pointed to the rusty sea-stained vessel alongside the quay and replied, 'I am just going to get on board ship.' None the wiser, Leakey and his passengers made their way towards what turned

out to be the *Thurland Castle*. 'I thought he must be out of his senses,'
recalled Leakey. But a surprise awaited him:

> We sailed towards this ship and received a nasty shock: looking
> down at the four of us . . . was the majority of our regiment, and
> there was much laughter and cheering. Then the CO poked his face
> over the side of the ship and asked where the hell we had been in
> the last 24 hours. I had forgotten to give our address when we left
> Cairo.
>
> 'Well, never mind where you have been, get moving. Go back
> to Cairo immediately and collect the truck we have left there for
> you. You will then drive to Tobruk and you have not a minute to
> spare.'

Lieutenant Colonel Brown, CO of 1st RTR, could not be accused of
exaggeration. Leaving the scene of 13th Corps' extraordinary triumph
in western Cyrenaica in February for a spot of leave in Egypt, Leakey
had been entirely unaware of the arrival of Lieutenant General Erwin
Rommel and the Afrika Korps.

Rushing back to Cairo, Leakey and Noel threw themselves into
the old Morris truck that had been loaded with their kit and immediately began their 350-mile journey to Tobruk. 'Taking turns,' Leakey
recalled, 'we drove through the night and never stopped.'

> By dawn the next day we were past Mersa Matruh, and fast
> approaching Libya. We now started meeting a constant stream of
> vehicles of every description driving in the opposite direction. As
> we came through Bardia, we saw dumps of petrol and other stores
> burning, and the number of vehicles that passed us had diminished
> considerably. A few miles to the west of Bardia we were stopped by
> a military policeman who said that the road to Tobruk had been
> cut and we could go no further. As the odd truck was still coming
> past, we decided to go on, and we had the road to ourselves. Several
> times we saw armoured cars in the desert to the south of us, but
> we did not stop to find out whether they were friend or foe.
>
> At about noon we saw the Tobruk perimeter wire, and the

gateway across the road, but still open. But as we drove towards it, we saw soldiers hurriedly start to push the heavy wooden beams across the gap, and a burst of machine-gun fire drew our attention to some German armoured cars which were approaching from the south.

'Come on in, you Pommy bastards,' shouted the Diggers as they pulled back the beams. They drove through, and once again Tobruk was surrounded.

4 » ROMMEL'S FIRST STRIKE

SS *Balmora* lay in Tobruk harbour loading men to be evacuated back to Alexandria as Rommel's troops rushed headlong for the town. Private Frank Harrison of the Royal Signals patiently waited for his turn to board. Smoke seeped skywards from the oil tanks of the shot-up half-sunk ship lying drunkenly against the shore. The smoke and booming artillery in the distance made for a strangely apocalyptic vision, but for Harrison and his mates it was all soon to be over, dust and desert left behind, the trauma of their awful retreat from the Gulf of Sirte a distant nightmare. They had not eaten, drunk or slept properly for a week.

A sergeant made his way through the crowd of quietly milling men. 'Jones! Leggat! Gauton and Harrison!' Answering reluctantly to their names the four soldiers elbowed their way to the front of the throng. There was something ominous in the precision of the sergeant's voice, but its authority had been strangely comforting. The terse instruction that came next was all too familiar: 'Right, you lot, collect your kit and come with me!' For Harrison this was an easy command to obey; the last he had seen of his kit had been in a fiercely burning armoured car south of Mersa el Brega. But when the sergeant led them to a small open-topped truck depression set in. It was clear that they were not going to board the *Balmora* after all. Their signalling skills had been deemed important enough for them to be retained in Tobruk. Did this mean that the town, port and defensive perimeter were to be held?

Silent in their misery, the four men bounced around the back of the 15-cwt truck grinding slowly up the heavily potholed Via Balbia. As the road reached the top of the first escarpment, the vehicle turned half-right, following the track south-west in the direction of Fort Solaro. Still no one spoke. Alexandria with its hot baths, clean sheets, pretty women and Shafto's open-air cinema now seemed remote. But Harrison's mood was lifted by what came next. Through the rattle of metal and grinding of gears came the sound of singing.

A truck overtook us, smothering us with its dust. It was open like our own and filled with infantrymen. They were wearing tin hats like our own and had their rifles propped up beside them; they were singing and they didn't seem to be giving a damn, not for the dust and not for the crashing of the truck springs and certainly not for the thunder claps coming from out west. They broke their singing to curse us with strange oaths and to bless us with stranger signs, and then they were gone with their cloud of dust. . . . They were Australians of course, sons of the southern sun, and something strange happened at that moment, which I have never forgotten. I quite lost my sense of despair. I realized that whatever I was being asked to face I could not be in better company to meet it.

As the Australians rattled away in the direction of Fort Pilastrino, the signallers' truck drew up on a high piece of ground dotted with low rocky outcrops. This was Fort Solaro, a network of cunningly sited deeply sunk concrete bunkers, gun positions, infantry trenches and anti-aircraft emplacements. A short scramble down the rocks and buried deep within the walls of the escarpment on the seaward side lay an extensive complex of caves and underground corridors. These were to become the headquarters of the Tobruk garrison and Harrison's home for the next eight months.

Frank Harrison looked back along the road they had travelled. As the dust slowly settled he saw the sea glinting through the haze hovering over the harbour. Turning half-right he stared across at the runway of the El Gubbi airfield, which straddled the Via Balbia. Hurricanes in European-theatre camouflage were taking off and landing. A number of wrecked planes had been pushed casually to the side of the runway. Horribly exposed to air attack, El Gubbi enjoyed few natural defences and would not last long under siege. Due south the desert stretched away towards the next high ground, 7,000 yards away and 450 feet above sea level, where the reserve perimeter – the Blue Line – would one day be prepared.

The men joked that whereas the Red Line, the forward perimeter, was indeed thin, the Blue Line was so threadbare as to be almost non-existent. The important thing, Harrison observed, was that the plateau between El Gubbi and the Blue Line was dead ground to the enemy: that is, from their positions outside the perimeter Axis troops could not look directly onto the plateau. To observe this area the enemy had to use their slow-flying and inadequately protected reconnaissance aircraft (nicknamed Betty Henschels by the Allies), a dangerous task for the Luftwaffe with thousands of itchy Australian trigger fingers below. A quarter-turn right lay the imposing pile of rocks that represented Fort Pilastrino. The road from where Harrison stood at Solaro ran via Pilastrino out through the perimeter to Acroma. Looking due west he could see the long black strip of the Via Balbia wriggling its way across the roof of the western plateau on its journey to Derna and beyond.

The four men were quickly apprised of the task expected of them. Tobruk was indeed to be held. Men, tanks, aircraft and equipment of all kinds were being salvaged from across Cyrenaica to be brought into the perimeter, including every remnant of armour that had survived the previous fortnight's fighting. This cobbled-together force would retain the title of the 3rd Armoured Brigade, the once-proud formation that had fought through northern France in 1940 but which had been so poorly prepared in Cyrenaica. The remains of one of its regiments – the 5th RTR – was to form the nucleus of the new formation. Colloquially dubbed the Tobruk Tanks, Lieutenant Colonel Henry Drew – erstwhile CO of the 5th – was given command. Drew's instructions to Jones, Leggat, Gauton and Harrison were brief: 'Work my signals for me. I want one wireless set on twenty-four-hour watch taking reports from the armoured car patrols. We'll arrange the rest as and when we need it.' Frank Harrison observed that these were the only orders that he received, or indeed needed, in the first six months of the siege of Tobruk.

In the early days of April, before the Tobruk perimeter was sealed, soldiers and equipment had poured in from all points of the compass.

Infantry units, artillery, tanks – all converged in a tangle of confusion; men and machines racing to avoid being cut off by Rommel's scything attack through Cyrenaica. The last battalion of Morshead's division – the 2/48th – had slipped in during the early hours of Thursday 10 April, only hours before Prittwitz's abortive attack along the Derna road, while into the grateful arms of Drew's 3rd Armoured Brigade fell the twenty-six cruisers (a mix of battle-worn A9, A10 and A13s) and the fifteen light tanks of B and C Squadrons of 1st RTR. One bit of luck was that four of the majestic Matilda II tanks from 4th RTR had also been on the SS *Thurland Castle*. These 'queens of the battlefield' might have been, as Peter Cochrane described them, 'antediluvian' when compared to what was to come and outgunned by the 50- and 75-millimetre main armaments of the panzer Mark IVs, but the heavily armoured beasts were a substantial enhancement to Tobruk's defences. These forty-five tanks were supported by the armoured car veterans of the King's Dragoon Guards, together with fragments of other regiments: the 3rd King's Royal Hussars and the tank-less men of the 6th RTR. These, in concert with twenty-four 2-pounder anti-tank guns mounted on the backs of 30-cwt trucks, comprised the Tobruk commander's mobile reserve. Against him at this time Rommel could field well over one hundred tanks.

At noon on Tuesday 8 April Leakey drove down through Tobruk's three descending escarpments to the harbour, to meet up with the remainder of 1st RTR disembarking from the SS *Thurland Castle*. The race was on to get the tanks serviceable and up to the front line as quickly as possible. This was far from easy. All vehicles had suffered heavily during Operation Compass. Many had been in pieces in Cairo workshops and then been rushed by barge to Alexandria for transportation to Tobruk. Few had working radios. Worn-out guns had not been replaced and new weapons lay greased up in their factory crates. But, fully operational or not, armour was required on the perimeter defences to help resist the pressure of Rommel's vanguard. Leslie Morshead's plan was to group the tanks together at Fort Pilastrino and King's Cross, from where they could counter-attack as and when required.

By 4 p.m. on Tuesday 8 April the first of the 1st RTR tanks were, in Leakey's words 'more or less fit for action'. Their initial task came two days later when Prittwitz attempted to rush the perimeter from the Derna road. Leakey took his tanks forward although dust and smoke made navigation extremely difficult. However, Australian soldiers guided the tanks to the battle area, where the cruisers were able – with the guns of 51st Field Regiment – to assist in halting Prittwitz's speculative attack. This was Leakey's first exposure to the Australians of the 2nd AIF. Like Frank Harrison, he was impressed. 'In the months to come,' he recorded, 'I got to know many of the officers and men of this division, and they were second to none.'

*

The death of Prittwitz during his foolhardy assault along the Derna road on the morning of 10 April and the failure of the attack had in no way lessened Erwin Rommel's determination to find a way into Tobruk. 'We probably tried too much with too little,' he remarked nonchalantly to Johannes Streich after the latter's outburst that after-noon. 'Anyway,' Rommel concluded, 'we are in a better position now.' At this point the Germans still had no maps of Tobruk and were obliged to attack blind, knowing nothing of the defences facing them and driving against sections of the wire in the hope of finding a weak spot. Nevertheless, all the evidence indicated that the defences around Tobruk were more strongly held than anything recently encountered by the Germans. Reconnaissance completed, Rommel drove back to his HQ, which had been set up on the evening of 9 April in a concrete villa situated along the main road to the west of Tobruk. Known thereafter as the White House, telephone wires connected it to the Italian fort at Acroma. The rest of Rommel's staff hid themselves and their vehicles in a nearby wadi.

On the morning that Prittwitz was killed Rommel took his open-topped Horch Kfz.15 staff car and, accompanied by Schmidt and an armoured escort, began a tour of Tobruk's perimeter. Travelling first to Acroma along a dusty desert track, the party turned left towards El Adem. They had not gone far before well-aimed British artillery fire landed among the vehicles. No one was harmed. Despite several scrapes, Rommel was to enjoy a charmed life in the desert. Reaching the high ground to the north of El Adem they came across companies of recently arrived German infantry of Lieutenant Colonel Gustav Ponath's 8th Machine-Gun Battalion preparing for an imminent attack. But their vehicles remained an inviting target to British artillery observation officers, some of whom remained on the escarpment at El Adem until the following day. Schmidt fell into conversation with a namesake of his he had met before. 'While the general talked, a salvo of enemy shells fell among us. A young lieutenant was killed, and my friend Schmidt lost an arm.'

Moving on another two miles, they came across Streich's HQ concealed in a wadi. The Tobruk batteries had followed them, and once again a salvo of shells came down. Rommel's final instructions to Streich were to waste no time punching a hole in the Tobruk defences. He wanted an attack the following afternoon – Good Friday, 11 April – when more artillery pieces would have arrived to support Streich's division.

*

To the exhausted crews of 1st RTR the first few days of their time in Tobruk proved a debilitating round of urgent responses to threatened penetrations of the perimeter. The night following the repulse of Prittwitz's force British tanks were kept constantly busy rushing – as fast as the lumbering vehicles could manage – to protect endangered sections of the line. On Good Friday morning Leakey's squadron found itself opposite Acroma in the south-western corner of the perimeter, called to deal with an encroachment by enemy tanks. 'Off we went to deal with them and we were delighted to find that they were the little Italian two-man tanks which had not been seen for many months. They were now being used as flame-throwing tanks, and we soon disposed of them.'

Rea Leakey thought he had to have been the last to make it into Tobruk, but late in the evening of Wednesday 9 April, twenty-four hours after his arrival, a long convoy of 300 vehicles comprising the whole of the 107th Regiment, Royal Horse Artillery (South Nottinghamshire Hussars), a pre-war Territorial Army artillery regiment equipped with 25-pounders, made it through. German patrols had cut the road to Bardia some twenty-four hours before, and the arrival of the regiment was nothing short of miraculous. But Rommel did not have the strength to close the road until the arrival of Knabe's motorcycle detachment the following day. Four days before, the Hussars had been conducting artillery practice at Kabrit Camp in the Nile Delta.

On 4 April their CO, the fox-hunting Lieutenant Colonel William Seeley, had received orders to make best speed for Tobruk. It would be a far from easy task. Their destination lay in Libya, over 700 miles across the desert via a single rapidly crumbling tarmacked road. On Sunday 6 April, with the lights of Cairo beckoning in the distance, Seeley paraded the whole regiment. Bombardier Ray Ellis of 425 Battery recalled that he told them what they had been tasked to do, warning there was every chance of being dive-bombed en route. It was imperative that they succeeded in getting the precious 25-pounders into Tobruk. If attacked by panzers or Stukas they were under strict instructions to press on with whatever equipment survived.

Escorted by military police with sirens wailing, Sunday night saw the convoy pressing forward through Cairo's suburbs to their overnight stop at Mena Camp near Alexandria. Tuesday found the regiment driving on through the now deserted Mersa Matruh. It was clear something had gone badly wrong in Cyrenaica. Ellis recalled:

> The deeper we got into the desert, the more alarmed we became. We began to meet columns of lorries laden with troops and equipment, and also many ambulances, all of them travelling at speed and heading eastwards . . . There was more than a hint of panic in the air, and the further west we travelled the more disorderly it all became. It was soon obvious that the British Army of the Nile was in headlong retreat; everybody seemed to be sharing but one thought, and that was to put as much distance between themselves and the enemy as possible.

The convoy drove virtually non-stop, only halting to refuel from dumps of petrol which were blown up after them. As they drove through Buq Buq dispatch riders raced along the length of the convoy carrying stark notices reading: CLOSE UP. DRIVE AS FAST AS POSSIBLE.

Nerves were fraught during the last eighty miles between the

Egyptian frontier and their destination. In each vehicle men shared the driving, concentrating on the bumpy surface rather than the German tanks and armoured cars that they knew had already reached the road or the Axis planes ranging along the coast. Private Reg McNish recalled, 'The drivers were changing over without stopping – they used to get out one door, nip over the bonnet and back in the other door. We just kept going.' As the miles to their destination diminished, night settled over the desert and the sky ahead was lit up with bright flashes like lightning from a tropical storm. To the south flickers denoted German forces on the move across the vast desert floor. Sergeant George Pearson was praying that he wouldn't come across any German tanks. He did, but they would leave him alone: 'By the middle of the afternoon a few tanks appeared on the escarpment side. I was watching them, they were German tanks, and they kept pace with us, following along and I was shaking in my shoes thinking, Oh my God, please, please, don't make me have to drop off! Luckily they didn't attack but I had a distinct looseness of the bowels when I thought of what might have happened.'

As the wire along Tobruk's eastern perimeter approached, flashes briefly illuminated the scene accompanied by the delayed reports of explosions. Major Robert Daniell, a regular army officer in the RHA attached to the South Notts Hussars as second-in-command, insisted that the vehicles drove with their headlights blazing, to intimidate the few Germans who had so far reached the Via Balbia. It worked. On Wednesday 9 April with about two hours to midnight the remaining 'quads', limbers and guns raced into Tobruk. Australian sentries hastily relaid the wire and mines on the road behind the exhausted, jubilant gunners. They were in, but for how long?

After spending a confused night at the El Adem crossroads (known to both Londoners and Sydneysiders as 'King's Cross') 426 Battery of the South Notts Hussars moved into its position along the El Adem road the following morning. Three miles from the Red Line, its main task was to provide artillery support to the Australian 2/13th Battalion. The newly arrived Territorial Army gunners of the 107th mixed with the men and guns of the regulars of the 1st RHA. The Germans were already aggressively probing the perimeter. Before the first rounds were fired that morning Ellis recalled seeing Colonel Seeley walking

calmly up and down in front of the guns. He appreciated the gesture.
The 107th RHA didn't need the order that came down later in the day
that Tobruk was 'to be held at all costs'; they were the South Notts
Hussars. The men were all friends, who had lived, worked and trained
together for years before the war as part-time soldiers. They would
stand up to the Germans, come what may. During that day – Thursday
10 April – artillery support was called for over the field telephone
by the infantry on the perimeter and the armoured reconnaissance
cars of the Kings Dragoon Guards (which remained outside until
the following day) and continuously provided, the gunners sweating,
heaving and firing almost constantly under the burning sun. It was
these guns that had followed Rommel's party on his perambulations
round the perimeter that morning.

*

Erwin Rommel was impatient to see action and had instructed Major
General Streich to attack with his 5th Light Division in the El Adem
sector on the afternoon of 11 April. His eagerness to move against
Tobruk resulted in a sorry little affair in the Acroma sector of the
perimeter early on the morning of that day. At first light on the 11th
the Afrika Korps commander drove from the White House back along
the dusty track to Acroma, where he paused to observe Tobruk's
defences far to the east. Several miles off on the horizon stood the
ramshackle buildings that denoted the half-complete Fort Pilastrino.
Was the artillery fire he had experienced the previous day a desperate
bluff by the British to disguise virtually non-existent defences? Could
pausing while the extra tanks and troops of the 5th Light and 15th
Panzer Divisions were brought up have been in fact a strategic error,
allowing the British to organize Tobruk's defences or even to mount a
second Dunkirk from the port? Four panzers waited in the early-
morning light under the command of Lieutenant Wahl. Standing there
alone with his binoculars, a pensive Rommel suddenly sprang into
action. Tobruk's defences were mere bluff. Initiative and aggression
would break them. Turning to Schmidt, Rommel declared, '*Herr Leutnant*, we're off! Tell that officer [Wahl] to follow with his panzers.'

Rommel drove away in the direction of Tobruk, and Schmidt ran back to deliver the orders. Wahl climbed aboard his panzer and grinned to Schmidt. 'Off to Tobruk!' It barely seemed sane. The corps commander in an unarmoured open-topped car followed by four tanks was apparently launching an attack to seize Tobruk without artillery, infantry or air cover.

Driving east for some miles, the little convoy drove through occasional bursts of incoming shellfire and passed an Italian artillery battery in a wadi, counter-firing against the British guns at King's Cross. Just beyond the battery Rommel stopped to examine his map. The Italian *bersaglieri* battalion that should have been there was nowhere to be seen. The panzers trundled laboriously up behind him, throwing up a cloud of dust that attracted more artillery fire from Tobruk. Halting the tanks in a shallow wadi, Schmidt ran forward to join his general:

> I find Rommel lying on the ground with shells exploding left and right. He is all alone . . . I watch Rommel as he lies on his belly, intently studying the ground ahead through his glasses. His firm mouth is tight-lipped now; his prominent cheekbones stand out white. His cap is perched on the back of his head. 'Fort Pilastrino!' he mutters.
>
> I glance quickly at his map before I crouch down behind a heap of stones and also survey the terrain ahead. The ground slopes down ahead of us, and then slopes upward again equally gradually. On the crest is a triangular-shaped ruin of stones surmounted by a close network of barbed wire. Considerably farther back is a higher mound of stones. I surmise that this is Pilastrino and an enemy observation post . . .
>
> The huntsman's urge seems to take possession of Rommel. '*Leutnant!*' he commands. 'Orders to the panzers! Attack the stone ruins ahead – two panzers through the northern wadi, two through the southern wadi close to the ruins.'

Schmidt dodged back through the whistling shrapnel of incoming artillery. Given the importance of his task the bursting shells seemed of little consequence. Orders received, Wahl smiled calmly, lowered the cupola on his turret and trundled off towards Tobruk with his three companions. Schmidt considered it almost criminally insane:

> We watch the charge of the panzers. They obey orders and get close to their objective – the ruins. Then an unexpected and murderous fire falls around them. A few moments later the fire of several batteries is directed at our own observation post. We race for shelter along the slope . . . Shells drop among the battery of Italian artillery. One gun and its crew are wiped out by a direct hit. All hell is let loose until sundown, when the shellfire ceases. We drive back to advanced headquarters near the White House. The panzers do not return.

Far from being chastened, the loss of Wahl and his four panzers seemed to spur Rommel to greater efforts. Schmidt recalled that, during April, their commander had only one phrase on his lips: 'Every man forward to Tobruk!' The 5th Light Division had by now been brought up to strength, and forward units of Prittwitz's 15th Panzers were arriving at the front, some infantry units being flown directly into the airfield at Derna.

*

As they finally took the opportunity to dig their guns in during Good Friday afternoon and construct some semblance of protection for themselves and their guns, the men of B Troop were gathered together by Captain Graham Slinn. All the men admired Slinn – recalled by Bombardier Ray Ellis as the 'perfect gentleman' – who treated everyone with courtesy. 'Everybody liked him,' said Private Ted Whittaker. 'He was one of those chaps you'd have followed anywhere. Great tall chap, well over six foot, thin . . .' Bill Hutton agreed: 'Slinn was very, very good at his job.' Slinn warned them that, though morale was high, the next few days would prove a severe test for them all. They would face a massive onslaught by German and Italian forces determined to overwhelm Tobruk in order to secure their advance on the Nile. If Egypt fell, the Middle East and its oil wealth would be lost and the British empire cut in half. 'He said that the fate of England and the free world was in our hands that day, and we must not fail. Captain Slinn concluded his stirring little talk by quoting the final passage of the speech of Henry V before the battle of Agincourt: "You know your places, go to them, and God be with you." '

Slinn's timing, said Ellis, was impeccable as within minutes of this homily 'all hell was let loose'. Rommel's first major attack on Tobruk had begun. With calls for artillery support coming from troops in positions to the west of the El Adem road, before long the sky was black with smoke and the guns of the RHA were glowing red. But like Prittwitz's attack the previous day on the Derna road and Wahl's suicidal advance opposite Acroma that morning, the attack on the afternoon of 11 April against the sector held by Brigadier John Murray's 20th Australian Infantry Brigade was entirely speculative, the product of Rommel's belief that Tobruk possessed nothing more than a perfunctory defences. Rommel later admitted that he knew little of the scale of the defences at this time, assuming his troops would break though somewhere along the extensive perimeter. While the Brescia Division attacked in the west, Colonel Olbrich's 5th Panzer Regiment and Lieutenant Colonel Gustav Ponath's 8th Machine-Gun Battalion, reinforced by two companies of the 605th Anti-Tank Battalion, were ordered to assault the perimeter on the left of the El Adem road. Once Ponath's infantry had made an opening in the wire, suppressed the defences and cleared the area of mines, Olbrich's tanks would pour through the breach, fanning out left and right along the perimeter to roll up the Australian positions from the flank.

Half a mile from the perimeter, hidden by a localized sandstorm, 800 German troops debussed from their trucks and moved into assault positions. Then, to Ponath's dismay the wind suddenly dropped and the sand settled, exposing his advancing infantry to the view of the waiting Australians. The Germans were clumped together rather than spread out, as if not expecting serious opposition. Their objective was the area of ground between outposts R33 and R35, which were defended by two companies of the Australian 2/17th Battalion. With clear visibility the British 25-pounders now began dropping shells in their midst while heavy machine-gun fire from the 2/17th pinned the Germans down some 400 yards forward of the Australian positions.

'We just mowed them down,' one Australian officer admitted to the British journalist Jan Yindrich. Ponath's attack had come to a grinding halt. At the same time Olbrich's tanks were hit by Bristol Blenheims flying out of Egypt, and Hurricanes from El Gubbi launched attacks on vehicles moving along the El Adem road, machine-gunning them from fifty feet. Half an hour later, the RAF strafed around a hundred Italian trucks on the Bardia road and other vehicles around Acroma.

The scale and intensity of the resistance surprised the Germans. Even Rommel admitted the attack 'seemed to be meeting more difficulties in the open desert than I had anticipated'. Axis forces had advanced so quickly along the coast road and across the Cyrenaican desert that reconnaissance around Tobruk had been negligible. Some units had got hopelessly lost, and had taken several days to round up after Mechili had fallen.

The blitzkrieg that Rommel had unleashed had one primary objective: to dislocate the British and Australian forces in Cyrenaica. If he could persuade Wavell and his generals that resistance was futile Rommel was certain he could push the British all the way back to Egypt. But the only way he could do this was to maintain a furious tempo, routinely surprising the British commanders, encircling and cutting off their troops, and sowing despondency wherever he could. The loss of confidence – perhaps even panic – would serve to defeat the British more decisively than conventional battle.

But here on the El Adem road the enemy had refused to budge, even when threatened with overwhelming force. Under the hail of Australian machine-gun fire and British artillery it was clear to Ponath that, despite Rommel's expectations of quick victory, there was going to be no easy way into Tobruk by this route. Ponath and his men were desperately exposed, reduced to digging into the sand and rock with their hands, bayonets and helmets. But the wind now rose again, lifting the dust, reducing visibility and making accurate Australian sniping impossible, although the British artillery continued its barrage. Ponath was rescued from his predicament by the arrival of Olbrich's Panzers, advancing across the open ground towards the Australian wire.

Gunner David Boe of the South Notts Hussars found himself in an unenviable position, sitting in a recycled 44-gallon drum atop a telegraph pole just to the rear of the Australian defensive positions. Constructed by the Italians, the pole had metal rungs running up it and a 'funk hole' dug into the ground at its base should the artillery observer need to seek protection from incoming fire. The pole was the only place elevated enough to spot for the guns that lay hidden from enemy view in dead ground several miles back near King's Cross. On the afternoon of 11 April Boe's perch came into its own: 'Up there I could see German tanks advancing supported by their infantry. I was able to direct gunfire onto them and saw some hits. But as they got closer I was forced to get down and shelter in the dugout.'

The arrival of panzers opposite their positions came as no surprise to the men of the 20th Australian Brigade. Tanks had been expected and the troops thoroughly briefed on what to do. But the sheer number of steel leviathans was enough to dent the confidence of the strongest man. At least ten medium tanks – perhaps more – were advancing in clouds of dust amid the awful, clanging percussion of their tracks and engines, punctuated by the ominous staccato beat of machine guns. The Australians possessed no effective anti-tank weapons, just rifles, Brens, bayonets and grenades, and a smattering of the puny Boys anti-tank rifles, which had little chance of stopping panzer Mark IIIs. Apart from raw courage and their determination 'not to allow the Hun to pass' all that the inexperienced young Australians had to call on were the guns behind them of the RHA and the weakened resource of Drew's Tobruk Tanks.

Suddenly the German tanks halted. To his surprise, Olbrich was confronted by an anti-tank ditch. In some places along the line the ditch was only a feeble eighteen inches deep but, only able to view this obstacle from their periscopes, Olbrich and his tank commanders could not see this nor judge just how serious a threat it was. With the sheer volume of Australian fire now hitting the tanks it would have been suicide even to open a turret for a closer look, let alone reconnoitre on foot. So Olbrich turned his tanks to the right, and drove along the side of the ditch, seeking an entry point, his vehicles peppered by bullets. The Australians thought that the noise of their rounds hitting the hulls of the Panzers might alone be sufficient to demonstrate their determination not to surrender.

But Olbrich's tanks presented a very serious threat to Tobruk's defences. When the first of the Mark IIIs emerged out of the dust 400 yards away, Brigadier John Murray immediately called HQ 9th Division on the north side of Fort Solaro for armoured support. He told them that he faced at least ten enemy medium tanks. As part of Morshead's plan for the defence of the perimeter Drew had two ad hoc squadrons available for such emergencies. If the forward defences (Red Line) defended by infantry in the Italian-built posts, the barbed-wire fence, anti-personnel mines, artillery and the anti-tank ditch was penetrated by tanks, the forward infantry were to stay put and deal with the infantry who were expected to follow. The Tobruk Tanks would deal with the enemy armour, assisted by the truck-mounted anti-tank guns of the 3rd RHA. Based along the El Adem road, the RHA were supported by the 2-pounders of the 2/3rd Australian Anti-Tank Regiment. Between them these two units boasted forty 2-pounder guns.

The 1st RTR tanks had been evenly divided between Major George Hynes's B Squadron and Major Rea Leakey's C Squadron. Both had a mix of five A9, A10 and A13 cruisers, together with eight light tanks, while Leakey retained the four Matilda IIs. When the call came through from the signals caravan in the 3rd Armoured Brigade (manned by the young Frank Harrison) Hynes's squadron was closer, in the dead ground south of Pilastrino. After a busy night countering potential threats across the perimeter Leakey was leaguered near King's Cross alongside the guns of the RHA. When it received Lieutenant Colonel Drew's call, Hynes's squadron at once moved off southeast, climbing over the escarpment and away from the protection of dead ground, before following the slope's gradual decline towards the perimeter in the direction of the El Adem road. From his open turret Hynes could see nothing through the dust and haze as he neared the front line. Then, approaching the rear of R32 and R34, he suddenly saw not the reported ten Panzers but thirty. Fortunately none had yet broken through the wire, though that was clearly their intent. The only tanks that could offer an equal contest to the German Mark IIIs and IVs were his five cruisers. The squadron immediately closed down, hatches clanging shut, turrets swivelling ninety degrees to engage. They had travelled with a round 'up the spout' and now began to fire at Olbrich's tanks. A short exchange took place, in which B Squadron claimed three hits and suffered none themselves. The panzers continued to travel along the ditch towards the El Adem road, probing unsuccessfully for a way through the anti-tank ditch.

While this brief fight was taking place Rea Leakey had brought C Squadron forward alongside the El Adem road. No sooner had they breasted the final escarpment than he saw ten panzers directly ahead. This was the vanguard of Olbrich's force which, finding no way to cross further to the west, had now almost reached the El Adem road. After closing turret hatches, Leakey's cruisers and Matildas immediately opened fire. A tank battle then ensued lasting thirty minutes. This encounter was very different from the previous battles with Italian tanks. Although the British cruisers and Matildas could shoot on the move, whilst the German tanks had to halt before firing, the panzer Mark IIIs were far better than the British cruisers. Leakey recalled:

> We opened fire on them when they were within 800 yards of us, and we were disturbed to see our 2-pounder solid shots bouncing off their armour . . . We were one side of the perimeter defences, and the Germans were the other; the Australians were in the middle, and we could hear them cheering us on. We were very relieved to see the Germans start to withdraw as already they had brewed up three of our tanks, and we had only accounted for one of theirs. It was painfully obvious that we were outgunned by those tanks.

Hynes, whose B Squadron had now moved towards the El Adem road to join the fray with Leakey, now received a succession of hits on his tank. His driver, Trooper Knapton, was killed and the vehicle immobilized. Hynes ran to a second tank, which was also hit and put out of action. He later told an Associated Press journalist in Tobruk that German anti-tank shells seemed to slice through the British cruisers like butter. Hynes's tank 'continued firing, although hit four times, but when hit a fifth time, it burst into flames. The first shot hit the track, stopping the tank, but the gunner continued firing. A third shot went through the floor and a fourth through the back, but the fifth hit the ammunition racks, setting the tank alight. One man was killed and another wounded.

Unable to cross the anti-tank ditch, Olbrich reluctantly withdrew. Leakey had not seen the wrecked panzers and believed the engagement to have been very one-sided. In fact Olbrich's 15th Panzer Regiment had left behind four casualties: a wrecked Mark III, two Italian M13 tanks and an L3 tankette. Only one had been destroyed by Leakey's gunfire; the rest by Hynes's squadron. 1st RTR had lost two tanks. Throughout the battle Second Lieutenant Roy Farran and his fellow Hussars, now reluctant infantrymen following the loss of their Italian M13 at Msus, manned a selection of Bren guns, Boys anti-tank rifles and pistols at Pilastrino, ready to fight off any German breakthrough.

Olbrich leaguered his regiment five miles to the south of the site of the battle, but his tanks were then bombed by a flight of Blenheims from Egypt. The withdrawal of the panzers left Ponath's men 400 yards forward of the Australians, and they were forced to remain there under constant small arms and artillery fire until darkness gave them some respite. Furious at Olbrich's failure to penetrate the Australian positions, Rommel turned on Streich. 'Your panzers did not give of their best and left the infantry in the lurch!' he bellowed. Streich blamed the anti-tank ditch, but Rommel was having none of it, accusing Olbrich and Streich of 'irresolution'. That evening he confided, 'Tobruk's defences stretched much farther in all directions, west, east and south, than we had imagined.'

This second day of action within the Tobruk defences now drawing to a close, Leakey took his squadron back to the crossroads at Fort Pilastrino to collapse into an exhausted sleep. Respite did not last long. Within minutes the fort's heavy anti-aircraft guns had opened up, dragging the exhausted tank men back to consciousness. Desperate calls were also now being received from the perimeter in the area of the Bardia roadblock:

I called up the tank commanders, and gave out my orders, and then we were on the move, slowly picking our way across the rough ground in the darkness. There was nothing we could do until dawn, but we had to keep moving about as the noise of our tanks always had an adverse effect on the enemy. Once again the Australian infantry had stood firm, and the enemy withdrew, leaving a number of dead behind him.

On the El Adem front both attackers and defenders did all they could to dominate the night action. Brigadier Murray sent fighting patrols through the wire from both of his forward battalions while Streich dispatched combat engineers to construct a crossing through the anti-tank ditch. Some of the German troops were dispersed by Australian patrols, and as the night drew on, parties of Australian troops laboured feverishly to sow mines in front of their outposts in expectation of a renewed attack by the panzers in the morning. Likewise, the darkness brought no respite to the RHA at King's Cross. German artillery observers in light aircraft searched for the British gun positions using the flashes of the guns as they fired, while incoming rounds probed for targets and sprayed the desert with shrapnel. Axis aircraft dropped flares and bombs.

At first light on Saturday 12 April, the third day of battle, four Hurricanes were sent up from El Gubbi to see just how close the Germans had managed to get to the perimeter during the night. These low-level reconnaissance flights and the strafing attacks which followed were dangerous and much disliked by the pilots. Hurricanes of No.73 Squadron had flown thirty-six sorties on Thursday 10 April and twenty-three strafing sorties on Good Friday. The Squadron's war diary recorded that ground attacks were leading to the loss of 'too many machines which we can ill afford'.

But for most of Saturday a sandstorm raged, preventing a second attempt to break through the perimeter, though heavy artillery fire was traded between batteries. Early in the morning Bombardier Ray Ellis was ordered into the trenches to act as an observation post assistant, feeding information on fire orders and targets back by telephone to the guns in the dead ground of the escarpment behind. Ellis could not believe that, after playing war as a child in make-believe trenches, here he was in a real trench facing the Germans of his childhood imagination. Stumbling through positions manned by grim-faced Australian infantrymen armed with Lee Enfields, seventeen-inch bayonets fixed, and strung about with grenades, Ellis eventually reached his position. Few men had slept the previous night. Those not on sentry duty had either been on fighting patrols or out sowing mines. The crackle of machine guns echoed without pause, while shells burst further to the right. He took his place on the fire step and surveyed the ground with binoculars. It was crucial that he quickly became familiar with his surroundings to call in rapid and accurate fire from the guns.

*

In Tobruk's old Italian hospital Major John Devine had little time to contemplate the consequences of the strategic failures that had led to the evacuation of Cyrenaica. This was just as well. Retreat exacerbates feelings of inadequacy, sows confusion and depresses morale. In even the strongest units rumours abound, while discipline and order became more difficult to maintain. Combined with exhaustion and lack of food, even so-called strategic withdrawals can be a recipe for disaster. But the German and Italian pressure on the Tobruk defences was now providing the hastily assembled garrison with a rationale for resistance, a purpose which forced the men to concentrate on the task in hand rather than dwell on what might lie ahead. Battle was proving an antidote to depression.

On Devine's first day in Tobruk he had witnessed the first of a long series of Regia Aeronautica and Luftwaffe raids on the garrison, this one directed against the El Gubbi airfield on the plateau just above town:

> Puffs of ack-ack fire were all over the sky, machine guns rattled, and streams of tracer ammunition ascended. The enemy dive-bombers came over at medium altitude flying in formation. When almost over the target they broke formation, and flopped on it in almost sheer dives . . . When between five hundred and a thousand feet, they pulled out of their dive and flew away to sea, zigzagging furiously to avoid ack-ack gunfire and the rear gunner blazing away with his machine gun at everything on the ground.

Constant air attacks on Tobruk and the perimeter defences placed considerable pressure on the hospital. Naively, Devine assumed the hospital would be immune from attack. Though there were no red crosses on the roof it was a well-known landmark, but during the siege there would be several instances when the Geneva Convention relating to hospitals and hospital ships was deliberately flouted by the Luft-waffe. Stukas were unleashed on the 11th against the port, bombs falling uncomfortably close to the hospital. Devine was working in a large tunnel under the half-destroyed Admiralty House on the north shore of the harbour. A large concrete building, its west wing long demolished and with a huge bomb crater marring its entrance, its subterranean tunnels offering a degree of safety unavailable elsewhere in the town:

> All the night before there had been air raids, and many bombs had dropped so near that the blast could be felt rushing along the passages and the air raid shelters. I was in the operating theatre when there was first a loud bang, and then a crash that almost blew us off our feet. Plaster fell down off the ceiling, and the two operating-room orderlies jumped under the table. As I was remov-ing plaster from the patient's wound, news came that a bomb had hit the hospital itself . . . killing a number of people including a nursing orderly and the medical officer at his post. Yet another medical officer had been killed when planes bombed and machine-gunned the beach section of the hospital.

Sunday 13 April saw heavy aerial bombardment of Tobruk. Gunner S.C. Hankinson of 152 Anti-Aircraft Battery recalled that when told that they were surrounded and would have to fight to the last man, the soldiers had taken the news sombrely. Realization that the situ-ation was extremely serious was accompanied by the heaviest air raids so far. Jan Yindrich watched the Stuka raids on the port:

> . . . at 8.30 this morning about thirty black Junkers dive-bombers escorted by Messerschmidts staged the biggest raid so far of the siege. For over an hour they flew over the defences and the harbour, bombing the harbour installations and machine-gunning the troops manning the defences.
>
> I saw eight in line dive down on the harbour, drop their bombs, then wheel to the right and fly along the outer line of defence, at about fifty feet, their machine guns blazing.

'We fired 291 rounds,' recalled Hankinson. 'Eleven planes were brought down – three by Hurricanes and eight by ack-ack. Our site claimed one plane.' There were repeated Stuka raids on the vintage British hospital ships SS *Vita* and SS *Devonshire*. From his vantage point at Fort Solaro Hankinson saw the *Vita* 'making her way towards the harbour – it could have been no more than three or four miles from our site. Suddenly it was dive-bombed by a number of Stukas.' Gunner Leonard Tutt witnessed the incident from his battery on the cliffs overlooking the Mediterranean at the north-east corner of the perimeter:

> From our position a curve in the coastline hid the harbour from our sight. We could see all the air activity that went on in the skies above it, but had to guess what success the Stukas were having by the amount of smoke and the volume of noise generated by their attack.
>
> ... a white-painted hospital ship came around the headland at our feet. She was hugging the coast and so close that we could have thrown a stone at her. She was plastered with red crosses from stem to stern and there was no possibility that she could have been mistaken for anything other than what she was.
>
> As she twisted and turned the planes harried her unmercifully. We could see the bombs discharged and begin their wobbling flight before straightening out and screaming down at their target. At times the ship was completely hidden from our view by the giant geysers of water thrown up by the near-misses.

The Stuka was a fearsome weapon. Leonard Tutt described coming under attack:

> They were stub-winged, almost ungainly in appearance. They looked rather slow-moving in flight until they went into their dive. They came down like a stone, holding their course until it appeared that they were going to dash themselves to pieces on their target, then they would pull out of it with such suddenness that you felt their wings would be torn away.

Under attack, one seemed to have been chosen as their sole target. You could see the bombs leave their racks, wobble hesitantly then straighten up as they gained the velocity. We were encouraged to fire at them with our rifles; I think this was solely to help us with our morale. I saw a Stuka that had been brought down by a Bofors team and the area around the pilot was as armoured as a light tank. No rifle bullet could have penetrated it.

Roy Farran had been ordered to make his way to the harbour the following day with the 72 officers and 1,149 tank-less men of the 3rd Armoured Brigade to be evacuated on the SS *Barpeta*. He was trapped in the Stuka attack that accompanied the attacks on *Vita* and *Devonshire*. Caught in the open when sixteen Stukas attacked, Farran lay face down in the mud as two bombs landed fifty yards away, near a leaguer of the Indian cavalry brigade which had escaped the demise of the 2nd Armoured Division at Mechili. 'Great hunks of clay showered down around me and then, as if slightly delayed, the front part of an Indian's foot plopped onto the marsh in front of my eyes.' Glancing skywards, he could see that the Stukas were coming round for a second pass, and he rushed across a road to an old Italian air raid shelter, a little ahead of two Indian soldiers with gaping wounds in their bodies. Inside the already crowded shelter, he did what he could to help the wounded soldiers while the walls were rocked by continued explosions.

When *Vita* was damaged by a near-miss, the two accompanying Australian destroyers HMAS *Waterhen* and HMAS *Vendetta* came to her aid. While *Vendetta* circled protectively, *Waterhen* came alongside the wallowing hospital ship to embark her patients and staff. Early the next morning *Waterhen* sailed for Alexandria and safety. 'We were all appalled by these attacks,' declared Gunner Bill Green of Right Troop, 153 Battery based on the promontory north of the harbour. They seemed to demonstrate that battles with the Germans would be more vicious than the previous campaigns against the Italians.

On 13 April Major John Devine observed an unequal dogfight between the fighters of No.73 Squadron and the large numbers of Luftwaffe Messerschmidts that now filled the skies:

Not often were they able to get up in time to catch the enemy, and when they did they were outnumbered by never less than twenty to one. Those Hurricane pilots were the gamest people on earth.

On this day they managed to get up in time, and sailed straight into a vastly superior number of Messerschmidt fighters and Stuka dive-bombers. Way up in the sky little specks were twisting and turning, and faint zooming noises, as engines were tortured by each dive, came to us alternately with deep purring roars as the planes climbed steeply. A noise like the tearing of calico told us when the Hurricanes were firing off all their machine guns at once. German fighters, which were fitted with cannon, made a *pop-pop-pop-pop* noise, each cannon shot sounding separately, and quickly after the preceding one.

Gradually the fight came lower, and close within view came one plane twisting, turning and diving steeply as it was pursued by two others ... The planes passed into the distance, with the pursued one still twisting and turning violently. We heard later that it was a Hurricane that was being pursued, and that it had been shot down.

These aerial contests held a morbid fascination for men on the ground. Devine recalled another occasion when from high in the sky a burst of black smoke appeared:

The black plume circled downwards, and as it came lower and lower it could be seen to be issuing from a plane. Pieces of the plane dropped off, the smoke got denser, and finally it struck the ground where there was an explosion. A tremendous column of black smoke obscured everything.

*

It was on the late afternoon of Easter Sunday – 13 April – that Streich launched his second attempt to break through the defences along the El Adem road. Swirling dust had enveloped the whole area during the morning, a leftover from the storm of the previous day.

Though visibility had been poor it was sufficient to enable both the Luftwaffe and Regia Aeronautica to launch attacks against the southern perimeter all morning. But it was the heavy artillery bombardment late in the afternoon which was to give away German intentions. Manning the anti-aircraft guns at Fort Solaro, Gunner Hankinson recorded in his diary, 'We can now see our own field artillery firing on the horizon. We can also see quite a few air bursts close to the ground about four miles south of our site. We assume these are made by German 88s in action against our ground troops.'

Hankinson was right. Under the cover of direct fire from the 88-millimetre guns of Hetch's 18th Anti-Aircraft Regiment, one infantry battalion and two panzer battalions of 5th Panzer Regiment, together with the divisional combat engineer battalion, moved forward. To the west the Brescia Division artillery bombarded the defenders, leaving Morshead worried by the threat of a multiple breach. Obscured by sand, Ponath's infantry led the way, in an attempt to create a passage across the anti-tank ditch for the massed panzers waiting half a mile to the rear. It was a dangerous assignment for the exhausted German infantry, most of whom had now been in continuous action for more than two weeks.

Learning a costly lesson from the attacks two days before, the Germans moved forward differently this time, advancing not in extended line but in small groups covered by machine-gun fire from their Spandaus. Crouching with Captain Charlie Bennett of the South Notts Hussars and Major Loder-Symonds of 1st RHA in the trench that also served as artillery OP, Bombardier Ray Ellis knew that a desperate struggle lay ahead:

> I could see the black crosses on the German tanks as they came thundering across the rocky terrain in a headlong assault with all their guns blazing. It was a terrifying sight, and as we put down fire among them we could see that the infantry were following up close behind. I saw men moving, running in little bursts from one piece of cover to another, and I could hardly believe that I was actually standing there, under shellfire, watching the German infantry advancing towards me.

As the Germans reached the wire, the young Australian soldiers of the 2/17th Battalion, with a calm precision belying the fact that most of them had been civilians only months before, opened fire with machine guns and rifles. If the German tanks did manage to get through the wire and cross the ditch, the Australian infantry were instructed to allow them to pass through. They were not to panic or run but remain where they were and engage the enemy infantry following behind.

Though the perimeter was relatively well protected with mines and newly strung wire, it had not been possible to remove the tons of drifting sand which daily filled up more of the Italian-built anti-tank trench. Following reconnaissance conducted by his divisional engineers on the night of 11/12 April Streich now knew that the ditch presented no significant obstacle to the panzers. Nevertheless Ponath's infantry was finding it difficult – if not impossible – to penetrate the Australian defences unaided. Unsupported by tanks the first infantry attack had failed. It was during this attack on the afternoon of 13 April that Corporal Jack Edmondson won a posthumous Victoria Cross, the first awarded to the 2nd AIF. A sergeant in R33 recalled that a party of Germans had made it into the anti-tank ditch. The Australians had difficulty engaging the group with fire . . .

> So our patrol commander Lieutenant Mackell led a fighting patrol which drove them back at the bayonet. He took with him Corporal Edmondson and five others. They charged the enemy in the face of heavy machine-gun fire and Edmondson was mortally wounded but he kept on and bayoneted two Germans and then saved Mr Mackell's life by bayoneting two more who had Mr Mackell at their mercy.

A bloody hand-to-hand stabbing contest ensued, in which the Australians demonstrated a fighting fury that took the Germans entirely by surprise. The twenty-three-year-old Lieutenant Austin Mackell later described Edmondson's gallantry to the journalist Chester Wilmot:

> Jack Edmondson had been seriously wounded by a burst from a machine gun that had got him in the stomach, and he'd also been

hit in the neck. Still he ran on, and before the Germans could open up again we were into them. They left their guns and scattered. In their panic some actually ran slap into the barbed wire behind them and another party that was coming through the gap turned and fled. We went for them with the bayonet. In spite of his wounds Edmondson was magnificent. By this time I was in difficulties wrestling with one German on the ground while another was coming straight at me with a pistol. I called out – 'Jack' – and from fifteen yards away Edmondson ran to help me and bayoneted both Germans. He then went on and bayoneted at least two more.

Edmondson was carried back to R33, where he died shortly afterwards. Left in command of the outpost when the patrol went forward into the anti-tank ditch, the platoon sergeant was certain that Lieutenant Mackell's aggression had made a decisive impact on the Germans. 'Those enemy who escaped were driven back through the wire. But for this they would probably have surrounded our post and with their superior numbers made a wide gap in our defences. As it was they didn't make another push for several hours.

Mackell, back in his post, telephoned Major John Balfe, his Company Commander, to report 'We've been into them, and they're running . . .' At about half past five in the afternoon a new attack was launched, and a party of Ponath's men managed to establish themselves behind R33 as the German combat engineers struggled to prepare a crossing area for the waiting tanks. Bitter hand-to-hand fighting took place right across the perimeter that night. Lance Corporal Maccles, who only six months before had been a commercial traveller in Sydney, was informed at 10.30 p.m. that about forty Germans remained inside the wire. On his own initiative he decided to remove them. 'I took six men, in order not to weaken the post too much, and we crawled out of our post,' he told Jan Yindrich:

As we were under machine-gun fire all the time, we went at the double, then lay down. The enemy were about a hundred yards away . . .

Our people behind were blazing away over our heads, to give us cover. Then we tore into them with bayonets. I got the shock of my life, because not one of them wanted to fight . . . I bayoneted four, but my bayonet stuck in the fifth. He was the only bloke that showed any fight, because he grabbed my rifle and pulled me down on top of him. Another Jerry was coming up behind me, but my corporal finished him off. He undoubtedly saved my life. I bashed several other Germans over the head with the butt of my rifle until it broke. Then I picked up a stone. Thinking it was a hand grenade, the remaining Jerries grovelled . . . I must have killed about twelve Germans.

Illuminated by the flash of explosions, isolated struggles continued throughout the night along the perimeter defences, with German troops developing a new-found fear – and respect – for the Australians. But the Australian infantry could not prevent exploitation of the gap by Olbrich's armour. At 5 a.m. on Easter Monday he ordered his two panzer battalions through the breach in the wire and into the fortress. As the tanks made their way over the half-filled anti-tank ditch Bombardier Ellis laid his guns closer and closer, until fire was falling on his own trench. 'I was never to witness such a situation ever again,' he recalled '. . . where an OP party brought down fire upon themselves.'

Back on the gun lines at King's Cross, Gunner David Tickle could hear Captain Bennett's orders coming over the radio: ' "Target me!" We thought, crikey, what's happening? He kept shouting "Target me!" Then it dawned on us what had happened.' The guns scored several direct hits on the tanks, but on they came, mincing the barbed wire behind them and driving through the forward trenches. The German infantry followed into the maelstrom of rifle, machine-gun and artillery fire.

When the first German tanks burst across the ditch to advance up towards his outpost the Australian sergeant in R33 recalled that his men did precisely what they had been ordered to do. With the darkness illuminated only by the moon and the white flashes of explosions . . .

we sat tight and watched them go by, as we had been told not to attract attention by firing on them. But it wasn't a very encouraging sight. We had no communication with our other posts and we didn't know if we had been overrun. But we'd been told to stick there and we did.

About forty tanks went through and then we came up and engaged the German infantry and gunners who were trying to bring their guns through the gap. These were easy meat. We shot up their crews before they could get into action, and every time the infantry tried to get through the gap we drove them back with Bren guns and rifles. After the tanks went through no guns and no infantry got past us.

Busy directing his guns over the telephone, yelling over the noise, worried that a shell might break the telephone cabling that ran back to the guns at King's Cross, Ray Ellis had no time to get involved in the fight. He was an island in the midst of a storm – calm and untouched as the desperate battle unfolded. Rifles fired, grenades exploded and bayonets stabbed. Men screamed and shouted, the concussive *whumph-whumph-whumph* of nearby British and German artillery shells exploding an ever-present sensation. Ellis remembered: 'Over to our right we could see men fighting desperately, hand-to-hand, with bayonets, and it was altogether a heart-stopping experience.'

Olbrich's panzers were now well past the perimeter, and Ellis found himself also calling down artillery fire behind him. Gunner David Boe recalled the 'fearsome moment when we heard the tanks rumbling over the roof' of his foxhole as they moved up the gradual incline of the slope. But the darkness proved a serious handicap for the tanks. Once through the wire they could see nothing and there was a considerable risk of losing individual tanks to enemy action in the dark. The two tank battalions of 5th Panzer Regiment therefore adopted a cautious approach, electing to leaguer together and wait out the couple of hours that remained before daybreak in a wadi half a mile behind the perimeter. This was a terrible mistake as at a stroke it negated the German success in breaching the perimeter, and handed back the initiative to the defenders. If Olbrich's tanks had continued through to the town the shock of finding scores of tanks behind and among them would undoubtedly have seriously – possibly decisively – shaken the defenders, especially if the port had been reached.

But the situation for Morshead and the defenders of Tobruk was still extremely serious. German tanks were inside the perimeter, and Rommel felt sufficiently encouraged to believe that the end of the siege was in sight. That night he scribbled some quick lines to Lucie:

> Dearest Lu
>
> Today may well see the end of the Battle of Tobruk. The British were very stubborn and had a great deal of artillery. However, we'll bring it off. The bulk of my force is now out of the desert after a fortnight of it. The lads stuck it magnificently and came through the battle, both with the enemy and nature, very well.

It was at 1.30 a.m. the next morning (Easter Monday, 14 April) that the exhausted Rea Leakey, leaguered with his tanks near Fort Pilastrino, was woken from a fitful sleep and called to his cruiser. Clasping the radio headset to his ears, he heard Lieutenant Colonel Henry Drew telling him that Germans had breached the Australian perimeter to the west of the El Adem road. He was to take his squadron east immediately and guard the heights of the escarpment where it dropped down into the wide plateau on which stood the gun lines and – further back – El Gubbi airfield.

Things were now critical. If the panzers took the heights there would be nothing to stop them overrunning the gun positions and making their way into Tobruk, splitting the defences and seizing the port. There had been hardly a moment's respite since the siege had begun four days before and the strain was now affecting officers and soldiers alike. Ordering his men to mount up, Leakey found himself confronted by a commander's nightmare; a junior officer showing signs of cracking:

> He was very young and had not been long with the regiment. I had noticed that, like quite a number of the tank commanders, he was beginning to feel the strain. All might have been well if we could have given each man a day off, but we had no men to spare, and on this occasion one tank could not go into action as it had no tank commander.
>
> I grabbed the young officer and pulled him aside; he was

shivering and whimpering like a child. I tried to calm him down, and told him that as an officer he must set an example to the men. But he went on repeating, 'I can't go into this action because I know I will be killed.' Time was slipping by, and I knew only too well the effect on the men if this officer did not go into action; they were just as tired and frightened. I gave him a drink of neat rum, but it had little effect. I tried being kind and gentle to him, but this made him worse. It was a most unpleasant incident, and I knew I had to settle it there and then.

I tried the last resort, and it worked. I drew my revolver, cocked it and pointed it at his temple. 'All right,' I said in a very stern voice. 'Either you get into your tank or I shoot you for cowardice in the face of the enemy.'

He turned and went back to his tank, and I heard him giving his orders. Even after all these years I have nightmares connected with this incident.

It proved an extremely demanding night for Leakey's squadron, and the young officer, together with his crew, did indeed die when his cruiser received a direct hit and was engulfed in flames. It took several hours for the squadron to reach the road leading up the third escarpment, which then fell away to the perimeter. They did not arrive until dawn, by which time the battles on land and in the air had reached a crescendo.

As Leakey reached King's Cross a mechanical scream above made him jerk his head skywards to see what he thought would be his last view on earth. A stricken Hurricane – smoke blackening its silver frame – was hurtling down, the pilot clearly dead. It appeared to be falling directly onto his tank but Leakey had no time to order avoiding action. The plane missed the cruiser by a mere six feet, the impact and explosion bouncing his twenty-ton vehicle like a rubber ball. The aircraft had been piloted by Sergeant Pilot H.G. Webster of No.73 Squadron. Webster and Flying Officer George Goodman had been flying two of the eight serviceable Hurricanes at El Gubbi and had already completed an early-morning patrol over the perimeter, shooting down a German Henschel. Shortly after returning to El Gubbi,

Webster was ordered to join another patrol of four aircraft and attack a group of Stukas bombing the harbour. Two Germans were promptly shot down, but while attacking a third Stuka from the rear Webster was himself engaged by two Italian Fiat G50s, a fast all-metal Italian fighter. He died in his cockpit.

Leakey's intense shock was overcome by someone yelling to his right, 'For goodness' sake, turn right and come to our help! My battery's being attacked by enemy tanks and guns are being overrun. Look! They're only 500 yards away.' In the half-light of morning Leakey turned to see some forty Panzers advancing towards the gun lines from the escarpment.

As dawn permeated the inky blackness, Olbrich had ordered his tanks forward in the direction of King's Cross. As they began their advance they came under attack to their left from the truck-mounted 2-pounders of 3rd RHA. Ignoring these bee stings the tanks drove on, the growl and clatter of their approach providing due warning to the gun batteries lined up on the desert floor ahead. Leakey's tanks had arrived in the middle of what would otherwise have been an unequal battle. The RHA's 25-pounders had fired first, immediately destroying two panzers, but within minutes the guns themselves were under heavy tank fire. Sergeant Major Reg Batten, commanding one of the 1st RHA guns, recalled that with machine guns and the German tank cannon 'the air was lit with tracer shells and bullets until it looked like Blackpool illuminations'.

Lance Sergeant Harold Harper and Lieutenant Ivor Birkin of D Troop, 426 Battery saw the tanks come over the escarpment. 'The firing was almost incessant,' recalled Harper. 'It was rather like going to a cup tie – when you knocked a tank out everybody cheered.' In the absence of armour-piercing ammunition Batten's crew was forced to fire high-explosive shells at the oncoming tanks. He saw his first shell fall short, and then the sparks on the panzer as the second shell struck home. Then, just as they were about to fire again, 'a 75-millimetre shell hit us square on the shield. The gun was knocked out and all the crew, except myself, were either killed or wounded.'

By the time Leakey arrived the panzers were almost on the gun lines. There was not a moment to lose:

We swung right into battle line. I handed Milligan his cigarette and told him to start shooting. There was no need for me to indicate the shot to him.

'Loaded!' yelled Adams, and away went another solid shot, tearing at the thick enemy armour. The fumes of burning cordite made us cough, and our eyes water, and soon the turret was so thick with smoke I could only just make out the figure of Adams as he loaded shell after shell into the breach.

Closed down in their panzers, edging forward through the smoke and dust into the glare of the morning sun, it took some time for the Germans to realize they were being attacked by tanks. One by one panzers erupted into smoke and flame and a number turned tail. Sergeant Major Batten managed to fire the round in his 25-pounder and was relieved to see the enemy tanks withdraw, as there was now almost nothing to hinder the panzers' continued advance. However, the Germans were now in some disorder, as tanks of the 2nd Panzer Battalion became entangled with those of the 1st, which had been paralleling their advance to the right. As these tanks moved south, they were struck in the flank by the wheeled 2-pounders of the Australian 2/3rd Anti-Tank Battalion, firing from their positions on the east side of the El Adem road.

Lieutenant Joachim Schorm recounted the confusion that resulted from the combination of heavy 25-pounder fire and armoured counter-attack: 'Now we come slap into 1 Battalion which is following us. Some of our tanks are already on fire. The crews call for doctors who dismount to help in this witches' cauldron. Enemy anti-tank units fall on us with their machine guns firing into our midst.'

But the Australian and British success had not come without loss. By the time the battle had turned in Leakey's favour, only three cruisers remained from the ten that had set out early that morning. Through his cupola periscope he saw one of his tanks explode, and the crew bail out. A seriously injured crewman was dragging himself along the ground, machine-gun bullets kicking up sand around him. Leakey immediately ordered his tank to turn left, to screen the wounded soldier. He would later admit it was a stupid move, as it turned the cruiser flank-side on to the German guns. They had his range, and shells began to find their mark. His tank stalled and began burning:

> 'She's on fire, sir,' shouted Adams, but he went on loading shells. At the same moment Milligan's head fell back against my knees, and looking down I saw that a shell had pierced the armour and removed most of his chest. He was dead.
>
> 'Bail out,' I yelled, and as I pulled myself out of the turret what few shells we had left started exploding, and the flames were already licking at my feet. I saw Adams get out safely, and we dashed round to the front of the tank to check up on the others. As we got round, the driver flopped out of his hatch, and Adams grabbed him and helped him back. I opened up the first sub-turret gunner's hatch and looked in, but I knew what I should see, as there was a neat hole through the armour where the gunner's head should be. He was dead, and already his clothing was burning fiercely.

The second sub-turret gunner was lying gravely wounded by the side of the tank, his right leg attached only by a small piece of skin.

> He was a big lad, and how he got out of his small hatch unaided and with only one leg has always remained a mystery to me. We were being machine-gunned. Somehow I got him over my shoulder and carried him back to where I found a shallow trench.
>
> The other two were there, and we laid him down, but he straightened up, looked at his leg, and said, 'Cut it off sir, it's no use to me.'
>
> I did so, and he then lay back smiling. At that moment up drove an ambulance driven by a large Australian. Within a few minutes this lad was in a Tobruk hospital.

The combination of tank, anti-tank and direct-fire artillery – and Olbrich's excessive caution, which had led him to wait in the wadi until daylight – had frustrated Rommel's armoured assault into the heart of the fortress. Some seventeen panzers had been destroyed or immobilized and the remainder, perhaps twenty-one vehicles, forced to retreat. Two of the RHA 25-pounder guns had been knocked out, along with two of its five truck-mounted 2-pounders. While this action was taking place the two Fiat G50s that had accounted for Sergeant Webster (one of which was piloted by the famous pre-war Italian acrobatic pilot Carlo Cugnasca) were themselves shot down by a Canadian member of No.73 Squadron, Flight Lieutenant James 'Smudger' Smith. Both Italian aircraft crashed close to Webster, on the El Adem road. Lieutenant Joachim Schorm recorded later in his diary, 'Above us Italian fighter planes come into the fray. Two of them crash in our midst.' Smith was also shot down and killed that day.

As Olbrich's two panzer battalions fought it out with the guns of the Royal Horse Artillery forward of King's Cross, Morshead had ordered counter-attacks against the German infantry and combat engineers who held the breach forward of R33 and R35. The Australians of the 2/17th reserve together with a further battalion – the 2/15th – mounted clearance and counter-attack sorties across the entire area of the breach, long sweeps of infantry clearing the ground with bayonet and grenade. They were joined by the cruiser and light tanks of Major Hynes's B Squadron of Tobruk Tanks. Meanwhile, gun batteries not engaging Olbrich's panzers over open sights continued to fire in support of the perimeter defences.

Olbrich's tanks now found themselves in headlong retreat, jostling to find the gap in the wire which they had confidently entered three hours before. The opposition inside the perimeter was overwhelming, and Olbrich determined to save what tanks he could. The withdrawing vehicles now headed towards the position along the perimeter where Bombardier Ellis's small OP was located. It was a terrifying experience:

> It is impossible to describe what it feels like to have a huge tank crunching its way towards you, and to be within feet of these menacing steel tracks, which could so easily grind you into the ground, and that is to say nothing of their machine guns spitting bullets in all directions. It was a great relief when they had lurched over our trenches and were making their way back into their own lines with our shells bursting among them.

Into the traffic jam of enemy tanks and infantry scrambling back through the gap in the wire 'We fired everything we had,' recalled one Australian sergeant, 'and the Jerries got their worst hiding they'd had to that time.' For Joachim Schorm, the experience was shocking:

> My driver says, 'The engines are no longer running properly, brakes not acting, transmission only with difficulty . . .' but the lane is in sight. Everyone hurries towards it. Enemy anti-tank guns shoot into the mass. Our own anti-tank guns and 88s are almost deserted, the crews lying silent beside them . . . now comes the gap and the ditch . . . the vehicle almost gets stuck but manages to extricate itself with great difficulty. With their last reserves of energy the crew gets out of range and returns to camp.

For Schorm, a veteran of both Poland and France, El Adem was 'the bitterest battle of the whole war'. He was to be awarded the Iron Cross by Rommel for his actions that day.

*

Early that same morning Lieutenant Heinz Schmidt had been ordered by Rommel to accompany Streich into battle in a second attempt to breach the perimeter. Streich had been commanded by Rommel to conduct the attack 'with the utmost resolution under your personal leadership', but the Desert Fox was not convinced his subordinate possessed the determination to retake the initiative and confided to his diary that 'the 5th Light Division had lost confidence in itself and was unwarrantedly pessimistic about my plan to open our main attack on the 14th'. Perhaps he believed Schmidt's presence would encourage Streich to follow his orders.

Unembarrassed by his task, Schmidt travelled with Streich up the El Adem road towards Tobruk before dawn on the morning of 14 April. The intention was for Streich to follow Olbrich's panzer spearhead into Tobruk and take command of the battle that would ensue. Together with the operational staff of the 5th Light Division, Schmidt travelled in Streich's Mammoth, one of the British Dorchester command vehicles captured at Mechili five days before. Streich wanted to stay on the road until forced to turn left through the gap and into Tobruk, but Schmidt was concerned lest they went too far and became entangled with the perimeter defences. Schmidt recalled what happened next:

> Before we realized what was happening we found ourselves in a real hubbub. Shell bursts, anti-tank missiles whizzing by and the *rat-tat-tat* of machine guns left us in no doubt that we had made a sudden appearance under the noses of the enemy. With lightning speed we leapt from the car and dived for protection behind the panzer. We clutched at it, hauling our legs up to avoid the burst of machine-gun bullets which were splashing knee-high against the caterpillars of the tank.

Dodging bullets in the half-light of morning they managed to make their escape back to the safety of a group of panzers. The poor light had saved their lives. Streich's attempt to follow Olbrich through the gap had failed before it had begun, with the Australian perimeter positions aggressively defending their line. As morning dawned, they learned that Olbrich's attack had failed and a large number of Ponath's infantry had been lost. Making their way back to Rommel's position, Streich and Olbrich reported the sorry news at 9 a.m. Rommel was incandescent, ordering Streich to rescue Ponath's infantry. 'With what?' Streich is reported to have replied. Rommel promised that the Ariete Armoured Division would be available to assist in a further attack that afternoon.

As if to avenge this embarrassing failure on land, furious attacks were launched by both the Luftwaffe and Regia Aeronautica throughout Easter Monday. Axis aircraft were now able to operate from close to Tobruk, the airfields at El Adem and Gazala having been quickly pressed into service. Based on the promontory north of the harbour, Gunner John Kelly of 153 Heavy Anti-Aircraft Battery recorded that on Easter Sunday there had been only one dive-bombing raid, but the morning of the 14th saw fifty aircraft attacking the town, dropping over 300 bombs. 'Four bombs dropped on our site. Killed Nobby Clark and Watts, injured eight other men, and the colonel got a broken arm. Boris got a piece of shrapnel in his chest and is too ill to be moved.

Bert Fullick is not expected to live. Doug Marchant is still unconscious. The rest have been put aboard the hospital ship [SS *Vita*].'

Once the final panzers had made good their escape through the perimeter that morning, Bombardier Ray Ellis was replaced in the forward trenches by a relief OP team and returned to the gun line at King's Cross. But there was to be no rest, as the artillery continued to ensure that the Germans did not regroup for any further attempts on the perimeter. By this stage trucks of the Royal Army Service Corps were delivering ammunition directly to the guns, offloading in the face of the constant counter-battery fire aimed at the gun lines by Axis artillery far out in the desert. After four days of constant action, exhaustion was setting in.

> We were all absolutely worn out, not having slept for several days and nights. Food was snatched when it was possible and towards the end of the battle I remember someone handing round a bottle of whisky from which we all took long stinging gulps of the raw liquid. Our faces were masks of sweat and sand with little red slits which served for eyes. We staggered around the guns like robots, laying, loading and firing without proper conscious thought of what we were doing.

Mopping-up continued between King's Cross and the perimeter all morning. Major Robert Daniell recalled the ease with which the few remaining German tanks and infantry inside the perimeter now gave themselves up:

> One of their new Mark IV tanks had meandered across the waste land inside the perimeter early in the afternoon. As it approached our regimental headquarters, one of the driving tracks just broke. The young crew jumped out, dismayed beyond words, for they were all alone; there was no fight left in them. I walked over to them, directing them towards the rear, where no doubt someone would pick them up.

Forward of the perimeter the remaining German infantry in the anti-tank ditch were being dealt with. Rea Leakey dispatched a light tank under the command of Corporal Hulme to assist the Australians in clearing a long section of the ditch in which a number of men from Ponath's machine-gun battalion had taken shelter. Hulme positioned his tank so that he could fire down the length of the ditch. One long burst was sufficient to persuade the Germans to surrender. Bayonets fixed, Australian infantry advanced in a line to marshal the prisoners to the rear and Hulme judged it safe to open the turret of his tank. When he did so a German shot him in the chest with a sub-machine gun. Leakey noted that the 'soldier paid the penalty for his treachery': 'He had evidently not noticed the Australians coming up; they saw his action, and they saw red. He let out a squeal like a pig as three long bayonets squelched into his stomach.'

The young Australians were in no mood for German recalcitrance. David Boe witnessed the death of a German officer. In the fury, fear and adrenalin of the battlefield a young lieutenant was shouting in perfect English, 'I am an officer of the great German Reich – you will never win this war.' This was too much for his captor who, having survived the battle and witnessed the death of Corporal Hulme, required simple acquiescence. He promptly shot the German dead. There were more incidents that day. Robert Daniell went forward with the chaplain to give succour to the German wounded in the anti-tank ditch.

> We found that the anti-tank ditch, which was about nine feet deep, was absolutely crammed with German wounded who had crawled in there from the vehicles that our shells had set on fire. They were lying in the ditch. We started giving them water but while the doctor was attending one of the soldiers who was badly wounded, I saw a German rise up on his feet and have a shot at him with a revolver. I shouted to the doctor and the Reverend Parry to withdraw.

When Rommel returned to Streich's HQ at noon on 14 April to examine plans for a further attack, he discovered that nothing had been done due to continuing heavy British artillery fire. With the greatest reluctance he called off the assault. Inside the wire the whole area had been scoured of German stragglers and work begun to restore the perimeter defences. It was a devastating defeat for what in truth had been an over-optimistic and overconfident assault. Olbrich complained that faulty information had caused the reverse, recording that he had been told that 'the enemy was about to withdraw, his artillery was weak and his morale had become low'. In addition to the loss of 45 per cent of Olbrich's panzers Lieutenant Colonel Ponath had been killed in the infantry melee (his body was never identified or recovered). Of the 1,400 men of the 8th Machine-Gun Battalion who had begun the operation, only 300 remained. At least 150 had been killed. Many of the wounded found themselves in British hands, as did at least 250 other prisoners of war, who were unceremoniously bundled into the POW cage at King's Cross. One German survivor was surprised to escape the ambush inside the perimeter, considering the battle to have been 'the most severely fought of the war. The survivors call this day "Hell of Tobruk" ... Thirty-eight tanks went into action; seventeen were knocked out and many more were put temporarily out of action.' By nightfall German artillery and aerial attacks had petered out, signalling the end of Rommel's first serious attempt to break into Tobruk. The defenders lost 26 killed and 74 wounded.

The final action of the evening on the perimeter at the El Adem road cemented the relationship between the Australians and the British. Captain Bob Hingston watched two hopelessly lost German staff cars stop at the perimeter wire:

> Colin Barber engaged them very correctly in best Larkhill fashion with ranging rounds of gunfire. He did it brilliantly. The two cars were standing together not very far outside our perimeter defences when he landed a round of gunfire right on them and they both burst into flames. It was most spectacular because it was dusk and the sight of these flames shooting up – there were a number of Australians around us and they were cheering wildly at this. One of them rushed up and smote me heavily on the shoulder and said, 'You're the best bloody battery in the British army!' It was very good for morale!

The defenders knew they had done well. At least one German prisoner, a doctor, agreed. 'In Poland, France and Belgium,' he remarked, 'once the tanks got through, the soldiers took it for granted that they were beaten. But you were like demons. The tanks break through and your infantry still keep fighting.' As the men of the AIF could rightly riposte, this was not that surprising. The Germans were now fighting Diggers, who when faced by panzers stood and fought. 'Well done, TOBRUK!' trumpeted Lavarack's order of the day. His men had brought to at least a temporary halt the embarrassing success of Rommel's intervention in Africa. As night fell in the trenches, gun lines and tank parks, men fell into exhausted sleep, the barrels of their guns cooling in the night air.

5 » THE SUMMER BATTLES

The next two months saw increasingly desperate battles for the possession of Tobruk with Rommel repeatedly trying to break into the perimeter, and two attempts by Wavell – Operation Brevity in May and Operation Battleaxe in June – to lift the siege by means of offensive operations launched from Egypt. When Rommel had first sought to smash his way into Tobruk via El Adem, he had also sent the 3rd Reconnaissance Regiment on to Bardia, which was seized by von Wechmar on 13 April. At the end of the month Sollum and the Halfaya Pass, which were largely undefended, also fell. However, British armoured raids from the desert in the days that followed forced the Afrika Korps commander to divert tanks to the Egyptian frontier that he would otherwise have been able to use against Tobruk. He renewed his efforts, therefore, to overwhelm the garrison using the tactics which had served him so well in France and Cyrenaica – punching a strong armoured fist through and beyond the enemy defences, with the panzers closely supported by mobile infantry, aircraft and combat engineers, and supplemented by mobile anti-tank and anti-aircraft guns. Unsuccessful at El Adem, Rommel now turned his eyes to the western corner of the perimeter, where the slight rise in the ground at the ruined Ottoman fort of Ras el Medawar (Point 209) provided clear views as far out as Acroma in the west and the escarpment above Tobruk harbour way to the east.

Unwilling to provide the impertinent defenders with any pause for reflection and hopeful that another rapid assault would do the trick, Rommel ordered an attack using twenty medium and light tanks of the Ariete Division and a battalion of infantry and artillery from the Trento Division stiffened by German infantry, for the morning of

15 April. An initial breakthrough by the Italian tanks at the outer minefield and barbed wire north of Point 209 was immediately countered by a ferocious British artillery bombardment when the tanks reached the crossroads at Point 187, forcing the armour and its accompanying infantry to withdraw in disorder. Rommel dispatched one of his aides to find out what was wrong.

When Lieutenant Brendt returned, breathless, it was to say that the Italians were surrendering in droves. He had arrived on the scene to see a Bren gun carrier ushering a company of Italians inside the perimeter. He had immediately opened fire with a machine gun on the enemy vehicle, hoping to give the Italians a chance to escape. 'They had run,' Rommel later recorded in disgust, 'towards the British lines.' During the day repeated attempts by large groups of Italians to approach the perimeter were broken up by British artillery, and many groups of dispirited Italians surrendered. In the afternoon a further attack was thwarted by the busy guns of the 51st Field Regiment, after which three Bren carriers from the Australian 2/48th Battalion fired a few bursts over the Italians' heads and corralled a large crowd of them towards the Australian wire. As this mass surrender was under way twelve German tanks approached and fired into the throng, perhaps in the mistaken belief that it would induce the Italians to turn on their captors and escape. It did the opposite, enraging the Italians and hurrying them into the perimeter. At the cost of one man dead and one wounded, that day the Australians captured 26 officers and 777 men, virtually all from the same battalion of the Trento Regiment.

However, the following morning persistent German and Italian attacks on Ras el Medawar succeeded in penetrating the Australian lines, the Diggers having no anti-tank guns to prevent twelve tanks getting through the wire onto Point 209, held by Lieutenant Bryant's platoon of the 2/48th Battalion. The only thing capable of stopping them was landmines. Bryant recalled:

> The tanks came on through the shelling and forced their way over a broken-down part of the wire. One Italian light blew up on the minefield, and two more were knocked out by our anti-tank rifles before they got very far. The rest continued on and we couldn't stop them. One party of four or five tanks shot up our sangars on

209 and overran the 51st [Field] Regiment's OP, wounding its CO (Lieutenant Colonel Douglas).

Charging across trenches and infantry positions, where in one case a Digger had an epaulette torn from his shirt by tank tracks passing over his slit trench, the Italian tanks turned back and scattered, their momentum lost. As they lurched back towards their own lines they found themselves mistaken by German anti-tank guns for British vehicles. Rommel was furious, blaming the failure of the attack on the poorly trained Italian soldiers and their atrocious equipment, although this did not persuade him to desist from further attempts.

The attacks at El Adem on the 11th/12th and Ras el Medawar on the 15th provided many lessons for the British and Australian defenders. Leslie Morshead immediately ordered the construction of a deep anti-tank minefield forward of Bianca and the Australian infantry were provided with tank familiarization training to ensure that they were not overawed by the twenty-ton beasts bearing down on them. Lieutenant Alexander McGinlay of 7th RTR was involved:

> We wanted to prove to the Aussies that it was quite safe to lie low in a ditch or trench and let a tank drive straight over them . . . We had them dig trenches, lie in them and ran over them. This training paid off and when Jerry broke in . . . the infantry just laid low while the Mark IV Jerry tanks rolled over them, then came up, wiping out the German infantry following. This left the Jerry tanks completely cut off from their support.

Forward with his troops throughout these engagements, Rommel lost one of his fabled nine lives on 19 April after decorating von Wechmar with the Knight's Cross for his seizure of Bardia. That evening, with Rommel about ten miles west of Bardia returning to Acroma, Schmidt spotted two aircraft approaching rapidly at low level over the sand. 'Air alarm!' he shouted at the top of his voice. The vehicles braked just before the Hurricanes were upon them, their guns firing. Schmidt threw himself flat onto the ground. The British fighters circled to attack again and Schmidt desperately wormed himself into the sand.

When at last the aircraft broke off and flew away north towards
the sea, I picked myself up, bleeding from scratches on my face . . .
I counted over a dozen bullet holes in my car. The motorcyclist
dispatch rider travelling just behind me [Private Kanthak] had
evidently not leapt from his machine in time: he lay next to the
sprawling motorcycle. He had a bad head wound and was obviously
dying.

Corporal Eggert, Rommel's driver, had been struck in the chest by
a bullet, and was seriously wounded. He was later to die of his injuries.
The radio truck had been hit so severely that it had to be abandoned.
Rommel himself took the wheel of the Mammoth and began the long
drive through the night to his headquarters at the White House, which
the battered convoy reached in the early hours of the morning.

It was soon after this visit to Bardia that Rommel finally received
from the Italians two copies of a map of the Tobruk defences. Only
now could he appreciate the extent of the fortifications, this realization chiming with his experience of trying, over the previous fortnight, to batter his way in. He decided that he would focus his attacks
on the south-western area at Ras el Medawar.

In this area the Italian-built perimeter defences were strangely
flawed because they did not extend to a mound 700 yards to the west
(Point 201) which the Diggers came to call Carrier Hill. An enemy
could use Carrier Hill as a covered approach for attacks on Point 209,
and prepare in the dead ground beyond it. To prevent Rommel using
it to mount a further attack, the Australians launched a pre-emptive
strike against the hill at dawn on 22 April. Accompanied on the ground
by three Matildas of 7th RTR and overhead by a Lysander spotter plane,
the raid by ninety men of the 2/48th Battalion swept around the flank
of the enemy position and tore into the unsuspecting Italians from the
rear: 16 officers and 354 men surrendered after a fierce firefight for
the loss of two Diggers killed and seven wounded. Not all raids,
however, were so successful. On the same day two heavy raids against
Italian positions by the 2/23rd Battalion along the Derna Road faced
stiffer opposition, fierce fighting resulting in nearly twenty Australian
dead and as many wounded for the capture of 87 Italians with many
killed and wounded.

For the rest of April German and Italian troops pressed against the perimeter at various points, testing the defences for a weak point. Determined and aggressive Australian resistance, however, supported by British tanks and artillery, prevented any breakthrough. Australian fighting patrols, accompanied on occasion by British tanks, moved beyond the perimeter to disrupt and forestall Italian and German attack preparations. As Axis troop concentrations occurred, RAF bombers, flying in from Egypt, struck hard. On 16 April Lieutenant Schorm complained to his diary, '[The RAF] get on our nerves. Ten raids or more a day. No anti-aircraft, no fighter planes to meet them. We remain on the alert. At nights, two raids.'

Major John Devine was amazed by the courage of the Allied fighter pilots based in Tobruk, who went up every day in spite of the odds against them. 'Four or five of them go up again and again against hundreds. Even though shot down once or twice, they go up again until they are killed. No knights of old ever reached their peak of courage.' On 23 April he recorded a day of desperate dogfights over the harbour:

Every now and then from the clouds above planes would chase each other in steep dives, only to zoom up again into the shelter of the clouds. I saw one Messerschmidt on the tail of a Hurricane which dived straight down to the ground and burst into flames and smoke, but above we could see its pilot floating down to safety on a parachute ... Two Messerschmidts were hard on the tail of a fleeing Hurricane at a height of only a few hundred feet. The Hurricane was swerving wildly, and leading his pursuers around and around the Tobruk ack-ack gun positions. The gunners had to aim at the Hurricane in front to hit the Messerschmidt behind, and after many shots a red Bofors shell burst fair in the centre of the Messerschmidt's fuselage, and it crashed in flames. The Hurricane went off to land, and its pilot came back and collected the anti-aircraft gunner who had saved him, thanked him, and took him over to his mess for celebrations.

Gunner John Kelly saw the same action as Devine and rejoiced in the cool work of both Hurricane pilot and Bofors crew, but recorded that three Hurricanes were lost that day to seven German aircraft shot down. Private Alex Franks of 2/2 Ambulance Company RAMC saw the terrible moment during the April battles when a Messerschmidt 109 fighter swooped on a Hurricane gliding in to land at El Gubbi. The troops on the ground, seeing impending disaster, waved and shouted fruitlessly to the pilot. A heavy burst of staccato gunfire was heard over the roar of engines and the Hurricane dived into the sand a hundred yards away. Racing to the scene Franks found the pilot already dead. Shells had pierced the rear of the cockpit and passed through his body, burying themselves in the engine. Franks's horror at seeing the man die was matched by his disgust as he realized that a number of soldiers had turned up to stare and were helping themselves to the dead pilot's wristwatch and wallet. During late April and May 1941 the RAF was heavily outnumbered in the skies over Tobruk, the few remaining Hurricanes struggling against vastly superior numbers of Me 109s, which were able to fly from any one of six airfields enclosing the perimeter. Exhausted pilots would repeatedly go up until they were shot down.

The last Hurricanes were withdrawn from Tobruk on 26 April, No.73 Squadron having lost twenty-seven of its thirty-two aircraft during the preceding three weeks. Without Hurricanes in Tobruk the Luftwaffe and Regia Aeronautica could turn their full fury on the anti-aircraft sites around the harbour. At 2 p.m. on 26 April ten bombs were dropped on Kelly's position but they suffered no casualties, although at B site six men were killed and at D site thirty-six men were injured and six killed. At A site, waiting to fire, Gunner W.J. Green watched several Stukas peel off above him:

Our magnificent gun crews put up heavy fire and as they got closer fired short-burst shrapnel shells at them. These shells burst from two to five seconds after firing [it normally took a shell thirty seconds to reach its maximum height] with a great black cloud of smoke and iron balls and the Stukas didn't like them at all ... A lot of bombs fell around the gun site but outside the walls. Tragically they hit one of our open lorries on which a captured Italian Breda gun had been mounted as a mobile and Sergeant Hayes was killed.

Two hours later two high-flying JU 88s appeared to finish off the job:

> Then came the tense moment when the spotter called out, 'Bombs falling,' and four 1,000-pounders were on their way. They fell right across the gun site, which to give them their due was pretty good aiming, but once again they fell outside the protecting walls. A great cloud of dust and smoke completely obliterated the gun site and the wretched burial party down near the beach [burying Sergeant Hayes] thought we were goners for sure until through the haze, in their own words, they saw the finest sight they had ever seen, four gun barrels spitting flame and smoke at the receding aircraft.

The following day more than fifty Stukas attacked gun positions and on the 28th nine planes attacked in the morning and thirty-five in the afternoon. In fact, 677 aircraft took part in 52 separate raids on the harbour in the last three weeks of April 1941, of which 67 were shot down or destroyed by anti-aircraft fire.

It was clear from the continued pressure against the perimeter and from aerial reconnaissance that Rommel was preparing another attack on Ras el Medawar. Frantic efforts were made by the Australians in the western sector to re-sow minefields, replace broken barbed wire and restock with ammunition for the coming onslaught as the Luftwaffe daily pounded the forward areas between Point 209 and Pilastrino. Despite the setbacks in mid-April Rommel was still confident of a rapid victory – if he had sufficient German troops. Writing to his wife Lucie on the 23rd he recorded, 'Once Tobruk has fallen, which I hope will be in ten days or a fortnight, the situation here will be secure. Then there'll have to be a few weeks' pause before we take on anything new.' But two days later Rommel admitted his nervousness: 'I shan't be sorry to see more troops arrive, for we're still very thin on the long fortress front. I've seldom had such worries – militarily speaking – as in the last few days.' However, Axis troops and equipment were now rapidly concentrating behind Acroma, and by the end of April Rommel had 120 tanks available to launch what he was certain would be the final, decisive attack on Tobruk.

The British likewise rushed reinforcements forward during April – by sea. Private Jack Senior of the Royal Signals arrived with a group of fellow signallers in an ex-North Sea trawler in the days before Prittwitz's first attack on the perimeter. On the voyage from Alexandria he manned a Bren gun in case of attack by enemy aircraft despite complaining that he had never been trained on the Bren. 'Now is the time to learn,' came the response. As they arrived off Tobruk and entered the harbour they passed floating bodies, some face up staring lifelessly into the sky. A beached Italian cruise ship – the *Marco Polo* – belched black smoke. The trawler dodged around other wrecks in the harbour before disembarking the signallers, who then travelled by truck to a wadi on the west of the town. Settling down for the night on the rocky ground, they lay on their backs watching a high-level bombing attack on the harbour they had just left before falling fitfully asleep.

As the day dawned they were woken by shouts and a number of shots. A voice bellowed to them to report to a bell tent on the beach and to take with them what water and food they could grab. With no idea where either the beach or the tent were, they nevertheless stumbled after some others and found where they had been told to report. A Coldstream Guards sergeant major met them, issued them each with a bandolier of fifty rounds, shook hands and wished them the best of luck. They were dumbfounded. Finding his voice, Jack stammered out that they were Royal Signals personnel and had been sent to Tobruk for a 'special job'. 'Yes, that's right,' replied the Guards NCO. 'You are now Royal Signals Infantry and your special job is to stop the Germans from breaking into Tobruk.' A few minutes later their transport arrived: one weather-beaten Bren carrier belching smoke and a battered Italian ambulance. After thirty minutes bouncing across the rocky ground they reached El Adem beyond the southern perimeter, joining a number of Guardsmen in a wide anti-tank trench acting as a forward lookout post for a German column, which was expected at any moment. Their instructions were simple. 'When you see us running like hell, try to overtake us and get back inside the perimeter.' Fortunately for the dazed signallers, they were withdrawn well before any Germans appeared.

On 19 April 1941 Lieutenant Alexander McGinlay, reconnaissance troop commander of D Squadron, 7th RTR, was part of one of the first tank crews to be taken into Tobruk on one of the new and secret tank landing craft – known as A Lighters to disguise their purpose. They were flat-bottomed, and discharged their cargo via a bow ramp lowered onto the beach. Loading up at Mersa Matruh, each A Lighter conveyed three or four Matildas to Tobruk:

> We went in line ahead, and the first one ran foul of one of the many wrecks in the harbour. As number two in line, and having a fair idea of a good spot to beach, which was just under a huge crane, I helped guide our tank landing craft in, and we were off like a flash, headed up the three escarpments, guided into our leaguer positions [near Pilastrino] by members of the 6th RTR who had been there some weeks. We were shelled but not damaged, and soon settled in.
>
> We could not dig in, being on a very rocky ridge. We camouflaged our tanks as best we could and scraped shallow holes for ourselves. Many were the varied hideouts over the months which we thought up. Bits of wood laid across rocks, canvas sheeting over them, rocks on top of that, and there we were, completely hidden from the air.

They only had days to familiarize themselves with the battlefield. In the late afternoon of 30 April Rommel's expected onslaught against the western defences at Ras el Medawar began with an hourlong aerial bombardment of forward posts by two separate waves of twenty-five Stukas, followed by the heaviest artillery barrage the Australians had yet experienced. Four miles of this part of the perimeter were held by a single Australian battalion, the 2/24th, commanded by Lieutenant Colonel Allan Spowers. Morshead had a second battalion in reserve for counter-attacks, together with the support of three artillery regiments (51st Field, 1st RHA and the South Notts Hussars) as well as the Tobruk Tanks with a mixture of cruisers, newly arrived Matildas and armoured cars. Morshead's greatest problem was that he did not know whether this was the sole assault or if another penetration was to be attempted at El Adem. As the Stuka and artillery barrage came down, blotting out the late-afternoon sun with clouds of dust and debris, German troops of the newly arrived 2nd Machine-Gun Battalion, 115th Artillery Regiment, 104th Rifle Regiment and 33rd Engineer Battalion advanced to the perimeter, clearing lanes through the minefield and directing such heavy fire against the forward Australian positions that within forty-five minutes of the initial attack a successful breach had been achieved. Under cover of the bombardment small groups of German soldiers rushed through, crouching in the distinctive way troops do when they advance into the unknown, weapons clutched in clammy hands, stomachs knotted, faces scanning the ground ahead through the dust and smoke for their first sight of the enemy, ears attuned to the final screaming seconds of an incoming mortar or artillery shell. Behind the front waves, through the cleared lanes in the minefield (the Australians called the process of clearing a minefield delousing), rumbled the menacing panzers.

Back in Tobruk Major John Devine recalled in his diary, 'A day of great anxiety and alarms. All roads were blocked, and all military police issued with Molotov cocktails, made out of old Recoaro mineral-water bottles filled with petrol. Even the air raid siren was stopped so as not to reveal the position of the town. All day the artillery thundered, and as I write now in the evening everything shakes to a distant rumble.' In the docks Private Parish described the atmosphere around the harbour as a 'flat spin'. All the dock personnel were given rifles and organized into infantry sections for the defence of the harbour. Air attacks continued without let-up against the harbour, artillery and anti-aircraft positions, an anti-personnel bomb falling on 1 May between John Kelly's trench and his tent, riddling his greatcoat with shrapnel.

The 104th Rifles, part of the 15th Panzer Division, had arrived by air at Benghazi over the previous week. They had left their barracks in Baumholder in the Rhineland Palatinate in a thick snowstorm only days before, exchanging blinding snow for choking sand. Setting off on foot from the dusty ruins of Acroma, the troops of the 115th Infantry Regiment marched, heavily laden with machine-gun ammunition and grenades, towards the clouds in the distance thrown up by the artillery bombardment. Paul Carell described the attack:

> They passed the first smashed barbed-wire entanglements and saw the first traces of tank tracks. The noise of the battle grew louder. Ahead of them clouds of dust thrown up by the shell bursts. A wall of dust marked the front line . . . They saw the first dead British [sic] soldiers in this theatre of war; their faces had been swollen out of all recognition by the heat. The corpses were in such an advanced state of decomposition that the uniforms had burst. Three or four Australians lay close together. They must have been killed by a machine-gun burst.
>
> Soon they met the first German soldiers returning from the front line, covered with filth and mud. A sergeant major staggered past. He was bleeding from the shoulder. The first shells fell close to them. Take cover! In short sharp rushes they made their way forward. The battlefield was covered with dead. They could not have been lying there very long for the bodies had not yet begun to swell.

New to the Tobruk battlefield, as they advanced into the Australian fire the German soldiers looked in vain for signs of entrenchments and pillboxes of the sort they had seen in France. They did not realize until they fell in or went past them that the Tobruk defences had been blasted deep into the rock and were flush with the ground. The concrete-reinforced positions were extremely difficult to locate let alone overcome, and had been constructed by the Italians for all-round defence.

At the breach the German infantry and combat engineers peeled off north and south and started to work their way along the perimeter, attacking each sunken Australian post as they came to it. The 1st Battalion of the 104th Rifle Regiment began their attacks around Point 209 at 2 a.m on 1 May. The battalion's combat engineers were ordered to take R6. Crawling forward on their bellies as quietly as possible the men badly cut their knees and elbows on the rocks. The plan was that when Lieutenant Friedl Schmidt fired a white signal flare, a barrage from 88s, field guns captured from the French months before and a huge 21-centimetre mortar would fall on R6. However, when Schmidt fired his flare, watching it soar into the air before slowly falling away into the darkness, he provoked not the German bombardment he was expecting but a fusillade from the Australian defenders only yards to his front. Bullets ripped through the night and grenades exploded around the engineers in a blitz of light and sound, the Germans afraid even to lift their heads. The diminutive and popular Private Sigrist was shot through the throat; amazingly the bullet exited his neck without doing any more damage than making a hole, and the young sapper was back on duty a week later. But that night they could make no headway against R6, and before first light, under cover of a thick dawn fog, they crawled back the way they had come, pulling their wounded behind them, Australian shots directed at the slightest sound.

German losses that night were heavy. Lieutenant Cirener, winner of the Knight's Cross in France a few months before and a company commander in the 33rd Engineer Battalion, was killed. The 104th suffered 50 per cent casualties. The CO of the 1st Battalion, Major Faltenbacher, was mortally wounded in the stomach, and the commanders of the battalion's four rifle companies were also wounded, one mortally. The Australians had refused to be intimidated by the force of the German assault, and doggedly held their ground. But German infiltration tactics meant that each Australian post had quickly found itself cut off from its neighbours and as the fighting continued throughout the night neither side had a clear idea of the overall situation.

During the night Spowers counter-attacked in an attempt to regain control of Point 209 and make contact with any of his troops still on the now cut-off rise. The darkness, smoke and confusion made it difficult to know precisely where the enemy were, preventing the British artillery from providing accurate counter-fire. Consequently the infantry counter-attacks made little progress. The breaking dawn and lifting fog on 1 May revealed at least sixty Axis tanks on Point 209. Seven Australian posts around the rise had been overwhelmed during the night and a German salient a mile and a half wide established. The Axis were now pouring in reinforcements and supplies from Acroma to enable them to punch through the remaining defences into Tobruk. That at least was the plan.

At first light at least forty of these German and Italian tanks began to roll eastwards in the direction of Tobruk along the Acroma road in a repeat of the Italian attack of 15 April. In their path was a thin minefield located forward of the rearmost Australian company guarding the crossroads at Bianca, hastily laid on Morshead's instructions following the Italian breach two weeks before. In addition there were the twelve First World War 18-pounders of the 51st Field Regiment and the twenty-four 25-pounders of the 1st and 107th RHA, which had been firing all night, the gunners exhausted and the guns hot from incessant use. A few Australian 2-pounder anti-tank guns in the north and some belonging to 3rd RHA in the south were the only purely anti-tank units in the threatened area. Around Pilastrino were grouped the Tobruk Tanks: the cruisers of 1st RTR and the 3rd Hussars, the few Matildas of 7th RTR brought up by sea and the ancient armoured cars of the King's Dragoon Guards.

Setting off from Acroma at 4.30 a.m. Lieutenant Joachim Schorm, leading his troop of four Mark IVs of 6 Company of the panzer battalion commanded by Major Hohmann, drove through a barrage of artillery fire at the perimeter breach. With the other tank companies detailed to deal with continuing Australian resistance on both Point 209 and the perimeter posts to the south, Schorm's company continued east as the vanguard of the advance into Tobruk. Soon afterwards he heard over the radio that his company commander's tank had struck a mine. Then an explosion rocked his tank, and 'things happened suddenly. Artillery shell hit? No? It must be a mine. Immediately send a radio message: "Commander Schorm on a mine. See if you can turn around in your own tracks." Five metres back. New explosion – mine underneath and to the left.' The entire company had struck Morshead's hastily laid minefield. Leaving his disabled panzer, Schorm climbed aboard another. 'Back through the artillery fire for 100 metres. Wireless order: "Panzers are to retire behind ridge." The men of the mined tank are all right. Enemy is attacking with tanks, but must be put to flight. Retire carefully . . . Nine Mark IIIs and three Mark II tanks of the company have had to abandon the fight owing to mines. Of course the enemy goes on shooting at us for some time. I move back through the gap with a salvaged tank in tow.'

Captain Peter Gebhardt, commanding the rearmost Australian

company of the 2/24th Battalion overlooking the minefield, watched with relief as the twelve German tanks of 6 Company – together with four from another – were brought to a shattering halt. Relief was immediately tinged with frustration as those tanks not destroyed were recovered by the Germans and dragged to the rear. The only weapons Gebhardt had to counter this activity – at a range of about 500 yards – were his Lee Enfields and a single ineffective Boys anti-tank rifle. Not having anti-tank guns covering the landmines was a serious mistake. Nevertheless the minefield, combined with British artillery, had by 9 a.m. destroyed or disabled some twenty tanks across the German salient and decisively thwarted Rommel's attempt to smash his way into Tobruk. As during the El Adem battles two weeks before, the German tank men were astounded by their Australian opponents. They had expected them to run when confronted by tanks and were thoroughly disconcerted when the Diggers fought back with grenades and bayonets. Their tenacity had a significant effect on Rommel's plans as, instead of concentrating to break through en masse, the German tank crews time and again peeled off to deal with the widely scattered pockets of resistance across the salient. This dissipated the panzer effort, negating its supreme virtue – concentration of force.

In the meantime the remainder of Major Hohmann's panzer battalion was busy fighting through the Australian posts to the south of Point 209. Groups of four or five tanks attacked each in turn. The tanks were followed by parties of forty or fifty German infantrymen, who would make the final rush on a trench with sub-machine guns, bayonets and grenades. The first to fall was R1, which Major Hohmann reported was occupied by twenty-four Australians. 'In the course of this operation,' he wrote, 'Obergefreiter Schaefer displayed conspicuous courage by leaping into the fortified position with hand grenades and taking several prisoners.' The fighting was fierce. When unsupported by tanks the German infantry were cut down in their scores by well-hidden Australian rifles and machine guns. The ground was too hard to dig slit trenches to shelter from the artillery fire, which fell like rain, and whenever heads were raised above the rocks behind which the attackers found shelter, they were shot at by the Australians. To the Germans' discomfort the Australians were extraordinarily good shots. During the day the men were forced to lie still in whatever shallow protection they could find for fear of taking a bullet, eating and carrying out all other necessary activities only when darkness fell.

Over the following three days the battle degenerated into a struggle by small groups of desperate men for isolated pockets of rocky desert. Few of the defenders knew what was going on elsewhere on the battlefield but fought on resolutely, counter-attacking fiercely when the enemy managed to take all or part of a bunker, refusing to give in. Signaller Frank Harrison spoke to a Digger on 5 May. Of course he had been scared, the Australian replied when asked, 'scared to bloody death, mate'. His strongest memory was of not knowing 'what the 'ell was going on and who the 'ell was doing it'.

At R4 Corporal Bob McLeish and his colleagues in the 2/24th were forced to defend themselves as best they could. As the Germans drew closer the Diggers opened fire, which forced the infantry to go to ground but did not stop the advance of four tanks:

> Their machine guns kept our heads down and their cannon blasted away our sandbag parapets. The sand got into our MGs and we spent as much time cleaning them as we did firing them, but we sniped at the infantry whenever we got the chance. Our anti-tank rifle put one light tank out of action, but it couldn't check the heavier ones, which came right up to the post. We threw hand grenades at them but these bounced off, and the best we could do was to keep the infantry from getting closer than a hundred yards.

Likewise, at R8 Sergeant Ernest Thurman and his shrinking band of men were able to keep up the unequal struggle because two German Mark IVs – having destroyed the 2-pounder anti-tank guns of the 3rd RHA – refused to advance across a non-existent minefield fifty yards in front of the post. 'They raked the top of the post with machine guns and cannon, and the crews even stood up in the turrets and threw stick bombs into our communication trench. But we still kept firing at both tanks and infantry. We'd take a few pot shots and then duck before their machine-gun bullets thudded into our sandbags.'

The defenders were not averse to taking on the panzers with little more than their bare hands. Trooper Bob Sykes of 6th RTR found himself a temporary infantryman and honorary Australian in the Tobruk defences. He was awoken just before dawn on 1 May with the news that German tanks had broken through:

> I staggered out to our Morris truck while in the darkness figures were loading up: petrol, bombs, grenades, guns, ammo, the lot. After travelling a long way we came to a barbed-wire barricade – a section was slid apart and we went through. In the distance a small war was going on.
>
> Tanks were moving away from us and we went after one that seemed to be behind. It was a German tank and some of the Aussies raced off behind it and jammed steel rods [metal fence pickets] between the tracks. Petrol bombs lit up the tank; grenades and shots rang out. We swung the truck close to the tank, which was well alight, and the raiding crowd jumped aboard. We had very minor casualties but tension remained very high.

Fighting continued south of Point 209 during the afternoon and evening. The Luftwaffe mounted heavy raids in an attempt to silence the devastatingly effective British artillery. In his diary Schorm reported, 'Dive-bombers and twin-engine fighters have been attacking the enemy constantly. Despite this, the British repeatedly counter-attack with tanks. As soon as the planes have gone, the artillery opens up furiously. It is beginning to get dark. Who is friend and who is foe? Shots are being fired all over the place, often on our troops and on panzers in front which are falling back.' It seemed to the Germans that the Allies had so much ammunition that individual soldiers were sniped at with artillery. When Lieutenant Friedl Schmidt went to visit Lieutenant Wettengel in a neighbouring position he came under fire from a lone gun. Moving in short rushes, he dived to the ground as the whine of an incoming shell warned him that it was nearly on him. During his journey he came across a slit trench. It was occupied. Crawling over the lip he was greeted by an overpowering stench. Eyes staring skywards, the lifeless body of the regimental doctor lay crumpled at the bottom, rapidly decomposing in the desert heat.

Small groups of British tanks helped to respond to local threats, the Matildas acting as mobile pillboxes and attracting the attentions of the Stukas and Messerschmidt fighters that roamed above the battlefield. Major George Hynes of B Squadron 1st RTR narrowly escaped death when a bomb dropped by a Stuka struck the ground next to his cruiser without exploding. In the late afternoon a fierce battle near R6 took place between panzers and the Tobruk Tanks. A mixed force of five Matildas of 7th RTR and a handful of cruisers of 1st RTR, nosing forward to ascertain what positions had been captured by the enemy and what continued to be held by the Australians, came under attack first from fifteen panzers to the front. Then, responding to the radio calls of their comrades, eight more panzers emerged from the direction of the wire to the left and shortly thereafter another fourteen appeared from the north-east. 'Jerry tanks seemed to attack us from all sides,' recalled Sergeant Stockley of 1st RTR, pleased he was in a Matilda rather than a cruiser. 'One cruiser was disabled and the other, because of its light armour, had to withdraw leaving us four to fight it out ... We were hit many times, but our heavier armour saved us and we kept the Jerry tanks off until it became hard to tell theirs from ours in the half light.' During the battle Alexander McGinlay, commanding his Matilda, felt a hard knock on his right leg:

I thought it was my loader/operator, and yelled at him to 'mind his bloody feet'. I should have noticed that at the same time the two cupola lids had flown open.

It wasn't until after the action, as we were rallying, that I looked down and saw sunlight streaming in on the floor of the turret. Now sunlight is the last thing one expects to see there. What had happened was that we had received a direct hit from an enemy 105-millimetre gun at very short range. The whole of the thick armour all along the side of the tank had sprung open, about three or four inches. That shows how tough these Matildas were. All we noticed was a kick on the leg from a 2-pounder shell dislodged from its rack and a puff of wind.

In fact, both McGinlay and Stockley were lucky. Of 7th RTR's five Matildas two were totally destroyed and two badly damaged. Two cruisers were also written off. The destruction of the hitherto indestructible Matildas by panzers mounting the powerful 50-millimetre gun came as a considerable shock to the British crews who were used to enjoying a measure of invulnerability in their queens of the battlefield. By nightfall on 1 May five British tanks had been destroyed or damaged (three of them Matildas) from a total complement of thirty-one.

The tank battle was a victory for the Germans, but they failed to exploit it. Unaware of the devastation wrought on the British and that the 1st and 7th RTR tanks were entirely out of ammunition, the Germans broke off the engagement at last light, withdrawing back through the breach to replenish and refuel at Acroma. They could have continued on to Tobruk unopposed, had they continued their advance. But Rommel's armour had also suffered that day. German and Italian tank losses were severe: the 5th Panzer Regiment had gone into action with eighty-one tanks on the morning of 1 May and ended 2 May with only thirty-five; most had been destroyed or disabled by mines. Many, however, were recovered from the battlefield, repaired and pressed back into service.

*

To the north the German had rolled up the Australian posts for a thousand yards from the centre of the breach at Point 209. Across the entire salient, extending by nightfall to three miles wide, the Germans and their Italian allies had captured fifteen Australian posts, but at great cost in lives and armour. At the end of the day an exhausted Schorm jotted in his diary, 'We cover until 2345 hours, then retire through the gap. It is a mad drive through the dust. At 0300 hours had a snack beside the panzer. Twenty-four hours shut up in the tank, with frightful cramp and thirst as a result!'

Flame-throwers, artillery, tanks and close assault by infantry were employed systematically to attack and reduce each perimeter post in turn; machine guns, Stukas and artillery keeping the heads down of the Australians in neighbouring posts attempting to provide support to their comrades. An Australian counter-attack by two companies of the 2/24th during the night of 1/2 May along the Acroma road from near Bianca advanced with great gallantry, but in the darkness it proved impossible to control and withdrew after two hours in the face of heavy fire, having suffered fifty-four casualties.

The following morning the weather came to Tobruk's aid as a heavy khamsin hit the coast, forcing the Germans to consolidate their bridgehead around Point 209 rather than attempting a further break-through. The storm allowed Morshead to bring up reinforcements and construct defences to plug the gap in the perimeter. All the while the British guns pounded the newly won German positions, further hindering Rommel from exploiting the salient that he had established. The following day – 3 May – using two infantry battalions, Morshead counter-attacked the German bridgehead, one battalion advancing from the north along the perimeter and one from the south. In support of one of these thrusts Lieutenant Tony McGinlay, commanding his troop of Matildas, nosed forward, peering through the smoke, dust and semi-darkness, trying to locate enemy tanks:

> Peering desperately for something to shoot at, suddenly I was confronted by what looked like a huge flaming ball. It was frightening. I asked my troop sergeant what the hell it was. He replied it was some sort of flame running along the ground. We then agreed to machine-gun back along the line towards the source next time it happened. Sure enough, it did, and as the action progressed with no more flames, we got on with pushing Jerry back outside the wire.
>
> After it was all over the Aussies brought in a dead Jerry with two large canisters strapped on his back. This was the first any of us had ever seen of a flame-thrower.

Although some territory was regained, despite the expenditure of 10,000 artillery rounds in two and a half hours and 134 Australian casualties the Germans remained in control of the salient.

Throughout the May Day battles German and Italian aircraft pounded Tobruk for all they were worth. Though not under Rommel's direct control, Axis aircraft nevertheless conformed to his plans. This meant that from the outset the danger was not confined to the perimeter trenches and defences. The port, tank parks, artillery positions, headquarters and, despite the Geneva Convention, the two hospitals all came under sustained air attack. In the 82 days between 9 April and the end of June 1941 there were 787 separate raids against

Tobruk involving over 6,000 German and Italian aircraft. This meant that on average 73 enemy aircraft were in the air over Tobruk every day. Because of their success against Rommel's tanks during the Easter battles the British artillery positions were prime targets for the dive-bombing Stukas and the higher-flying Savoia 79s and Heinkels, as well as for Italian and German artillery fire. 'The dive-bombers made repeated attacks on the guns,' recalled Ray Ellis of A Troop, South Notts Hussars in the 25-pounder gun position near King's Cross:

> and the scream as they went into their bombing dive was a familiar sound. They usually dropped five bombs: four in a circle and one in the middle. It was very frightening to crouch in a trench and watch the plane screaming down from directly above, to see the bombs leave as the pilot pulled out of his dive.
>
> Sometimes we had to watch as the dive-bombers attacked B Troop and for me that was a dreadful ordeal, almost as bad as if I were under attack myself, because my brother and all my best friends were there. They were about half a mile away, over to our right.

On 5 May he watched in dismay as plane after plane roared down to deliver its deadly load, the whole area becoming obscured under a huge cloud of smoke. Among the dead was his good friend Jim Smedley:

> During the raid he like everybody else had dived for cover into a slit trench. Had he remained there he might have been spared. But Jim was not the man to lie shivering in a trench, and as the raid progressed he noticed that the Bren gun was not being manned to provide protective fire. Without a thought for his own life he jumped out of his own trench and ran towards the Bren gun pit, but alas he did not make it.

The Stukas did not always have things their own way. On one occasion, hearing them head towards his leaguer after a noisy attack on the town, Lieutenant Alexander McGinlay ran to man a machine gun on a Mark VI in his squadron. 'We all blazed away at the low-flying planes as they flew over us, and I heard above the other clatter the heavy slower *rat-a-tat-tat* of my point-five heavy machine gun. These light tanks carried an ordinary Vickers 0.303-inch and a 0.5-inch coaxially mounted. Then we heard terrific cheering as one of the planes came down in flames.'

Between 9 April and 31 May forty-nine enemy aircraft were shot down by anti-aircraft fire, and at least forty-two others were severely damaged but not seen to fall. It was every man's dream to bag a Stuka. Gunner Jack Daniel of 153 Heavy Anti-Aircraft Battery recalled that when they came over 'everyone would be firing, 303s, revolvers, anything. We could almost chuck bricks at them as they came whizzing by.'

In the air and on the ground the fighting had been intensive. Schorm wrote in his diary, 'Captain Prossen and the other officers who served in the Great War are all saying, 'Yes, it was like that in 1916–18. What we experienced in Poland and the Western Front was only a stroll by comparison.' By the end of four days of fighting the Australians had lost the equivalent of a battalion of men: 797, of whom 352 were from Spower's 2/24th Battalion, which had borne the brunt of the fighting during the first two days. Four hundred and fourteen had been killed or wounded, and 383 were missing, most of them captured during the methodical reduction of the perimeter posts and marched into captivity. Four German Me 109s had been shot down over Tobruk for the loss of one Hurricane. The Germans and Italians had sustained 1,398 casualties. 'Our troops and particularly officers have suffered heavy casualties from infantry and anti-tank fire,' reported an officer to Rommel. 'Most units have 50 per cent casualties, some even more.'

Rommel had again been surprised by the stubbornness of the Tobruk defences, noting in his diary that the defenders had 'fought with remarkable tenacity. Even their wounded went on defending themselves with small-arms fire and stayed in the fight to their last breath.' He was particularly struck by the sight of fifty or sixty Australians being marched into captivity on 1 May – 'all immensely big and powerful men, who without question represented an elite formation of the British empire, a fact that was also evident in battle'. For the first time in two years of war the German offensive steamroller had been checked. 'Our opponents are Englishmen and Australians . . .'

recorded Joachim Schorm, 'men with nerves and toughness, tireless, taking punishment with obstinacy, wonderful in defence.' The Germans found the fighting far tougher than anything that they had hitherto experienced. The CO of a German infantry battalion reported:

> The Australians, who are the men our troops have had opposite them so far, are extraordinarily tough fighters. The German is more active in the attack but the enemy stakes his life in the defence and fights to the last and with extreme cunning. Our men, usually easygoing and unsuspecting, fall easily into his traps.
>
> Enemy snipers have astounding results. They shoot at anything they recognize. Several NCOs of the battalion have been shot through the head with the first shot while making observations in the front line. Protruding sights in gun directors have been shot off, observation slits and loopholes have been fired on and hit as soon as they were seen to be in use.

In summary, although Rommel had created a salient in the western corner of the perimeter the Axis offensive had been contained by a vigorous and obstinate defence. Rushing forward troops and equipment to the Western Desert, a relieved Wavell signalled to Morshead, 'Your magnificent defence is upsetting enemy's plans for attack on Egypt.' With memories of other sieges in the recent history of the British empire clearly in the forefront of his mind, Churchill told Morshead by telegram, 'The whole empire is watching your steadfast and spirited defence of this important outpost of Egypt with gratitude and determination.' On 4 May the siege, for that is what it now was, had lasted for twenty-four days, and Morshead and his mixed bag of Australians, Britons and Indians had reason to be pleased with their efforts. They could not know it had 218 days left to run. On the Axis side, Rommel now knew what he was up against. 'The Australian troops are fighting magnificently and their training is far superior to ours,' he wrote to Lucie. 'Tobruk can't be taken by force, given our present means.'

*

The considerable resources expended by Rommel on attacking Tobruk meant he was not able to advance into Egypt, the division of his forces between the siege and the frontier between Sollum and Capuzzo preventing him from striking for the Nile. His losses in the battles around Tobruk also disconcerted Berlin, whose original intention had been that he should not by this stage have moved much beyond the capture of Benghazi.

Pressed relentlessly by an impatient prime minister to counter-attack in Libya, Wavell instructed his forces in the Western Desert on 1 May to draw up plans for the recapture of Sollum/Halfaya and Capuzzo to provide a launch pad for a more ambitious offensive to join up with the Tobruk garrison. This was Operation Brevity. Shocked by Rommel's offensive into Cyrenaica and the disaster which had befallen 13th Corps, Churchill had immediately dispatched a convoy of five ships to Egypt with Britain's last remaining reserve of tanks – which he codenamed his Tiger Cubs – to enable Wavell to mount an armoured offensive against Rommel and thus defend Egypt. These 238 tanks (one ship was sunk by a mine with the loss of 57 tanks) – 21 Mark VIs, 82 cruisers in various states of repair (including 67 of the new, untried Crusaders) and 135 Matildas – arrived in Alexandria on 12 May, but took several weeks to prepare for use and in any case were far too late for Brevity. For this the British had only the 55 medium tanks (29 cruisers in 2nd RTR and 26 Matildas in 4th RTR) of Strafer Gott's 7th Armoured Brigade. In addition, and separate from the tanks, which British doctrine deployed independent of other arms on the battlefield, the British had three trucked infantry battalions together with a field regiment of artillery, and the divisional support group containing the 11th Hussars and a further two trucked infantry battalions.

One of the primary reasons for launching Brevity was a misreading by Churchill of signals between Berlin and North Africa concerning the state of the Afrika Korps. Rommel's spectacular though unauthor-ized advances had prompted concern in Berlin that he was overreach-ing himself and, following his failure to break into Tobruk in mid-April, the OKW dispatched Lieutenant General Friedrich von Pau-lus (who was to surrender Stalingrad to the Soviets in early 1943) to the region on a tour of inspection. At the end of April von Paulus sent a signal to Berlin, picked up by the British at Bletchley Park, to the effect that Rommel was to limit his operations in Cyrenaica, await the arrival of the 15th Panzer Division and not contemplate offensive operations beyond Bardia/Sollum until the Afrika Korps had had a chance to recover after its recent exertions. This information was seized upon by Churchill with glee as evidence that Rommel had shot his bolt and that a quick offensive from Egypt combined with aggressive counter-attacks from Tobruk would force the Afrika Korps back on the defensive *before* the 15th Panzer Division was operational. That Churchill believed that Wavell could do this with only fifty-five tanks was the least of his misjudgements. London's real failure was to understand the nature of much of the signals traffic that travelled between Rommel's headquarters near Tobruk and Berlin. When Rommel said that his troops were 'exhausted' and 'thin on the ground', it did not mean that they had run out of fight and would run at the first sign of a British attack, merely that he wanted more troops and was dissatisfied with the performance of his Italian allies. As for von Paulus's advice, Rommel simply ignored it and continued to do what he believed to be operationally expedient.

At the beginning of May Rommel had only limited forces on the Egyptian frontier but these included a mixed force of Italian and German artillery, most notably a battery of German 88s. However, in the days following the end of the salient battles in western Tobruk Rommel pushed reinforcements up to the border area including a further battalion from the Italian Trento Regiment, Major Hormann's panzer battalion (which included Leutenant Joachim Schorm) and a motorcycle battalion of the 104th Rifle Regiment.

Operation Brevity began before dawn on 15 May, and a surprise assault on the Halfaya Pass by Major Miles's C Squadron of 4th RTR was immediately successful. The lack of a preliminary artillery bombardment took the Italian defenders by surprise, catching most in their pyjamas or at breakfast, although gunners managed to destroy or disable seven of the slow-moving Matildas. Seeing their 47-millimetre anti-tank shells bouncing off the thick hides of the advancing Matildas, the Italians had the presence of mind to fire at the tracks and underbellies of the leviathans as they climbed over the low rock wall which skirted the position. Defenceless without Halfaya, Sollum then fell quickly.

*

German guns likewise put up strenuous resistance at Fort Capuzzo against the nine tanks of A Squadron, 4th RTR, disabling seven, although that fort also fell briefly. Running tank battles during the morning of 15 May in the region of Fort Capuzzo between 2nd and 4th RTR and Major Hormann's panzer battalion rapidly reduced the British tank strength to such an extent that they were forced to withdraw to their start positions, although retaining Halfaya with nine Matildas of 4th RTR and the 3rd Battalion Coldstream Guards. By now 4th RTR had only six runners available for action from the twenty-nine that had started. By the end of its first day the British offensive had run out of steam: an ill-conceived attempt to recover control of the frontier and perhaps drive an armoured wedge through to relieve Tobruk had been swept aside by the vastly superior numbers of German tanks and their more skilful deployment. Hormann's panzers reached Sidi Suleiman well inside the Egyptian frontier late on the 16th, although he withdrew soon after coming under attack by the remaining cruiser tanks of 2nd RTR. During the operation the British suffered 160 casualties (100 of whom were taken prisoner); five Matildas were destroyed, thirteen damaged, and at least six were captured after breaking down on the battlefield. After repairing them and painting crosses on the sides, the Germans pressed the Matildas into their own service. Combined German and Italian losses totalled 653. Importantly for German–Italian cooperation the hand-picked *bersaglieri* who defended Halfaya under Colonel Montemurro fought tenaciously, doing much to repair the poor impression Rommel had of his Italian allies. 'Many Italian officers had thought of war as little more than a pleasant adventure,' he wrote, 'and were, perforce, having to suffer a bitter disillusionment.' Rommel, unprecedentedly, recommended Montemurro for the Iron Cross First Class. 'The German soldier surprised the Italian soldier,' Rommel told Montemurro, 'but the *bersaglieri* surprised the German soldier.'

The British offensive had been weak, its tank strength not sufficiently concentrated to deal with German armoured counter-attacks and too concerned with irrelevant tactical objectives. Unlike German units, British tanks, artillery, infantry and aircraft failed to coordinate their operations, with the result that such tactics as artillery masking enemy anti-tank guns while tanks advanced, or infantry accompanying tanks to clear and hold ground were unheard of. Instead of holding Halfaya, for instance, and then masking Bardia and Capuzzo while making a strong armoured dash to Tobruk, the British were concerned with the piecemeal reduction of the forces opposing them. With the limited assets the British possessed they never had a chance of overcoming all the forces deployed against them in Cyrenaica using such tactics, and Rommel was able to defeat each attack in turn.

News of the failure of Operation Brevity was received in Tobruk on 16 May with consternation. It was clear that relief was not imminent, despite the rumours that had run like wildfire through the garrison during the preceding days. The garrison had attempted to play its part by launching attacks from within the perimeter designed to force Rommel to keep his tanks at Tobruk. The ubiquitous Captains Leakey and Benzie took two cruisers on an armoured fighting patrol 800 yards west of S15 – parallel with the Derna road – to harass the Italians, and a further show of tank activity was made between Bianca and Pilastrino in full view of the bemused German defenders of Ras el Medawar, although there is no evidence that either diversion successfully secured Rommel's attention for more than a moment.

Wavell tried to allay any concerns in London about the failure of his offensive by telling Churchill that he had instructed the 13th Corps commander to 'mobilize the Tiger Cubs as soon as possible and try again'. The initiative, however, had passed to Rommel. On 26 and 27 May, in Operation Skorpion, Rommel, concentrating a force of seventy Panzers from Colonel Hans Kramer's 8th Panzer Regiment supported by the 15th Infantry Motorized Battalion, the experienced troops of von Wechmar's 33rd Reconnaissance Battalion (based in Bardia since mid-April) and a battalion of the 104th Rifle Regiment, launched an overwhelming attack on the poorly defended Halfaya Pass. Meanwhile, west of Fort Capuzzo Major Hormann's panzer battalion feinted south-south-west to convince the British their desert flank was under threat.

At Halfaya, its defences reduced to two Matildas (from nine) by the morning of the 27th and with the Coldstream Guards having lost a hundred men, the British withdrew, pulling back to Buq Buq, only one Matilda making it to safety. The jubilant victor, Colonel Maximilian von Herff, reported that the battle had netted him nine 25-pounders, seven Matildas, two other tanks and much other booty, including forty prisoners. Rommel was delighted, recommending Colonel Kramer for the Knight's Cross and signalling his men, 'Congratulations to you all for your successful attack . . .'

The loss of the Halfaya Pass proved expensive for the British, given subsequent efforts in June to regain it. However, Operation Brevity had forced Rommel to divide his forces: one group masking Tobruk, one holding the frontier at Sollum/Halfaya and a third forming a mobile armoured reserve to prevent a future British offensive turning Tobruk's southern flank.

Urged almost daily to commit his newly arrived Tiger Cubs to battle, Wavell now rushed to launch Operation Battleaxe, Churchill in London seemingly unaware of the amount of work needed to 'desertify' the tanks and to prepare and train their crews, many of whom were going from light tanks to mediums for the first time, and most having never fired a 2-pounder in action before, let alone in training. The British plan would once again dilute its impact by striking in three columns rather than, as Rommel was doing, attacking with a concentrated armoured fist. It also aimed to attack the German fortified frontier positions, rather than bypass them and allow them to wither on the vine. One column, on the right, would occupy Sollum after the centre column, consisting of the 4th Armoured Brigade (2nd and 4th RTR), two artillery field regiments, one medium battery, one anti-tank regiment and the three infantry battalions of 22nd Guards Brigade, would advance south of the escarpment, cross the frontier well to the south of Sollum – thus avoiding the enemy's prepared defences – and then turn north and capture Musaid, Bir Waer and Capuzzo. A detachment would be sent to capture Halfaya. On the extreme left the 7th Armoured Division (less 4th Armoured Brigade), with cruisers, was to advance further south of the escarpment to protect the left flank of the centre column and attack enemy tank forces wherever encountered. From Tobruk an armoured force plus the 18th Australian

Brigade was to break out south-east to occupy the high ground on the Ed Duda ridge, which dominated the road in the shallow valley below, the Trigh Capuzzo, the old Ottoman route that ran all the way through the desert to Bardia and Rommel's vital supply line to the east.

Although he now had far greater resources than he had enjoyed with Brevity, Wavell was still nervous about his chances of success, given the light armour of his Mark VIs, the slowness of the Matildas, the propensity of the cruisers to break down (especially the new Crusaders) and the inadequate training of his troops. He told London that he could not accept battle 'with perfect confidence'.

Disastrously for the British, Rommel had long appreciated the importance of the Halfaya Pass as the gateway between Cyrenaica and Egypt and from the moment of its capture on 27 May had rushed to transform it into a fortress. By the time Battleaxe was finally launched – on 15 June – the pass was defended by 900 hand-picked Italian and German troops with five 88-millimetre anti-aircraft guns deployed in the anti-tank role, four Italian artillery pieces and a battery of 155-millimetre captured French guns. Even the turrets of captured Matildas had been converted into fixed strongpoints. The overall commander was the new CO of one of the 104th Rifle Regiment battalions, Captain Wilhelm Bach, forty-nine-year-old erstwhile pastor of the Evangelical church in Mannheim. It was as formidable a position as the British were ever to encounter in the war, as resistant to British offensive aspirations in mid-1941 as Tobruk was to Rommel's. Equally disastrously and despite warning signs over previous weeks, the British remained oblivious to the effectiveness of the 88 in the anti-tank role and implemented no new tactics to counteract the extraordinary power of this weapon. Mounted on a wheeled trailer, it could throw a 20-pound shell a mile, more than twice the distance any British tank could throw its puny 2-pound projectile. By now too, the remainder of the 15th Panzer Division, under the half-Scottish Colonel Walther Neumann-Silkow, had arrived outside Tobruk and was spoiling for a fight.

The British attacks on Halfaya and on Point 208 (Habata Ridge) began before first light on Sunday 15 June, a day when temperatures reached an impossibly hot 50 degrees Celsius, and inside the tanks 60 degrees or more. At Halfaya a distant rumble warned of the British advance, tanks being observed through binoculars by the commander of Bach's 1st Company, Lieutenant Richter, when the first of the twelve Matildas was still 3,500 yards away. The truth was that the Germans had known as early as 6 June that a substantial attack was impending, in major part because of appalling British radio discipline. Most commands, especially once combat began, were sent in clear and assiduously picked up and acted upon by German commanders. The day before Battleaxe British commanders had been told in clear that 'Peter' would begin the next day. Rommel correctly assumed this was the code for the offensive and every man in the Afrika Korps was ready. Biding their time, waiting until the British tanks were on the edge of the minefield only 300 yards in front of their position, and after a heavy British artillery bombardment had fallen harmlessly into an empty wadi to the rear, the five hidden 88s opened fire simultaneously on Pastor Bach's hand signal. The British tanks had been supposed to be accompanied by a battery of 25-pounders, but these had got stuck in soft ground and never made it to the start line.

The opening salvo produced bloody devastation in the advancing armour of Major C.G. Miles's C Squadron, 4th RTR. The heavy shells tore whole turrets from the chassis of the Matildas. One hit blew up a tank's ammunition, the armour peeling back in a flash of smoke and flame like the petals of an opening flower:

> Abruptly, through the distant comfortable-sounding mutter of our tanks [recalled one British tank man] there came the vicious *whip-crack* of high-velocity shot. Instantly, three of the leading tanks stopped and burst asunder, as it were, in billows of red flame and black oily smoke. The *whip-cracks* continued, unhurried, deliberate, and almost with each one it seemed another tank burst into flames. Horrified, we realized our Matildas were no longer invincible. The Germans had a gun which fired shells that cut through their armour like a hot knife through butter. It was shattering. In that moment I knew our attack was doomed, that the whole operation must fail.

The lighter 20-millimetre German and 47-millimetre Italian anti-tank guns under the command of Major Pardi aimed at the tracks and underbellies of the slowly advancing vehicles. Within moments, and under the awed but jubilant gaze of the waiting German infantry, seven Matildas lay destroyed and burning fiercely in front of their positions.

In the minutes before his own Matilda was hit and he was killed, Major Miles managed to tell his CO over the radio, 'They've got large-calibre guns dug in and they're tearing my tanks to bits.' At the coastal end of the pass five Matildas attempted to cross a minefield. Soon the dull thump of exploding mines could be heard over the screech of tank fire. Only one made it through but, seeing all the others out of action, reversed back across the minefield, following its own tracks. Unable to get any closer to Halfaya – now nicknamed Hellfire by the British – the 2nd Battalion Cameron Highlanders formed up to assault the pass but were torn apart by the machine guns and artillery of the largely untouched defenders before being counter-attacked by tanks. Five separate attacks over that day and the next failed to budge Pastor Bach. The only good news on the northern front was that the Guards Brigade had taken its objectives at Musaid and Sollum.

Meanwhile the vanguard of the 7th Armoured Division advanced through Capuzzo to threaten Bardia. Here, the battle only went Rommel's way because a single 88, brought out hastily from Bardia by Lieutenant Tocki of the 33rd Reconnaissance Battalion, destroyed three Matildas in quick succession, halting the advance of the remaining forty-seven. This provided time for the panzers of Kramer's 8th Panzer Regiment to reach the scene from their leaguer outside Bardia. Captain Johannes Kümmel, CO of the First Battalion, leading in a Mark IV panzer equipped with a 75-millimetre gun, ordered his tanks to form a wedge and advance directly against the British. Stopping only to fire, two companies engaged the stationary British tanks while the other two companies drove through them. A fierce tank-on-tank struggle ensued in which, after several hours, the British were forced to concede ground and withdraw, thwarting their ambition to reach Bardia.

While the struggle for Hellfire Pass was under way Rommel's other defences prepared themselves to the west at Hill 208, at Fort Capuzzo and Sidi Omar. Hill 208 on the Bir Hafid ridge was occupied by a mixed force of Italians and German troops from the First Oasis

Company under the command of Lieutenant Paulewicz. Paulewicz had overseen the fortification of the hill – 600 yards long by 500 yards wide – the ubiquitous 88s playing a significant role in his plans. Lieutenant Ziemer, commander of the 88-millimetre troop, had ensured the huge guns were so well dug in and protected by stone walls that the barrel of each projected no more than three feet above the ground. Walking forward to the minefield the previous day, Ziemer had turned around and to his satisfaction observed that none of his guns was visible even at one hundred yards.

Paulewicz was shaving in the dark the next morning – Monday 16 June – when the sound of approaching armour led him to drop his razor in the sand and race to Ziemer's position. 'Under no circumstances fire until the enemy infantry and tanks are on top of us,' he ordered rather superfluously, as his men had constantly rehearsed their tactics over the previous days. As dawn broke thirty tanks could be seen in the distance, clouds of dust billowing behind them as they advanced towards the ridge. Returning to his trench and recovering his razor, Paulewicz completed his shave. Firing too early would warn the British, who would counter with an artillery bombardment. As at Halfaya, the trick was to remain unobserved until the enemy tanks filled the whole of the gun sights. As the tanks grew nearer Ziemer calmly counted seventy of them. Finally, when only a thousand yards distant, the four 88s fired, and within moments eleven new Crusaders of 6th RTR lay burning on the battlefield. The attack was broken off.

A second attack was launched in the afternoon, but this too suffered heavily at the hands of the 88s, eight cruisers being destroyed. Captain Cyril Joly, who had rejoined 2nd RTR after leaving Tobruk several weeks before, engaged with his squadron a group of twenty panzers on Hafid Ridge. At 850 yards his tank opened fire. 'Through the smoke and dust and the spurt of flame I watched intently through my binoculars the trace of the shot in flight. It curved upwards slightly and almost slowly, and then seemed to plunge swiftly towards the target. There was the unmistakable dull glow of a strike of steel on steel.' Suddenly his own cruiser was hit:

There was a clang of steel on the turret front and a blast of flame and smoke from the same place, which seemed to spread into the turret, where it was followed by another dull explosion. The shock wave which followed swept past me, still standing in the cupola, singed my hands and face and left me breathless and dazed. I looked down into the turret. It was a shambles. The shot had penetrated the front of the turret just in front of King, the loader. It had twisted the machine gun out of its mounting. It, or a jagged piece of the torn turret, had then hit the round that King had been holding ready – had set it on fire. The explosion had wrecked the wireless, torn King's head and shoulders from the rest of his body and started a fire among the machine-gun boxes stowed on the floor. Smoke and the acrid fumes of cordite filled the turret.

Tongues of flame licking across the floor of the vehicle, Joly and the other surviving crew member managed to bail out and make the safety of some nearby scrub before the tank exploded. Lying on the sand he saw the three tanks of the neighbouring troop, commanded by his friend Egerton, burning fiercely, columns of black smoke and flame pouring skywards like Roman candles. They scrambled back to safety and the news that the regiment had lost ten cruisers in the engagement.

German losses were two men slightly wounded and one gun put out of action, although 88-millimetre ammunition was running short. When he asked to see what had caused so much devastation a captured British officer remarked, 'It doesn't look too hot, but nothing can be done against it. It will prove the undoing of the Mark II [Matilda].'

By this time Rommel had reinforced Point 208 with the tanks of the 5th Light Division, which now counter-attacked into the flank of the 7th Armoured Brigade, and after a tank-on-tank exchange towards the evening of the 16th the British began to withdraw. The German commander now combined his armoured forces from the 5th and 8th Panzer Regiments to execute an outflanking move against Sidi Omar and Sidi Suleiman on the British southern, desert flank, entirely collapsing the Allied front. By the evening of the 17th Wavell had decided to withdraw his remaining troops and armour back to their start lines. Operation Battleaxe had been an expensive disaster. After repairing their 'crocks' the British had lost 64 Matildas and 27 cruisers against German losses of 12 panzers. The Axis suffered 1,277 casualties and the British 969, but Hellfire and Point 208 on the Hafid Ridge remained firmly in Axis hands.

Inside Tobruk plans for the breakout were quietly dropped. Harrison recalled an order of the day 'worthy of any advertising agency.' It read:

1. In yesterday's fighting in the Frontier area severe losses were inflicted on the enemy and 800 prisoners were taken. In the air our fighters shot down 12 Stukas and 6 fighters during a dive-bombing attack on our forward troops.

2. Considerable reinforcements have reached the enemy and following our capture of Capuzzo, numerically stronger forces operating against the left flank of our attack have succeeded in stopping it.

3. The operations contemplated [by Tobruk] ... are accordingly postponed for the present.

They would be placed on hold until November.

*

Wavell's ambitious offensive had been undone by the stubborn defence of Halfaya Pass and the Hafid Ridge, the lethal 88 and Rommel's concentration of his two panzer regiments at the decisive moment on the 16th and 17th to strike at the British flank. Rommel's counter-strokes had been facilitated by British commanders unwittingly giving away their plans on the radio. Strangely, the crucial role of the 88-millimetre, so clear to the jubilant Germans, was overlooked by the British, who ascribed German success exclusively to superior tanks and did not develop tactics to deal with this gun for many months to come.

Rommel's success in destroying Battleaxe did not, however, enable him to strike into Egypt. From late June he was forced simultaneously to contain the Tobruk garrison and secure the Capuzzo and Halfaya defences while bringing up reinforcements from Tripoli and Benghazi to prepare for new offensives. Assiduously polished by his PR staff and the Nazi Party, Rommel's star was in the ascendant in Berlin (although not necessarily in the corridors of the OKW), while for his inspired defence of Halfaya Pass Pastor Bach received the Knight's Cross from Rommel's own hand. In London Wavell's reputation had reached its nadir. His signal on 17 June regretting the failure of Battleaxe proved to be his final act as C-in-C Middle East. Within four days he had been sacked by Churchill and sent to 'sit under a Pagoda Tree' in India. Meanwhile the Australians, Britons and Indians within besieged Tobruk settled down to a hot summer under the watchful attentions of an emboldened enemy eager to end their tenure of this disputed stretch of rocky desert at the earliest possible opportunity.

6 » SIEGE RATS

The end of Battleaxe signalled the end of the fleeting opportunity the British had of relieving Tobruk by land. Now, with the high summer fast approaching, the besieged garrison (reduced by the removal of 'useless mouths' to some 14,000 Australians and 10,000 Britons) was forced to settle down to an arduous struggle that was to last until the garrison broke out in December, a full five months distant. The struggle was not only military, but against the extraordinarily harsh environment – rocky desert, baking sun and limited water.

Tobruk was not one battle but a series of distinct and separate contests. Along the perimeter the infantry defended their trenches and strongpoints, dominating the area outside the wire by aggressive patrolling; further back the tanks and guns supported this battle, although by July limited supplies of fuel prevented anything other than emergency counter-attacks by the tanks. At sea the Royal Navy and Royal Australian Navy ran a nightly gauntlet of submarine and Stuka to bring in supplies and reinforcements and remove the wounded, POWs and those considered unnecessary to the defence. Around the harbour and along the coast the gunners of the anti-aircraft batteries faced their own daily battle to survive and defeat the relentless Axis aerial assault. To many who fought in it the siege was a strange sort of war. Corporal 'Bunny' Cowes, an anti-aircraft gunner who arrived on HMS *Griffin* on 22 September to join 192 Heavy Artillery Battery, had no contact at all with the troops on the perimeter. It felt to him as if they were all fighting separate little wars.

As the garrison settled into the routine of siege life the most basic task for many was to master the challenges presented by the natural environment. These were many and considerable. The first, for those unable to enjoy the doubtful pleasures of Italian-built strongpoint, underground bunker or cave, was improvising somewhere to live on the hostile rocky crust of Tobruk's wide desert. This was primarily a problem for the men of the field and anti-aircraft artillery batteries, who had to construct shelters as best they could, close to their guns, wherever they found themselves.

For those able to get their hands on abandoned Italian munitions, the solution was easy. Lieutenant Alexander McGinlay found numerous mines scattered around the harbour, intended for the Italian navy. 'We used one of these per tank. They were about the size of a red pillar [post] box in this country. Having dug a small trench, we rolled in a mine, blew it up, and just drove in the Matilda, covering it with long poles and netting.' This was a dangerous game for the unwary. Ray Ellis was digging a new gun position when the two men digging in the next gun pit wandered away:

> These two were not renowned for their intellectual prowess and we joked that they had decided to walk to Cairo to buy a drink. Some time later they returned carrying a huge unexploded German shell between them. When we enquired the purpose of their errand, they said they were going to use the shell to blast a hole in the rocks to save them digging. Some minutes later there was a tremendous explosion, and when we looked across, they had disappeared. We never did find more than the odd bit of them: they had blown themselves to pieces. We seriously wondered if they had fitted the shell into position and then struck the firing pin with the back of a shovel.

For those with no explosives it was often impossible to dig anything more than shallow scrapes in the surface of the desert, although digging was easier in some areas. The usual solution was to build rock shelters around these superficial holes. Leonard Tutt of the Essex Yeomanry made himself as comfortable as he could in a narrow trench alongside his 25-pounder near King's Cross:

> My hole in the ground was about seven feet long, four feet wide and five feet deep. In bed at night it felt rather like a cosy coffin.

'Bed' sounds a bit pretentious but it had become de rigueur for other ranks to have a bed made of a pole framework with a couple of groundsheets laced across them and resting on four petrol cans.

The ground was a cheesy kind of sandstone in this area and was easily carved out with a jackknife. All along the walls at the side of my bed I had carved out shaped holes to take my personal possessions: mess tins, mug, book and reading lamp – a tobacco tin filled with paraffin and a piece of frayed cord for a wick. It was just enough to read by when I had pulled the old piece of tarpaulin over the whole to keep out the cold and shield my light.

As the months went by, elaborate constructions sprouted up. Lieutenant John Hurman was proud of his desert home near the town:

Some Aussies with a pneumatic drill made me a wonderful dugout in the rock, over which we placed an upturned lorry body piled up with sandbags. Some steps went down one end and an air duct at the other was made of several petrol tins soldered together and a cowl lined with metal gauze to turn into the wind. I also had a fly-proof door made of metal gauze. I found an Italian two-tier bunk bed which, with a mattress and mosquito net, made a comfortable bedroom. Well-surrounded with sandbags it could withstand all but a direct hit and my second lieutenant, Jock Yuill, was happy to share it with me.

At Fort Pilastrino during the Easter battles Major John Devine lived in a dugout ten feet by four, sleeping on a stretcher. The dugout was about four feet deep, and covered with a single layer of sandbags as protection against shell splinters. There was no ventilator as this would have let in dust, yet even so it was necessary for him to sleep with his glasses on and a towel around his mouth. In the morning he had to scrape away the dust from round his eyes, take off his glasses and brush off the rest of his face. His first night in the dugout introduced Devine to a persistent problem in Tobruk – rats:

I retired to bed early on my first night and started a losing fight against the rats. They fought and chased each other all around so much that they shook the dugout, and when flashes of anti-aircraft fire, searchlight beams and the sheet lightning of bomb explosions showed that Tobruk was being stormed, the rats were making such a row that I could not hear the bombs.

They had a playful habit of running round on the parapet just under the dugout roof, and when one was soundly sleeping they would scratch down dirt and dust. One night I woke with pain in my finger, and found that it was bleeding from small bites. A thirsty rat had been gnawing it. If a water bottle were left within reach, the rats would gnaw away the cork for the moisture it contained.

Bill Green, a British anti-aircraft gunner, would wait in his dugout for the rats to poke their heads out from holes in the walls and then jab at them with a bayonet. 'They were very crafty and quick, but we sometimes scored a bullseye.'

John Devine's first few nights in the desert near Pilastrino in April 1941 introduced him to some of the other of Tobruk's many plagues. On his first night in the open he encountered the scourge of the desert – fleas. They were ubiquitous and resilient to most known forms of eradication. Army-issue insecticides and kerosene were ineffective and they were a pestilence to both friend and foe. Over two days in late September Bunny Cowles took great pleasure in killing twenty-three between his fingernails. Having no flea powder, he resorted to soaking the sand of his dugout with diesel: it stank like the sump pit of a garage, and the diesel offered only temporary relief. 'The fleas were so bad that on waking in the morning one's pyjamas were spotted all over with one's blood,' Devine recalled. 'We tried everything – airing all our bedding, spraying it with kerosene, covering everything including ourselves with insecticide, lighting fires on the ground – but nothing seemed to do the slightest bit of good.' The fleas were no respecters of rank. Rommel fought a constant battle against biting bugs. To his wife on 27 August 1941 he wrote:

Dearest Lu

Nothing new. The heat's frightful, night time as well as day time. Liquidated four bugs. My bed is now standing in tins filled with water and I hope the nights will be a little more restful from now on.

The only thing that appeared to work was pyrethrum powder, a natural insecticide extracted from chrysanthemums, which finally reached the defenders in October, although there was never enough of it. Fleas were only one problem; it was no surprise to anyone in Tobruk that flies had constituted one of the ten plagues of Egypt. There were millions of them. Appearing from nowhere, they went for moisture, especially the eyes, nostrils and mouth, spoon, mess tin and mug. The intense heat combined with the constant flies caused great strain, a few men succumbing to cafard, desert madness: one Northumberland Fusilier even tried to shoot the flies with his revolver.

Considerable effort was expended on devising methods for their destruction. Of the many games played to alleviate boredom one was to see who could catch and kill the most flies. Many and varied were the methods used; scores were kept, and league tables run up. Bombardier Mick Collins of the Royal Wiltshire Yeomanry described one solution:

> One method was to smear treacle on the disused electric light cables suspended from the ceilings of the billets and after dark when the flies had gone to roost on the cables it was simple but very messy to run one's hands down the cable collecting hundreds of the things. Whilst eating one's meal and in order to escape the attention of the fly hordes it was expedient to get under our mosquito nets, but this meant having to carry one's net round with you everywhere.

Private Alex Franks, in the 2/2nd Motor Ambulance Company driving old Morris Commercial trucks and earning two shillings a day (Australian soldiers received six shillings, a source of envy for the Britons), came across a novel solution one day. He noticed that one of his fellow drivers in the 'blood wagon' always had far fewer flies around him. On being questioned, the man revealed his secret: a pet chameleon tied to a piece of string. 'He doesn't have to go out looking for flies,' Alex was told. 'An ambulance is the next best thing to a fishmonger's slab.

Where there's wounds there's blood, and where there's blood there's flies. They come in looking for grub and he just shoots his tongue out and grabs them.'

From April through to September the heat from the sun was powerful, and while most men browned evenly others were tortured by sunburn. It was an offence not to wear a shirt and get burnt, but most men ignored these instructions and turned a golden brown. Along the coast a refreshing breeze off the sea took the edge off the heat, although underground or in a slit trench temperatures were still stifling.

The disturbance to the desert floor from the movement of thousands of troops, hundreds of vehicles and relentless bombing increased the number and intensity of the duststorms which raged over the summer months. Thirst was compounded by the dust, a gritty all-pervasive substance that swirled in the air and gathered in every cranny, particularly the working parts of rifles and machine guns. Regular cleaning of weapons with a lightly oiled rag became an almost religious ritual: a single jammed round at a crucial moment could mean the difference between life and death. The local duststorms could be just as dangerous and disorientating as the massive khamsin. Reginald Cooper recalled, 'Some of the sand was so coarse that when the winds reached 50 miles per hour or thereabouts it would strip the camouflage paint off the vehicles.' A sandstorm could last for two hours or two days and the wisest course was to sit tight and wait for it to pass. George Porter remembered one man who 'left the gun park in a sandstorm in the morning and took a slightly wrong bearing so that he missed the rest camp. He wandered for an hour or so looking for the camp and then decided, as he had his bedding with him, he would lie down and, wrapping himself up in his blankets, wait till the wind dropped, only to discover that he was within a stone's throw of his own bivvy.'

Other examples of such a mistake had more serious consequences. Some time in May 1941 Lieutenant Peter Massey of 7th RTR was travelling forward in a truck to arrange a location for his three Matildas with one of the Australian battalions on the Red Line. Driving forward of the battalion HQ to meet a recently returned patrol, Massey found himself in a sandstorm. After a while, having driven for some distance in the blinding sand, the Australian driver said to Massey, 'Are there any Free French around here?' 'No,' replied Massey. 'Why?' 'Well, there are some bloody queer-looking helmets outside,' came the reply.

They had driven through the wire and blundered into a German position. Peter quickly told his driver to take off his slouch hat and hid his own black tank beret, waving to a German who tried to stop them, but it was no use. They were taken prisoner. Within a few minutes they were brought before a German officer, who to Massey's amazement continued to have his boots polished by his batman as he stood addressing the two prisoners. To the Digger he said little, but realizing from his insignia that Massey was from the Royal Tank Regiment asked him how many tanks were in Tobruk. All he got in return from Massey was name, rank and number, so the German tried the Digger with the same question. 'Bleedin' thousands,' was the reply, a response that was rewarded with a slap across the face.

The two men were then ordered to be taken back to the rear, and were led away by two armed guards. The sandstorm was still blowing fiercely. After a while it became clear the Germans were not sure of their bearings so Massey, leading the group, edged further and further left, with the guards following. He quietly alerted the Digger to the strong possibility that they might soon come across an Australian position, and that is exactly what happened. Out of the blizzard ahead rose some Australian infantry, challenging the group. Peter and his driver hit the ground yelling for the Australians to shoot the two Germans but in the sandstorm nothing would fire. In the confusion the two Germans took to their heels and disappeared.

*

The rats, fleas and flies, burning heat and swirling sandstorms added an unpleasant natural dimension to the continuing dangers of the battlefield. The violence with which the siege had begun in April never diminished through to its eventual conclusion in December, although it varied in subtle ways. While Rommel's pressure during April and May concentrated on the physical integrity of the perimeter, from June it was focused on attempts to starve the garrison into submission through an aerial campaign of unprecedented fury, supported by the attempts of German and Italian submarines to sever the sea lifeline – the famous 'Spud Run' – to Alexandria operated by the ships of Admiral Cunningham's 'Scrap Iron Flotilla'.

This meant that the siege never witnessed an entirely quiet day, nor was one locality more or less dangerous than another, although the fighting took different forms from area to area. Tobruk was the focus of the confrontation in North Africa and between June and November received the concentrated attention of Rommel's combined German and Italian forces. Shells fell every day; there was no let-up in the intensity of the aerial onslaught; and the rattle of machine guns and rifle fire was almost constant. Even when the perimeter was not under direct attack and the troops there could get down to a routine of sorts, aerial and artillery attacks continued without pause on the port, the town and particularly the artillery and anti-aircraft gun positions. The ex-French artillery piece in Bardia nicknamed Bardia Bill had long zeroed in on the dockside areas, and intermittently lobbed 159-millimetre shells into the port. 'High-level bombing became so commonplace, both by day and by night,' recalled Bombardier Ray Ellis, 'as to pass almost unnoticed unless the bombs were falling close by.' Captain Vernon Northwood described the pattern of each day:

First thing in the morning everyone stood to and expected – anything. Perhaps nothing happened; perhaps some shelling, some mortar ... Then about midday a heat haze would settle over Tobruk. Everything became distorted – a camel became a twenty-storey building. That was when you could move around safely, wander over to the platoons and have a talk to them. We encouraged the men to take their boots off and walk about barefoot in the sand – that's the only way we kept our feet clean. We took our shirts off and the sun baked the perspiration into salt, and we rubbed it off. You were always rubbing salt and dust off your body.

Inside Tobruk men adapted to routines that enabled them to survive, both physically and mentally. Along the Red Line the two front lines were closest in the Ras el Medawar salient. Here it was impossible to travel during daylight. Eating, exercise and wire, trench and parapet repairs could only be carried out under the cover of darkness. During the day the burning heat, sand and flies made real sleep an elusive dream. It was a strange mole-like existence. From May, Leonard Tutt's artillery OP was on the neck of the German salient at R11, or Nixon's Post. The salient was close by on three sides:

> It was very difficult to make any sort of move during daylight hours without calling down a hail of fire on one's head. Reliefs could only take place during the darkest hours of the night, and this was the time too when the OP officers and the acks changed over. Together with their rations, water supply and other odds and ends they were taken to about a mile from the post by truck, from which point they had to walk or crawl. To minimize the amount of movement above ground reliefs only took place every forty-eight hours. Even then they were very tricky affairs. The enemy fired star shells and brought down fire on the area at the slightest sound in the darkness.
>
> Life in Nixon's post was governed by the few brief hours between sunset and moonrise. This was the only time it was possible to move above ground and, even then, you had to be ready to take cover if a star shell or a flare went up.

In this environment the most precious commodity was water. The ration for each twenty-four-hour period was a mere one and a half pints, for drinking, shaving and washing. Everyone was constantly thirsty, hungry and dirty. Lips were swollen, split and bleeding from lack of moisture. Gunner Ted Holmes, cook of 425 Battery RHA, recalled dreaming 'about putting your head under the tap at home'. A man's personal ration was carried in the water bottle at his waist, so often exposed to the sun's rays and therefore always tepid. Normally, recalled Vernon Northwood, the troops had to clean, shave and wash their teeth in half a mug of water:

> You got a water bottle full of water per day for your own personal use. Tea was made when the food came up at night, so your breakfast and your lunch came out of your water bottle.

I had a little tobacco tin – I used to smoke a pipe then – and I shaved in it. Every man shaved every day in Tobruk. People don't believe that – but if they didn't, they soon got a skin rash. I wet my brush and I shaved in that tin. I cleaned my teeth and spat the water back into the tin – didn't waste any of it. I used the balance of the water for the sponge to wash my privates. A little piece of sponge that could absorb water – you hung on to that. That was very valuable to you.

Keeping clean was extremely difficult. Major Gerald Barry of 2nd Battalion the Black Watch – a First World War veteran and no stranger to dirt – complained bitterly in his diary, 'Really this is a filthy place! It is quite impossible to keep clean, and one's hair becomes a clogged mass of dirt. Washing one's head in seawater with soap is fatal, the whole thing congeals into a mass of semi-glue through which the comb will not penetrate – and when it does, it takes an hour to clean.' But cleanliness was hugely important. Sergeant John Longstaff of 2nd Battalion the Rifle Brigade insisted that his men shaved every day, 'even if it meant shaving out of a cup of tea, because it made you clean. If you felt clean, you felt your morale is good.'

When Tobruk fell to the British in January 1941 the Italians left behind many tens of thousands of litre bottles of Recoaro mineral water. Unfortunately, in the chaos of the first few weeks of occupation, much of this was wasted or destroyed; it was even used to wash clothes. What remained was stored for use by the hospital. A limited source of water was the native wells, which produced a brackish and evil-tasting liquid that could only be drunk after boiling and when made into tea. The wells were naturally contaminated by the rich oil deposits of the region, although neither side realized this, blaming each other routinely for the deliberate pollution of the desert *birs*. Water was occasionally brought in at great risk from Alexandria, and stored in tanks near the docks for use by the hospital. Rain was scarce. When it did fall men would rush about frantically trying to catch as much as they could in mess tins, helmets and whatever containers were to hand. When, on the morning of Friday 26 September the heavens opened, Bombardier Cowles and his mates stood outside in the downpour and used the opportunity to soap themselves down and then dashed around with containers, Cowles catching enough to fill a sixty-gallon tank. The following morning the troops were astonished to see the desert in bloom as a carpet of tiny colourful flowers emerged in response to the rain. A temporary though shallow lake startled Major Robert Daniell with the sight of hundreds of migrating ducks paddling around contentedly on its surface. He didn't have the heart to shoot any to augment his meagre rations.

Water was so hard to come by that the more ingenious built their own saltwater distillation plants to complement the two large Italian-built distillation plants near the harbour which, despite the best intentions of the Luftwaffe, remained operational throughout the siege. Private Alex Franks was one of many who built a makeshift distillery using the petrol tins which followed the British army on its travels. Seawater was heated and the fresh water condensed off, some two pints per hour, but even tea couldn't entirely mask the taste of the remaining salt and occasionally residues blocked the outlet pipe, resulting in a build-up of steam and, as Signaller Jack Senior once observed, a spectacular explosion.

*

Between June and November 1941 the air battle for Tobruk was fought between Axis planes and the garrison's anti-aircraft batteries. Rommel's aims were to make the port unworkable and to demoralize the defenders into surrender. Raids by Italian and German bombers, fighters and dive-bombers were an everyday affair, Stukas and Heinkels prowling the skies above the town, the former taking off from desert airfields often in sight of the defenders. John Devine described the daily Tobruk run by German Heinkels and Italian Savoia 79s:

> The raiders come over at medium height with protecting fighters just visible above them, buzzing to and fro like aphids. The bursting ack-ack sends up little balls of smoke which expand from a pinpoint to a snowball in the space of a second, like balloons being rapidly blown up. With puffs of smoke all around them, the bombers fly serenely on their course, the sun glittering on their metal wings, the glassed-in noses standing out clearly.

Over their target they break formation, and down they come one at a time in deep, flopping dives which, at quite low altitudes, flatten out with the simultaneous release of little clusters of bombs. These are at first visible, but vanish from sight as they increase their downward velocity. Then the planes are so low that red-tailed Bofors shells chase each other upwards, and just shave the bombers, which are wildly zigzagging at a height of a few hundred feet, striving to get away from the hail of machine-gun bullets and shells. Often one can see the rivets of the plane quite clearly, and even little bits of metal on the wings being flicked off by our machine-gun bullets. Now and then a plane, obviously hit, starts to smoke and lose height: the anti-aircraft fire has claimed another victim.

One night at the start of the siege Driver Bob Braithwaite, his supply company based forward on the perimeter, stood with his mates Alf from Yorkshire, John, a Geordie everybody for some reason called Jock, and Bill from Birmingham, watching an air raid over the harbour. The noise was accompanied by the red, green and blue hues of tracer bullets, the great yellow moons of star shells, the brilliant white of parachute flares, swinging slowly to and fro as they descended to the earth, the probing yellow beams of the searchlights as they pricked holes in the night, desperately seeking the bombers hidden in the darkness. Suddenly Alf said, 'Bloody hell! Listen.' They stood and listened, and heard what Bob described as 'a big one coming down'. The bomb left the aircraft and made a *ch-ch-ch-ch* sound as it fell, getting louder by the second. 'Bloody hell, they're dropping railway engines now!' Alf said.

They were laughing as they hit the ground. But the bomb didn't explode, burying itself in the rock nearby with a shattering thud. It was followed by many bombs that did detonate, however. The men hugged the ground, lifted and shaken with every explosion, shrapnel whistling overhead, destroying some of their dispersed and camouflaged vehicles. The next morning as it grew light, they could hear aircraft engines starting up at El Adem, about six miles distant. Through binoculars, they saw the German aircraft take off and circle north towards Tobruk. Now at least 300 miles from the nearest RAF unit, the Luftwaffe and their Regia Aeronautica colleagues had enjoyed mastery of the skies since the final Hurricanes had been evacuated from Tobruk in late April. Twenty-four Stukas bore down on the harbour, in which a number of ships were disembarking supplies and reinforcements. The anti-aircraft batteries began to fire as the Stukas peeled off one after another and fell towards the ground, sirens screaming. One of the aircraft was hit and continued into the ground, exploding in a ball of flame.

The air raids were continuous and wearing. Bombers exploited every wisp of cloud; Stukas screamed down from the sun; ground-hugging fighters – the most feared the Me 109 – darted over the desert machine-gunning at will, exploiting their speed to take unsuspecting troops by surprise. On occasions prowling Stukas went after individual targets. Private Richard Hill had decided to walk the two miles to a neighbouring battery one day and, having gone only a few hundred yards, heard the sound of an air raid on the harbour. He carried on, not giving the matter much thought:

> I was walking along the edge of the escarpment when a burst of engine power rushed at me. A Stuka was about fifty feet above me and a hundred yards or so ahead. It was coming straight at me, guns blazing. I looked for cover and was very lucky to find an old trench three parts full of sand, with old sandbags, threadbare and torn, around the rim. Without further ado, I threw myself down behind one of the bags at the same time as I felt a thud near my head the other side of the sandbag. I lay there as the Stuka thundered overhead.
>
> Rolling over onto my back, I saw this black giant bird, a swastika painted on each wing, go by, and a shadow follow, still only some hundred feet above me.
>
> After the Stuka had crossed the horizon, I went round the other side of the trench. There I opened my knife and dug a copper-plated bullet out of the sandbag.

Another morning the warning sirens sounded and a dozen Stukas appeared overhead. Private Alex Franks, thinking it was just another raid on the harbour, ignored them. The scream of Stuka sirens, however, made him look sharply skywards, to see that the aircraft were directly overhead and seemingly intent on attacking him. There was nowhere to hide. Throwing himself to the ground, he tried in vain to burrow into the unyielding terrain. His back seemed to grow to the size of a football pitch as, petrified, he prayed desperately in the last seconds left to him. He had only moments to live; he had seen too many mangled corpses and scattered body parts and was convinced he would soon be blown to many tiny pieces. The ground shook as the first stick of five bombs exploded, the blast sucking air from his lungs and filling the air above his prostrate body with flying shrapnel and debris, Franks waiting in terror for the next stick to arrive, and the next. But nothing happened. As the dust began to settle he gingerly raised his head to see the splintered tailgate of a nearby 15-cwt Bedford truck and five unexploded bombs. Later, as Australian engineers took them away for disposal, one exploded, killing some of them and wounding others.

The Stuka was heavily armoured and resistant to all but a direct hit by a large shell. For a while Gunner Bill Lewis manned an anti-aircraft Lewis gun, but the ancient weapon was worse than useless, his friend Harry Bradley shouting as its 0.303-inch rounds bounced harmlessly off the plane's armour plating that he wished that he had something bigger to 'stick up their arse'. Some of the enemy pilots even had the audacity to wave as they passed overhead. Major Gosling of 104th RHA (Essex Yeomanry) was an unconventional soldier, a bank manager in civilian life, who wandered around the battery position barefoot, in dirty grey flannels and always with a rifle over his shoulder. Whenever an enemy aircraft appeared he aimed his rifle skywards and loosed off some rounds. 'Good for my morale,' he would mutter, 'and it's loaded with one round of tracer and one round of armoured-piercing, just in case I should hit it!' Gunner Jack Daniel of 153 Battery had grudging respect for the German and Italian pilots:

You had to hand it to them. To get into an aircraft and nose it down through a barrage which could blast you to smithereens any minute, and dive through it and let go of the bomb and then race back for home with everything in the harbour going at you. Everyone would be firing – .303s, revolvers, anything. We could almost chuck bricks at them as they came whizzing by.

Occasionally the troops on the ground would get lucky. When not on patrol beyond the perimeter wire John Hurman would sit on top of Admiralty House in Tobruk town with a captured Italian Breda heavy machine gun and fire at the Stukas as they came over. 'They always went into a screeching dive to drop their bombs as this was the way they aimed. I must have damaged many, but on one occasion I could see my tracers well on target and smoke started pouring from the engine as it lost height rapidly and disappeared over the hill towards the German lines.'

Air attacks were often lethal. Mick Collins, based at a gun site on the escarpment above Tobruk hospital, saw two truckloads of newly arrived Australians caught in a dive-bombing raid. A bomb exploded near the leading vehicle, forcing it to lurch to a stop:

> The second truck smacked into the rear of the first one followed by sudden yells of anguish and pain. I . . . went down to see what help was needed and found the occupants of both vehicles very badly shocked. On getting them out of the smashed trucks we found one had a large chunk of shrapnel embedded in his chest and was obviously very dead . . . Another passenger was out cold and when we lifted him we discovered his hand had been severed at the wrist by flying shrapnel.

Fortunately many Stuka bombs failed to explode, recalled John Hurman. 'One fell in a trench close to me and broke a chap's leg but failed to go off. All the raids killed relatively few people, as everyone was well dispersed and dug in.' There was a reason why many German bombs failed to explode. An Australian infantry officer – Lieutenant Geoffrey Fearnside of the 2/13th battalion – recalled a 500-pound device that fell on his battalion's position on the El Adem road. It struck with terrific force and skidded 'crazily along the surface of the earth' before coming to a stop. When the ammunition disposal officer was eventually able to examine the device he was in for a surprise: 'When he took out the detonator a thin stream of sand spilled into his hand. A small hard object, borne like driftwood on a current, fell with the sand into his palm. He could feel that it was cardboard. He ventured to strike a match to satisfy an immense curiosity. On the

card was written in English, "From your friends in Czechoslovakia." '
For Private Bill Harvey the 'biggest danger to us in the higher parts of
the town was from falling shrapnel from our anti-aircraft barrage.
Pieces of shrapnel were anything between one to three inches in size
and all capable of inflicting considerable damage on any unfortunate
individual caught in the open. We soon found the most effective cover
was to dive under a lorry.'

Four ack-ack sites in Tobruk were manned by gunners of 51st
Heavy Anti-Aircraft Regiment with 3.7-inch guns. On the promontory,
at A site, was 153 Battery (Right Troop); on the Derna road below the
Solaro escarpment, at C site, was Left Troop of 153 Battery, together
with B and D sites, which belonged to 152 Battery. The positions were
protected by stone walls and wooden boxes filled with rocks. Temporary positions, to which the guns were moved periodically to confuse
the enemy, were known as Welz sites. Welz 1 was on the north coast
in a wadi running down to the sea, Welz 2 on the north side of the
Derna road, Welz 3 at Pilastrino, Welz 4 on the escarpment west of
King's Cross, Welz 5 at Solaro and Welz 6 on the north side of the
Bardia road, east of King's Cross.

On 27 May Gunner John Kelly recorded in his diary that since
15 April his position had fired at 1,000 enemy planes. The strain of
constant attack was intense. At the end of May 1941 Kelly wrote that
it was 'the worst I have ever experienced. Several times I thought all
my birthdays had come together . . . Most of the fellows are worn out
and skin diseases are very prevalent. Several chaps have been sent to
base because their nerves were broken. We are very short of men
through wounds and illness.' The intensity of night raids equalled
that of the daylight attacks and caused a steady stream of casualties.
On 2 June Kelly wrote, 'Two of No. 1 gun were killed today by a
premature bursting over their pit. I was in No. 3 pit at the time and
we were firing harbour barrage when I saw a great flame spring out
from No 1's ammo bays. A second later the bay on the other side of
the pit exploded.'

There were, however, reasons for optimism. The anti-aircraft
defence batteries not only bagged the occasional enemy aircraft, but
also, with their extraordinarily colourful barrages, forced the Axis
pilots to fear for their lives. John Kelly noted a change in the attitude

of the Stuka pilots as the siege progressed. Writing in his diary on 22 August:

> Two Stuka raids today. The first started just before noon. In this raid the planes went out to sea and turned back outside the perimeter on the Bardia road side. The second lot received a terrific barrage before they got anywhere near the town. We picked them up just south of us and set the ball rolling. The other guns started as they came within range and we finished up with the best harbour barrage I have seen for a long while.
>
> Many of the Stukas dropped their bombs in the sea. They went the same way as those of this morning but one of them turned in too quickly. He came heading for the site and we put up a shot in front of his nose which must have shaken him for he turned off very sharply and headed for his own lines as fast as he could.

Devine spoke admiringly of the calm professionalism of the anti-aircraft crews who, disdaining the shelter others sought, braved the falling bombs to lay their guns on the enemy planes and then fire. On one occasion he observed three Stukas single out a gun position and in what became a duel between gun and aircraft, the Stukas came off worse:

> [The Stukas] dived on it, machine-gunning as they went, bombs dropping from under their fuselage. Coolly, unhurriedly . . . [the gun crew] fired first one or two shots at one plane, then one or two at the other, and with the expenditure of five shots they brought down two out of the three planes. There was no hurried or frantic pumping out of shells to frighten off the planes; they carefully sighted their targets regardless of their own lack of protection and scored direct hits.

There were raids every single day of the siege. Some were of considerable size: a raid of over one hundred aircraft took place on 27 August. No one was killed but one anti-aircraft gun was destroyed and another damaged. Kelly grabbed a Lewis gun and managed to pepper a Stuka flying across his field of fire at 200 feet, and one aircraft exploded in mid-air. One hundred and ten aircraft struck on 1 September, the raid targeting the water points (points set up across the garrison to dispense water). The gun positions were always prime targets, and accordingly dangerous places to be. At mid-morning on Wednesday 8 October 1941 Bombardier Harry Wiles of the Essex Yeomanry was lying in his trench after a busy night when he heard the screech of diving planes. Dozens of dive-bombers were heading straight for his position:

Before I could grab my rifle they started machine-gunning us and bombing from a very low height. Everyone disappeared into slit trenches. The planes had evidently got our position pinpointed. The ground rocked and the walls of my bed pit shook and caved in. The heavy bombs came down one after the other, and the roar of the planes and the rattle of their machine guns deafened us. Then there was a pause and I dashed out and got five rounds off at them. They circled around and got ready to dive again. Then down they came and me on my belly again. Then the drone of their engines as they climbed away and moved off. I looked around and the position was a shambles. I saw flames coming from our gun pit, amongst the ammunition. I grabbed a shovel and helped throw sand on the flames. Then I moved to No. 3 gun, where the same thing was happening. I shouted to Sergeant Swansborough and we started to put that out. A great sheet of flame came flying out, but we managed to put the fire out before the ammunition went up. Then I heard that someone was hit near the latrines. I ran and got my first aid kit and doubled over fast. Gunner Webb and Sergeant Anderson were with Lance Sergeant Seabeck, who had got a piece of shrapnel in his ankle, breaking it. I put splints on it and we put him on a stretcher.

Then I had time to look around the place. It was in a mess. I saw a length of timber, several inches thick, which had served us as a tabletop ripped through against the grain by bullets . . . On our gun the shrapnel had ripped through the shield, smashed the dial sight and the telescopic sight. No. 3 gun was smashed about worse, so we took the shield off it and put it on ours; we got the spare dial sight and generally patched the gun up. Two 500-pound bombs had fallen just a yard or so from our gun pit. There were bomb craters all over the position and blast powder and shrapnel everywhere. Sergeant Goddard was hit in the arm and Dixie Dean in the leg.

Regularly moving the gun positions kept the enemy guessing. On the afternoon of 8 December Bill Green's troop was at Welz 4 and took a formation of sixty Stukas by surprise. The shooting was so deadly that the formation broke up in confusion, some being shot down and most jettisoning their bombs off-target. But at 8 a.m. the next morning they came back for revenge. While some took on the other anti-aircraft sites a hornets' nest of Stukas went for Welz 4. One bomb struck the top of the predictor pit wall, and another the top of the gun pit wall. In the gun pit Bombardier Dave Reed and Gunner Ernie Golding were killed outright, and there were some wounded in both pits.

The barrage of flak over Tobruk contributed strongly to the defenders' sense that the attackers were not having it all their own way, despite their air superiority over Cyrenaica, but the raids also demonstrated the limitations of German air power. When working closely with infantry and armour, dive-bombers could be extremely effective. On their own, however, in vast swathes of desert, they were almost entirely inconsequential unless they managed to score a direct hit on a truck, trench or bunker. Troops in well-prepared positions, dug deep into the rock and camouflaged well, rarely had any cause to fear the Stuka once they had got used to the fearsome noise of the siren the pilot switched on at the start of his dive. Considerable efforts were made to camouflage positions from air observation because if spotted they quickly received a visit from the sky. Every morning troops would check their positions and sweep away any telltale signs of human movement by brushing out footprints with camel thorn. Such tracks showed up clearly on aerial photographs. It was very different, however, at sea or in a built-up area. Out at sea there was nowhere to hide; the ships travelled slowly compared to aircraft and were therefore extremely vulnerable to attacks by dive-bombers. In built-up areas flying masonry and other debris was a more significant danger than the actual bomb explosions. Fire was also an ever-present danger.

One way of getting back at the enemy and overcoming any feelings of impotence generated by the relentless aerial onslaught was patrolling. Morshead's Australians turned it into an art form. The aim was so entirely to dominate no-man's-land that the besiegers were forced to accept that the terrain between the wire and their lines was unequivocally *terra australis*. Alexander McGinlay recalled that the Germans feared the Australian patrols, and one captured German officer wrote home to describe the constant stress in the forward trenches and the 'desperate state of nerves and lack of sleep because of the wretched Australians'. Patrols were often made up solely of volunteers. 'There was always a queue, and those picked had their faces blacked, sandbags wrapped around their boots, and when it was dark away they would go, most times returning with a few very angry German prisoners.'

In June 1941, with petrol rationing curtailing the role of the Tobruk Tanks, a bored Captain Rea Leakey approached Lieutenant Colonel Evans, CO of the Australian 2/23rd Battalion, with the request that he join the battalion for a period disguised as a Digger. Evans agreed and, equipped with Australian uniform, a Sydney address and an indifferent Aussie accent, 'Private Leakey', a NSW publisher's son, joined C Company on the perimeter. On his first night he went out on patrol into no-man's-land. 'From the time we left until the time we got back, they hardly stopped cursing me for my clumsiness and for my slow reactions. I was more frightened of the Aussies than of any enemy who might have been around.'

*

Planning for night patrols had to be meticulous to ensure that neighbouring units were informed and that all knew where fixed-line machine guns might be firing. The aims of each patrol were specific – to establish the enemy's position, to take a prisoner for identification, to extend the mapping of an area, to locate minefields or report any special features, noises or incidents. The route was drawn out on a map and bearings and distances noted. The patrol leader would search each man to make sure he carried no papers; watches and other objects that might glint in the dark were left behind; weapons were examined and care taken to ensure nothing was loose and would make even the slightest sound if jerked. Every man was given a particular task and, while the patrol was out, nobody spoke.

Leakey quickly graduated from the 'Australian School of Patrolling', and was involved in a series of skirmishes far forward of the perimeter, one of which, beginning on 19 August 1941, ended in a desperate battle four miles from help at a position nicknamed Jim, east of the El Adem road. The story is best told in Leakey's own words:

Many years ago the Romans had dug a number of water cisterns in the Western Desert, and even today the mounds of earth above each cistern provide some of the best landmarks in this featureless desert. There was one of these marked on our maps just over 7,000 yards from the perimeter, and it was chosen as a possible site for an observation post. I was told to go and try it out.

My party numbered about ten men, and we set out from the perimeter as soon as it was dark, laying a telephone cable as we went. We had no trouble in finding the mound, and we estimated that it was about 500 yards from the nearest enemy position. It stood some eight feet high, and must have covered an area of ten square yards. It had obviously been used as an observation post before because there was a shallow trench dug in the top. We enlarged this by scooping away the soft sand, and made a depression in which three men could lie. It would do.

The telephone was connected and I spoke to the battalion commander back in Tobruk, telling him that I intended to occupy the post. Corporal Hayes and Private Bennet stayed with me while the rest of the men went back, and they left us well equipped. We had a good supply of water and bully beef, a small sack full of hand grenades, a Bren machine gun, a Thompson sub-machine gun, my pistol and an ample supply of ammunition. The three of us lay down in our shallow hole and pulled the painted groundsheet over us.

It was always exciting to see what the dawn revealed from a new position, and this was no exception. Appreciating that the mound we now occupied was an obvious landmark and therefore a likely artillery target, the enemy had kept clear of it. However, there were a series of defensive positions almost all round it; in fact, only to the north of us along the route which we had taken from Tobruk was it possible to approach the place without running into an enemy position. The nearest position to us was 400 yards, which was not too bad. But what did disturb us was a watchtower 300 yards north of our mound. It consisted of a platform erected on the top of telegraph poles, and must have been some thirty feet high.

At about 9 a.m., when the sun was well up, three Germans walked across to one of the enemy posts and climbed onto the platform, and throughout the day they took turns in watching to the north through a pair of binoculars. They probably could just see Tobruk's perimeter. So long as they did not turn round and look south, we felt we were safe. We too had a grand view from our eight-foot-high mound. On all three sides of us there was a great deal of activity. Lorries drove up to the various positions and unloaded stores; parades were held; and long lines of men queued up at the cookhouse for their meals. I kept up a running commentary to Tobruk, and soon an artillery officer came on the line. He said he had moved some guns to the perimeter from where he could shell these enemy positions. Using my compass and judging the distance, I was able to give him fairly accurate locations of the groups of men. Soon the shells were landing in among them.

Two mobile canteen lorries drove up and stopped close to one of the positions. Through my binoculars I could clearly see the salesman open up his shutters and prepare for business. I plotted the position, passed on the information to the gunners and suggested that they wait until I gave the word to open fire. It was not long before a crowd of soldiers gathered round, and I could see that business was brisk. Then down came the shells and the crowd scattered back to their dugouts. But the lorry stayed on. When the shelling stopped an ambulance drove up, and I saw several bodies hoisted aboard. Then the crowd started collecting again and business was resumed. Three times I spoiled that man's trade, and in the end he gave up and drove away. His windscreen had been smashed by a shell.

Not far to the south of our mound I could see the bypass road which the enemy had built round Tobruk perimeter, and which his

20. British anti-aircraft gunners clean their 3.7 inch gun.

21. Australian infantrymen firing a captured Italian gun, without its sights, on 27 August 1941. These crews called themselves the 'Bush Artillery'.

22. British Bofors
anti-aircraft gunners
in Tobruk, 1 May 1941.

23. HMAS *Waterhen*,
sunk en route
to Alexandria,
30 June 1941.

24. Diggers returning
from a patrol outside
the perimeter,
August 1941.

25. German air raid on the harbour, 1 September 1941.

26. Tobruk under air attack, 12 September 1941.

27. British Mark IV Cruiser tanks inside Tobruk, 12 September 1941.

28. The 'Tobruk Tanks'. Matildas photographed on the same day.

29. British 3.7 inch anti-aircraft guns in action in Tobruk on 30 September 1941.

30. One of a battery of Italian guns that fired against Tobruk from Sollum, nicknamed 'Bardia Bill'.

31. Diggers of the 9th Division on their way out of Tobruk, courtesy of the Royal Navy, 24 October 1941.

32. A Digger reading a copy of the daily news-sheet *Tobruk Truth* aka 'The 'Dinkum Oil'.

33. A rare luxury in Tobruk: a bath.

34. A Polish soldier of the Carpathian Brigade manning a Bren-gun in the anti-aircraft role.

35. Men of the King's Own Royal Regiment man a Vickers medium machine gun shortly before the breakout, 10 November 1941.

36. On 24 November 1941, at the height of the breakout battles, lifeboats carry wounded men offshore to the hospital ship *Somersetshire*.

37. British wounded awaiting treatment and evacuation during the breakout battles in November and early December 1941.

38. Men of the 7th Armoured Brigade larking about in Tobruk at the end of the siege, in January 1942.

vehicles now used on their journeys to and from Bardia and the frontier. It was a busy road and it was normally free from interference by the Tobruk garrison, being well out of view. However, on this day any collection of vehicles that were travelling close together or happened to halt on the sector of road I could see received rough treatment from the Tobruk artillery. All day long I kept our artillery supplied with targets, and I was enjoying myself at the expense of the enemy. I hardly noticed the heat, the flies or even the slight duststorm that blew for about an hour at midday. I was so busy that I had no time to bother about food or even a drink.

About 3 o'clock in the afternoon one of the Aussies with me called my attention to the three men on the watchtower. It must have been painfully obvious to them that this area, which was normally never shelled, was now under close observation, and they in their turn were looking round for the observers. They must have examined every bit of scrub and every stone to the north of their tower, and they found nothing. Then they searched east and west, but still with no result. Now we could see them looking south, and we lay very still. One of them pointed down to where we lay, and the man with the binoculars focused them on us. Then the three of them climbed down from their perch and ran across to the nearest line of trenches. I phoned the artillery officer and asked him to be prepared to give us a little support when we were attacked, and he wished us luck.

We saw them the moment they left their trenches, and there must have been about fifty of them. They moved across the desert in extended order, and their bayonets glinted in the afternoon sun. Our shells fell close to them, but on they came, and soon I had to tell the artillery to stop firing as the shells were beginning to land close to our mound. The two Aussie privates were itching to open fire, and I had a difficult time restraining them. Then the enemy party split up into four groups and surrounded the mound. We lay very still and waited. Closer and closer they came, and there was no sound except for the occasional sharp word of command given by one of their officers.

When the nearest group was within fifteen yards of our

position, I gave the order to open fire. The effect was like a damp squib going off. The tommy gun fired about six rounds, then stopped. The Bren gun fired one round and stopped. The duststorm which had blown up earlier on had filled the working parts with fine sand. But these few shots were sufficient to make the soldiers drop to the ground, and I heard one man cry out in agony. Then the fun really started. Each enemy group had at least one machine gun, and these and the rifles sent a hail of bullets in our direction. For some reason I was not wearing my tin hat, and one of the Australians noticed. 'For heaven's sake, put your tin hat on,' he yelled. 'If you hold your finger up, you'll get it shot off, the bullets are coming so thick and fast.' And to illustrate the point he poked one finger up in the sky, only to pull it down with an oath less than a second later; the tip was shot off.

Although the trench in which we were lying was less than six inches deep, it was just sufficient to give us shelter from the ever-increasing stream of bullets that came at us from every direction, and we knew we were safe from a bayonet charge so long as these idiots continued to fire from all round our position. I ordered the two Australians to lie on their backs and start tossing hand grenades over the side of our trench. With the sack between them, they were soon busy pulling out the safety pins and deftly flicking the deadly grenades over the side, and each one rolled down the slope and burst among the enemy. Meanwhile I worked like a madman clearing up our two guns. I got the tommy gun going, and handed it back to its owner, who now set about the task of killing off the enemy one by one. Then both guns were working.

Some instinct made me turn my head and look in the direction where we thought the enemy were all dead. One bold man was charging up alone with his rifle at the ready, and the bayonet at the end of it was aimed at my stomach. I grabbed my revolver and fired at him. It was the best shot of my life: I hit him between the eyes and he fell back dead, not two yards from me.

All was then quiet. I picked up the telephone and Lieutenant Colonel Evans answered me. He told me that he had sent three Bren gun carriers to our assistance. I thanked him but told him that they would not last long in our present area, as every enemy soldier was by this time on the alert. Sure enough, as the three little tracked vehicles came charging down towards us, every gun that could bring fire to bear on them opened up. But on they came, and the three of us raised a hoarse cheer. They did not dare stop for a second, and we were relieved when they circled round a few hundred yards from us and disappeared back towards Tobruk. They were lucky not to be hit, and there are not many soldiers who would drive a vehicle through a barrage of fire such as these men faced that afternoon.

Then the enemy turned his guns on to us, and shell after shell exploded round us. If any of the fifty men were still alive, this shelling must have killed them, because they did not have even the protection of a shallow trench. About 1,000 yards to the south of us I could just make out a large number of the enemy moving slowly in our direction, and behind them was a tank. As the smoke and dust from the enemy shells closed in on us, we could see very little. Therefore we too would not be seen if we got out of our hole. By this time our telephone wire was cut, and later I was told that it was considered we would not be seen or heard of again after the damage we had caused.

Carrying our weapons and the telephone, we rolled down the little hill and joined the dead at the bottom. Here we exchanged our shallow steel helmets for the coal-scuttle type worn by the enemy. By this time the shelling had eased off, and in comparative safety we got to our feet and started staggering off in the general direction of Tobruk. We limped and held our heads and did what we could to convince the thousand eyes that were watching our every movement that we were survivors from the fifty-strong attacking party.

The shelling stopped and we walked on across the silent desert. As we passed beneath the watchtower, somebody shouted at us in a foreign language, and glancing to my right I could see two soldiers standing on top of a trench beckoning to us. I pretended not to see and limped on. My greatest desire was to start running, and one of the Australians suggested that we should do so, but I knew that once we started to run every gun would be turned on us. So very slowly, it seemed, we moved past one after another enemy post, and all the time we could hear the shouts as the occupants tried to attract our attention. I hope I never again have to experience the nervous strain of that walk.

We must have been about 500 yards north of the last enemy post when the first few bullets kicked up the sand around us, and only then did we start to run. Soon there were a number of machine guns firing at us, then they shelled us. Every pace took us closer to Tobruk and safety, but we had over 6,000 yards to cover and soon my lungs felt as if they were about to burst. At last the shelling stopped, and we were beyond the range of the machine guns. But still we ran. I knew there was still danger, and my fears were confirmed by the sound of clattering tracks and the steady hum of an engine. I shouted, 'Tank,' and tried to increase speed. Then I heard the scream of shells and the dull thud as they burst behind us. The Tobruk artillery was engaging our pursuer.

Just as the sun was setting, we saw the perimeter wire and heard the cheering of the men of our battalion. They walked forward to meet us, and helped us over the shallow anti-tank ditch. Somebody thrust a bottle neck between my parched lips, and I drank greedily. It was neat rum, and I had not had an alcoholic drink for many weeks. My knees sagged, and I crumbled to the ground drunk.

*

As the months went by food became a considerable problem for both sides, not so much perhaps because of scarcity, but its monotony had a direct impact on morale. Troops both inside and outside the perimeter talked about the subject endlessly. On 28 April Leutnant Schorm recorded in his diary:

We have now been away from Germany for two months and without butter, etc. into the bargain. Our principal food is bread, with something to spread on it. In this heat every bite needs a sip of water or coffee to help it down. There is no fat . . . Where would you find anybody in Germany who would drink water of this colour and taste? It looks like cocoa and tastes of sulphur.

By mid-summer 1941 for the inhabitants of Tobruk the staple of their existence was tinned corned, or bully, beef and hard, thick Army biscuits which the men swore were the same as those inflicted on the men of Nelson's navy. When Tobruk had fallen to the Commonwealth forces in February it was found to contain a cornucopia of supplies. There was enough good-quality canned food – meat, vegetables (tomatoes, peas, beans and carrots) and fruit (cherries, strawberries, pears, apricots) – not to mention vast quantities of Chianti and brandy, to support a garrison of 25,000 for two months. But this quickly ran out, and when it did so the garrison was forced to rely on its own rations, food intended to sustain men in combat for short periods but not form their staple diet. 'I distinctly remember that the contents of one of the tins of biscuits,' swore Reginald Cooper, 'were green and mouldy, and the tin labelled NOT FIT FOR HUMAN CONSUMPTION.' The best thing for the biscuits was to beat them into powder and add hot water to make 'burgoo', a form of porridge. The problem with much of the bully beef was that it had been allowed to sit in uncovered dumps in the desert under the sun. This melted and re-melted the fat in the tins until, in John Devine's words, 'It seemed to go a bit queer.' In this state it was only edible if 'covered by some such disguising fluid as tomato sauce'.

It did not take long for everyone to get heartily sick and tired of bully. Most unit medical officers tried to limit the men's consumption of bully because of its very high fat content but if there was nothing else available they had no choice but to force the stuff down. Gunner Bill Lewis came to hate 'Mr Fray Bentos', whoever he was. Tins of M&V (meat and vegetables) were sometimes available to vary the monotony, but until a new Crosse and Blackwell concoction arrived in October 1941 there was only a disgusting version which the men christened Muck and Vomit. Bunny Cowles found the only way he could eat M&V was to open the tin, throw away the meat and gravy, wash the vegetables and fry them in butter, and then mix them with a tin of herrings. For a few months there were tins of rice and prunes (Price and Runes) but little else. Signaller Jack Senior was exploring the ruined hulk of the Italian liner in the harbour when he came across boxes of tinned pineapple and sacks of rice in a storeroom, a discovery that gave him and his mates a much-needed change of diet.

Ascorbic acid tablets were issued every day to compensate for the lack of fresh fruit and vegetables, and thus prevent the terrible desert sores that otherwise took so long to heal. 'An attempt to provide some green vegetables by giving us dehydrated cabbage was a hundred-per-cent failure,' remembered Leonard Tutt. 'No matter how the cook prepared it, it always ended up looking and tasting like stewed gas cape.' The consequence of poor water was gippy tummy – diarrhoea – but the opposite problem – constipation – from the monotonous bully-beef diet was as big a problem, although, as Jack Senior asserted, a good Stuka raid cleared that up very quickly. Many attempts were made to supplement the rations. A favourite was fishing. Some used traditional techniques, while others adopted a rather more modern and rapid method. Mick Collins became a devotee of the cult of explosive fishing. This entailed standing by the shore, waiting for a shoal of fish to appear and then pulling the pin from a hand grenade, counting to three and throwing it into the water. 'After running like the blazes to avoid getting drenched, all we had to do was swim out and collect the stunned fish.'

The British field bakeries in Tobruk made small quantities of bread and continued to do so throughout the siege, although the amount they were able to produce diminished over time. When yeast was available the bread was edible despite the use of weevily Italian flour. Food became a serious morale problem. 'I dare not think of just how low my morale was at times,' commented Alexander McGinlay. 'It became very noticeable just before the breakout in November, when food supplies started to reach us. Most of us lost a great deal of weight over the months.' When there was a change of diet, morale soared. One of McGinlay's fellow troop commanders received regular gifts from his Russian girlfriend in Alexandria via the Spud Run – Klim tinned milk powder, sugar, cocoa and on one occasion a large cake. When the man was killed Alexander wrote to her with the news. Ludmilla continued to send the parcels, which he shared with his soldiers.

In Cairo, Betty, wife of Major Robert Daniell, found an ingenious way to send food and comforts to her husband. She filled an empty kerosene tin with whisky, tinned fruit, underclothes, socks and shoes, chocolate and cigarettes, sealed it and labelled it NAILS. She then charmed one of the officers on an Australian destroyer to take the tin up to Tobruk. He did this regularly until the destroyer was sunk. Occasionally the destroyers brought in long-forgotten luxuries:

> Once it was two fresh onions apiece: we ate them like apples. Another time it was an orange each, and it was like being a child at Christmas . . . Once an attempt was made to issue us with fresh meat, but it was from a nameless beast and badly butchered. The cooks were at a loss to know how to handle it and, when it was served up, we couldn't get our teeth into the tasteless, rubbery stuff.

Men became scavengers and sometimes thieves. Foraging on the Tobruk rubbish dump Cowles came across a two-pound tin of cheese and some Italian macaroni. The tin had perforated, but on opening its contents seemed to have matured from a Cheddar type to something like a fine-flavoured Stilton. He triumphantly cooked macaroni cheese that night to the great satisfaction of his mates. A few days later his friend Doug Woodward 'produced a dish of biscuits boiled to form a porridge flavoured with three quarters of a small tin of Bournvita and, for sweetening, quince jelly. Gunner Sleigh made bread and butter pudding made with layers of army biscuits and jam.' Scavenging sometimes backfired. Tutt recalled that one evening his friend Joe said he would add some dried spaghetti to the stew bubbling in the billy can:

> It proved to be cordite. We were still coming across all sorts of munitions every time that we moved. We were near a dump of charge bags for their guns. The Italians might have been able to tell the difference between cordite and spaghetti. We often couldn't. Cordite had taken the place of petrol for our brew-ups. There was so much of it available. Thrown under the can in small quantities it soon had the water boiling, but you had to be careful. Throw on too much at one go and there'd be a sheet of eyebrow-scorching flame.

Beer was an infrequent pleasure, bought up on the Spud Run by the Australian Comforts Fund or as part of NAAFI stores. When something did arrive there was never enough, and usually one can of fruit or beer had to go around three or four men, so the best way to share it out it was to draw lots. On one occasion some beer arrived for John Hurman's company, enough for one bottle between two men, but some neighbouring Diggers heard about the shipment and an ugly scene threatened when the Australians demanded their share of the golden nectar. Hurman explained that it was the first ration of beer his men had received during the siege, and the Diggers reluctantly agreed to wait for the next shipment. A fight was averted. The Royal Leicesters recorded a 'red-letter day' on 26 October when the NAAFI issued a tin of beer per man and a quart of whisky per officer. The scarcity of alcohol was disliked, but never caused serious complaint. The lack of cigarettes, however, did. Fifty per man were issued with the rations each week. Smokers carried little tin boxes to store their fag ends, breaking them up and re-rolling the tobacco until the last puff. They became a form of currency. Bunny Cowles, a non-smoker, used to barter his cigarette ration: haircuts, for instance, were commonly paid for with cigarettes.

*

Rea Leakey's relationship with his Australian hosts was characteristic of the close ties that developed within the besieged garrison between the forces of the nations represented in Tobruk: Australian, British, Indian, Free French and, from August, Polish and Czech. The bond was primarily one of shared danger and endeavour. McGinlay was not alone in speaking highly of his Antipodean comrades. 'They were completely raw, and unblooded,' he recalled, 'but what magnificent men they proved to be.' Leonard Tutt spent much of the time in his artillery OP with Australian infantrymen, and he was grateful for their generosity:

> Because of our isolation from all normal sources of supply quite simple things took on a value far beyond their worth. Tinned milk for a private brew, needles for running repairs, razors, tea and tobacco were always sought after. We rolled our own, using any paper we could scrounge. Fortunately the Australians were

always more generously endowed. Seldom did I do an OP duty with them and not come away with some cigarette papers and tins of tobacco.

Some British officers could not understand how relationships between officers and other ranks in the Australian army could be so relaxed without posing a threat to good order and military discipline. Captain Vernon Northwood explained to one British enquirer that 'there's just this sort of feeling between us . . . The blokes came from the south-west of Western Australia, a farming community, and they were the salt of the earth. I knew a lot of them from back home. You could go to a feller and call him Tom and sometimes, if he thought he should, he'd call you sir, and sometimes he didn't.'

There were some amusing encounters between the nations. As an ambulance driver Alex Franks had carried a rifle for two years but never actually fired it, even in training. His Lee Enfield was in his vehicle, but he never had any ammunition for it. Thinking he might soon be required to use the rifle in anger, he decided to get in some practice. He found a clip of five 0.303-inch rounds in the sand and, finding an empty patch of desert, he pressed the butt carefully into his shoulder, took aim at an empty flimsy and squeezed the trigger. The explosion was louder than he had expected and the rifle thumped back into his shoulder with unexpected force. But the most surprising thing was the loud cheer that erupted from behind him from an apparently abandoned armoured car. He had hit the can, and a group of Australians had been watching him, intrigued, from a trench. They could not believe it was the first time Franks had ever fired his rifle. 'We'll soon change that,' one of the Diggers said. Pointing at a Boys anti-tank rifle the Aussie corporal told him, 'Just you jump up here and have a go at this little beauty. But watch your step: it's got a kick like an angry roo. Pull it hard into your shoulder and you'll be OK.' Franks did so, fired and hit the flimsy a second time. The Diggers cheered. 'Bullseye, cobber' yelled the corporal. 'What'll you have? A fluffy teddy bear, a fancy hat or one of our best clay pipes?'

Stuck in a slit trench for days with an Australian Bren carrier driver, Bob Braithwaite was fascinated by his stories of life in Australia.

He learned of sugar cane cutting in Queensland, the hard work, snakes and the weekend sprees in the nearest town, where the boys would go and get 'blindo'. He found the Diggers pragmatic and irrepressible. When the situation allowed it, one of the tasks of Braithwaite's supply company was to drive Australian soldiers down for swim parades on the coast. On one occasion, near Fort Pilastrino, he went to pick up his charges, who were sitting having breakfast. Waiting for them to finish he suddenly heard the unmistakable whistle of an incoming shell. Throwing themselves to the ground they were all faster than one tall Australian infantryman who, with a mug of tea in one hand, his breakfast in the other and reluctant to drop either, was still standing when he disappeared with a flash and a bang as the shell struck him directly. Ten minutes later, the wounded taken off to one of the two hospitals in the town, the remainder were in the back of Bob's truck bumping happily down the escarpment to the coast, singing loudly.

As the siege began to stretch beyond days into weeks, and the weeks became months, the garrison did as much as it could to occupy itself. Despite the daily attacks from the air and artillery bombardments, the danger was boredom. When not fighting, the troops were kept busy. For Alexander McGinlay and the men of the Tobruk Tanks, 'maintenance of the tanks, guns, radio and keeping ourselves as clean as possible was all we could do'. Shortages of razors, toothpaste and scissors for cutting hair made keeping clean difficult, but for Leonard Tutt the lack of books was the greatest deprivation:

I begged them from all and sundry, some of them with wads of pages torn out for cigarette paper so that I had to use my imagination to fill the gaps. Because I was dependent on the reading interests of others my taste became a catholic one. I read *No Orchids for Miss Blandish* followed by *War and Peace*. *Das Kapital* was a strange companion for *The Pickwick Papers*. I still have by me the three utility, wartime printed Penguins by Adrian Bell: *Corduroy*, *The Cherry Tree* and *Silver Ley*, a gentle trilogy about the East Anglian countryside ... One glorious find was an omnibus edition of John Buchan's novels. That kept me going for a whole fortnight.

To keep themselves busy men became inventive. Alexander McGinlay occupied himself with making a guitar from the debris that littered the battlefield and getting a small orchestra started. In Tobruk town variety concerts were laid on every ten days or so in the hospital. Despite having to halt proceedings as many as five times a night to rush to the air raid shelters, they proved popular. John Devine was given responsibility for organizing these for a while, and was surprised at the previously hidden talent that emerged. 'Some of the Tommies had musical instruments and could sing and dance well . . . Of course there were many amusing incidents. Once a quartet of English wharf labourers gave an imitation of an air raid. While they were emitting shrieks and howls and reproducing crashes and the rattle of machine guns, there came the real whistle of a bomb, and the party broke up almost in panic.'

The only newspapers were those that came via the post, months late, or the locally produced news sheets like the *Tobruk Truth*, which the Australians nicknamed the Dinkum Oil, which were summaries of the nightly BBC news. The radio was a godsend. It was across the airwaves that the garrison heard on 19 October that their stand had surpassed the 186 days of the siege of Mafeking in the Boer War. 'Just as Malta has helped to keep the Mediterranean open for Britain,' Sir John Dill, chief of the Imperial General Staff told the garrison through the BBC, 'so the Tobruk garrison has been the bulwark of Egypt's defence. We are proud of you.'

German radio stations were judged to play the best music and were a favourite, especially when they broadcast the troops' (on both sides) favourite tear-jerker 'Lili Marleen', as were the English-language programmes broadcast on Radios Berlin and Belgrade, a regular feature of which were the speeches made by 'Lord Haw Haw'. For all his mocking irony, William Joyce displayed quite remarkable ignorance of the ability of the besieged to make light of their misfortunes, and to turn them psychologically to their own advantage. Indeed, the defenders of Tobruk derived much amusement from the ill-judged broadcasts of this famous Irish-American. Every day Lord Haw Haw (or Lord Jaw Jaw), as he had long been dubbed for his peculiar accent ('Jairmany calling, Jairmany calling'), pontificated in his excessively modulated tones on Radio Berlin to the diverse troops of the empire, braying that the rats of Tobruk would be sentenced to twelve years of road building in Libya when captured:

> He never failed to cheer us. Though we were often interrupted by air raids, any wireless receiver tuned into him was sure of a big audience. He told us month after month that we were to be exterminated. Month followed month, and still the warnings came, and still we stayed. He told our people not to worry, for we were all thirty feet underground and still digging. This amused us quite a lot, for it was very nearly true.

Recreation facilities were extremely limited. Throughout the entire siege the Salvation Army managed to run the semblance of a club in the town, although Gunner Bill Lewis, with unconscious irony, declared that how they did it 'God only knows.' They had a single room with a few games such as draughts and cards, plus a few books, a dartboard without the darts and a rackety old piano. 'Swimming was just possible, under strict control,' said Alexander McGinlay. It was a good way to relax, as well as to wash:

> There was one sheltered bay and beach, sheltered that is from direct enemy view and shelling. So at intervals, far too few, we were allowed down to bathe in batches of about fifty at a time. Scouts were posted, and when the alarm was given, usually when the Stukas were finished with their bombs and came over machine-gunning, those who were drying out on the beach would dive into trenches previously prepared for just this; those who were in the water and too far away from the trenches trod water until the planes came into view, then dived under the water until they had passed.

Bob Braithwaite recalled that the Australian swim parades were hilarious. Stripping off all their clothes even before they had left his truck, the Diggers looked as if they were all wearing white swimming trunks as they raced naked and shouting into the sea, ducking each other and behaving like larrikins on a picnic without a care in the world. It could have been Bondi rather than Tobruk for all these men cared, or at least that was the impression they gave.

But fear was never entirely absent. All were nervous at one time or another, although most managed not to show it. Experience of battle did not remove fear. In fact, it often made it worse, the thought occurring that at some time one's number must come up. The daily raids became harder to deal with the more one was exposed to them; being bottled up in Tobruk undoubtedly had a wearing effect. Braithwaite admitted that late on in the campaign, under a particularly fierce artillery barrage, he suddenly panicked and started running. His lance corporal calmed him down and within a few minutes, ashamed and angry at letting the side down, Braithwaite returned to his position. Nothing more was said. Over the many months of the siege Bob's courage had been gradually depleting, and it is hardly surprising that momentarily he panicked. 'I saw big men worn down to tears with the constant screaming of shells and explosives,' he recalled. A common corollary of artillery bombardment and sudden air attack, recalled Rudolf Schneider, even in experienced soldiers, was involuntary defecation. The *Wehrmacht* had a saying: 'Fear is brown.'

By mid-summer Leonard Tutt felt low:

I was trying to cope with dysentery and the difficulty of taking a walk with a shovel [finding somewhere to defecate] in an area which was liable to sudden bursts of shelling. I had about four desert sores, one of which had practically eaten its way through to the bone. I sat down on a piece of ground which housed a mean-minded scorpion which bit me on the back of the leg. This was the time too that I discovered that I had become an unwilling host to two grossly bloated camel ticks on my more private parts.

Some men did not cope well, but most found ways of dealing with the strain of constant action and deprivation. For some keeping busy helped, while for others exhaustion was added to stress and fear. On 17 July John Kelly recorded in his diary that morale in the gun pits was very low. 'Too many of the boys are sick, mentally as well as physically,' he wrote. For the anti-aircraft gunners morale improved when they scored a hit. On 13 August Kelly's battery caught a Ju 88 flying in at 17,000 feet from the sea. The first burst caught his port engine, which immediately started smoking, and he began to lose height, falling to 7,000 feet and disappearing, still smoking and losing height, into the distance over the desert. The men were jubilant and in the flush of success morale revived somewhat. On 14 August he observed wryly on the propaganda war between the sides:

> Jerry communiqué: 'The men of Tobruk are tired and worn out and we shall keep them besieged until the end of the war.'

> Our communiqué: 'The men of Tobruk are in fine fettle and are waiting for the word "Go." All the men in Tobruk have had a month's leave.'

> My communiqué: 'Dr Goebbels has been out-lied at last.'

It was inevitable there would be psychological casualties among the besieged. Bill Lewis's best friend, the happy-go-lucky Bill Barlow, committed suicide after losing his mind. He had been very ill with dysentery for several weeks, but then became nervous and frightened. During one Stuka attack his machine gun jammed and, panicking, he leapt from his gun pit and ran for the nearest cover, dodging the bullets as he ran. Afterwards he told everyone he was finished. The medical officer refused to send him to hospital, and one day the twenty-two-year-old walked out of his trench and shot himself in the stomach.

One antidote to fear was friendship. The comradeship of the team was everything. 'We came to love the desert,' Private Alex Franks asserted, 'because we were surrounded by our friends.' At nights, when off duty, Braithwaite would sit in his slit trench with Alf and Jock and cook up some bully on their Primus, and then yarn about home and sing a bit to keep their spirits up. 'Many prayers were said by me and most of the others those nights under the stars, wondering about the folks back home and your mates who had gone or who were in hospital.' One bad night, shellfire incoming, Jock, Bob and Alf fled their foxhole and ran over to the larger trench occupied by their friends Chris Garden and Bill Dainty and two boys from Birmingham. They trench was sturdy and well built, with heavy planks on top covered by several feet of packed sand and rock. 'They made us welcome and had a brew. Chris had lost his family in a German bombing raid at home but was always there with a joke, and Bill Dainty too. In the morning there were five shell holes around us within a twelve-foot circle and, sticking out of the top of the trench, the one we'd never heard: an unexploded shell!'

Those who couldn't cope might find themselves evacuated by ship, but the majority just had to grit their teeth and find ways to overcome their fear. Within a short period of time, recalled Ray Ellis of the South Notts Hussars:

We found ourselves able to deal with our problems and to accept them as part of a daily routine. We became wise in the ways of war; learned to distinguish between the sounds of enemy gunfire, when to dive for cover, and when to remain unperturbed. We taught ourselves to ignore the sound of any bombardment that did not immediately concern us. We discovered the art of sleeping through all kinds of noise and danger, and it became a common saying when settling down for the night: 'Don't wake me for anything less than three panzer divisions through the wire.' And so, gradually, a pattern of life emerged which allowed us to contend with the hardships, the perils and the boredom which were to be our constant companions for the next nine months.

Bombardier Cowles remarked that the downside to life in Tobruk was the constant danger from air attack, but the upside was no parades – being 'properly dressed' was an irrelevance and there was no spit and polish. There were no senior officers to bother the regimental officers, and many army rules and regulations went by the board. Normal attire was boots, socks, khaki drill shorts and, when in action, a tin hat. At night they wore shirts and, when cold, a battledress blouse.

When it got through mail did much to raise morale. Sometimes letters would be stamped SALVAGED FROM THE SEA, a reminder of the hazards of sea travel in general and of the Tobruk run in particular. Mail was always slow. A reply to a letter sent home at the beginning of May would not be received before September. Aerographs were introduced quite early on. The letter was written on a single piece of paper, photographed in Cairo with thousands of others and sent to the UK by microfilm, where it was printed out and sent on to the addressee. Ordinary letters could be sent by ship, including one 'Green' envelope a month containing a self-certified letter that required no censorship as it contained only personal information. All other letters were censored by regimental officers. Occasionally parcels arrived. Items Bill Green received included a fruitcake in an airtight tin, soap, toilet rolls, chocolate, sweets and Players cigarettes. Ray Ellis was amused to find in one packet from home, which had been delayed many months, some stale cake, chocolate that had turned white, two packets of balloons and a tin of salve sent by his father. The cake and chocolate were quickly discarded; the salve turned out to be a remarkable cure for desert sores; and the balloons were floated above the trench one day to the amusement of the Germans opposite, who potted away at them as if at a circus shooting gallery.

There was little personal animosity towards the enemy. Ellis had no ill feeling towards the Germans. 'It seemed to me that they were more or less in the same unhappy situation as ourselves,' he considered. 'This feeling was to some extent mutual, I believe, for one could often hear the machine-gunners from either side signalling to each other ... 'da diddley da da' from one side, which would be answered by a 'da da' from the other side.' For long stretches of the siege through the summer months, aside from the daily Stuka and artillery attacks, the opposing front-line troops had a tacit truce. Lieutenant Alexander McGinlay recalled how on one occasion he was detailed to supply an armed escort to some engineers who were out in front of the perimeter, laying mines:

So we formed a D a few hundred yards the enemy side of the sappers, and settled down to watch. The enemy sent over the odd shell, but no damage was done. Then they sent forward some eight-wheeled armoured cars, only so far and no further. The crews of these cars sat in their turrets and viewed us through binoculars. We did the same. Obviously no action was planned or anticipated. Came tea time, or whatever time the sappers packed in, and retired through the wire to safety, we were then free to do the same.

A casual wave of the hands towards the enemy produced exactly the same response, as they too retired. Funny war.

Similarly, one day Leonard Tutt was in a small forward weapon pit with some Australian infantrymen, observing for his guns. As the day dawned one of the Diggers went through the first-light task of seeing if anything had happened in the enemy-held area during the night:

This meant scanning the whole area with a periscope to look for the first giveaway that they were becoming ambitious: freshly turned earth, revealing that they were digging new earthworks or installing extra machine guns. Quite unexpectedly, one of their men climbed above ground, moved a few steps away from the edge of his trench and started to urinate. I waited for the Australians to open fire on him but, suddenly, there was a great laugh from someone on our side then two or three of them climbed out and began to do the same. It was contagious. In a few minutes there must have been about fifty men, friend and foe alike, relieving themselves, shaking out their blankets, trying to toss cigarettes across the intervening space, and generally enjoying a holiday from hate. This must have gone on for about six or seven minutes before the whine of a shell sent everyone diving below ground again and the war resumed.

For those forced to endure the long dangerous months of confinement, life in Tobruk during the siege was a strange combination of fear, hardship and pride. 'Not one who took part in the siege,' observed Leonard Tutt, 'can have remained unchanged by it. There was a "oneness" about our daily existence,' he recalled, a sentiment echoed by many others, whose voices echo down to us through the pages of their letters and diaries:

When I heard a burst of firing coming from one of the posts on our front I could see in my mind's eye the tall Australian with his battered bush hat, a finger on the trigger of his Bren. I could almost hear what he was saying to his Number Two: 'Come on, Bluey, let's give the buggers a couple of magazines full – let 'em know we're still here.'

I could make a pretty good guess too that his hand would have a dirty bandage around it. There had been a heavy attack the night before. He would have fired until his Bren was nearly white hot and must surely have burnt his hand when changing to his second barrel.

The danger and hardship created a brotherhood of weary warriors which still binds the survivors into old age. Life was not always enjoyable, but it was survivable and the 'Rats of Tobruk' took justifiable pride in their ability not merely to survive, but to thrive in their adversity. The irascibly irreverent Diggers had a word for it:

> This bloody town's a bloody cuss
> No bloody trams, no bloody bus
> And no one cares for bloody us
> Oh, bloody! Bloody! Bloody!
>
> No bloody sports, no bloody games
> No bloody fun with bloody dames
> This place gives me bloody pains
> Oh, bloody! Bloody! Bloody!
>
> All bloody fleas, no bloody beer,
> No bloody booze since we've been here
> And will it come, no bloody fear
> Oh, bloody! Bloody! Bloody!
>
> All bloody dust, no bloody rain
> All bloody fighting since we came
> This war is just a bloody shame
> Oh, bloody! Bloody! Bloody!
>
> The bully makes me bloody wild
> I'd rather eat a bloody child
> The salty water makes me riled
> Oh, bloody! Bloody! Bloody!
>
> With raids all day and bloody night
> The Huns strive with all their might
> To give us a bloody fright
> Oh, bloody! Bloody! Bloody!

SIEGE RATS

> Best bloody place is bloody bed,
> With blanket over bloody head
> Then they'll think we're bloody dead.
> Oh, bloody! Bloody! Bloody!*

Eric Lambert, an Australian infantry officer, observed his countrymen's stoicism and endurance with pride. He watched a patrol of Diggers returning from the desert in August 1941:

Down the wadi comes a file of men. They march slowly, out of step, and mostly in silence. The dull clink of their weapons is clear in the evening air. At first their faces look all the same, burnt deep, their eyes red-rimmed with the whites gleaming, cheeks hollowed, lips straight and grave. Their shirts and shorts are stiff like canvas with mingled dust and sweat, and streaked again with the sweat of the day. Their legs are bare and burnt and almost black; their boots are worn pure white. Some who still have them wear their tunic, for the air will soon be deathly cold, and their headgear is, as before, motley: a steel helmet, a crumpled slouch hat and an Italian pith helmet. Their packs, haversacks and ammunition pouches have become as white as their boots and their weapons gleam dully in the spots where they have become worn, for they had five months of use.

They are a strange spectacle. They were once ordinary men, but now they do not belong among ordinary men . . . Not one of them will ever be quite the same again.

* Written by Private Hugh Patterson, son of the famous Australian poet 'Banjo' Patterson and a driver in the 20th Brigade.

7 » RELIEF-IN-PLACE

The first thing that they were aware of was the flash of anti-aircraft guns. It could have been lightning from a tropical storm, the small grey clouds which followed detonations only detectable by day. The flares stayed alive longer, swinging down beneath their parachutes before flickering out. Along the coast searchlights stabbed into the night, occasionally picking out a bomber at high altitude, while the weaving aircraft sought to escape the beams.

The second thing was the noise. The dull, distant thud of exploding 3.7-inch anti-aircraft shells providing a screen against the Italian Savoia 79 bombers flying out of Tripolitania and the Heinkels coming in from Crete. There was always a delay between the flash of ignition and the explosion, the time between dependent on one's distance from the action. To the troops crouching on board the fast-moving destroyers the time grew shorter as the little convoy approached its destination. The heavy 4.5- and 3.7-inch weapons of the 51st Anti-Aircraft Regiment providing a protective shield around Tobruk's harbour could now be detected, but the smaller Bofors 40-millimetre single-barrelled rapid-fire guns of the light anti-aircraft regiments were only distinguished when the harbour was reached.

The third was the smell. Even at a distance – and with the breeze sweeping the smells of land far offshore – the unmistakable odour of this scruffy little North African port deep in the grip of a long siege was overpowering. For the British infantrymen of the 70th Division, crammed into every nook and cranny of the four Royal Navy destroyers making the dangerous twelve-hour run in from Alexandria, it would have been an adventure were they not due to take over the defence of the port and its environs from the gallant 9th Australian, which had been fighting there since April.

It was 11 p.m. on the evening of 18 October, and Lieutenant Philip Brownless, along with 264 other soldiers on board the six-year-old H-class destroyer HMS *Havock*, stared at Tobruk with fascination. The siege was now into its sixth month and as well known around the kitchen tables of Melbourne and Sydney, Colchester and Liverpool, as it was in Berlin and Rome. For weeks the 1st Battalion of the Essex Regiment had been preparing in Egypt for this moment.

Tobruk had only survived because of the plucky small ships of the Scrap Iron Flotilla, which operated a regular ferry service into and out of the beleaguered garrison from May 1941, bringing in food, ammunition and reinforcements and taking out wounded and POWs. It was on these destroyers that Brownless and the other members of the British 70th Division arrived in Tobruk and the bulk of Morshead's Australians were spirited away.

The experience of Bombardier Bunny Cowles of 192 Heavy Artillery Battery of the Spud (or Suicide) Run from Alexandria was shared by many thousands of others during the siege. On Monday 22 September Cowles's regiment, encamped in dirty transit billets outside Alexandria, was woken by reveille at 3 a.m. followed by a hot mug of tea. Then at 5.30 a long convoy of trucks took the 2,000 or so troops down to the harbour, arriving at 7.30. By 8 a.m. they were aboard and the destroyer HMS *Griffin* was steaming out of harbour with four other destroyers, the men packed tightly in wherever there was space. The sea was rough, and left everyone feeling ill. 'At times the ship seemed to go nearly under the water as it ploughed through the waves, drenching everyone on deck with spray,' recalled Cowles. During the afternoon enemy planes attacked the ships from 10,000 feet but did no damage, the destroyers making sharp turns to avoid the falling bombs. The convoy arrived in Tobruk at 10.15 p.m. in complete darkness. The deck cargo was quickly onto the quay and the men bundled into waiting trucks and taken somewhere within the perimeter, where the men dossed down where they could.

The night that Brownless arrived – 18 October 1941 – was moonless. Normally the Mediterranean moon shone like a street lamp, making the harbour a perilous place. If at all possible ships docked at Tobruk on only the darkest nights. Getting into the harbour was itself a tricky affair, and described by Lieutenant N.B. Robinson, anti-submarine officer on the destroyer HMS *Kipling*, who made dozens of such journeys:

We would get into a certain position by nightfall and from there we would rush for Tobruk at full speed, which was the best way of avoiding the attentions of the Luftwaffe. Within about five miles of the harbour, we had to slow down because of the mines. The essence of our plan was to unload all our food, oranges, lemons, ammunition and supplies piled up on the upper deck, with the utmost possible speed so as to get back before daylight to a point where we could expect air support as soon as it was light enough for the enemy bombers to come in . . . Needless to say, on moonlight nights when enemy aircraft could spot us, the journey became an extremely dangerous one and we used to undergo some terrible bombing. Our casualties reached such proportions that the journey was eventually abandoned altogether during the three days on either side of the full moon.

From the sea, Tobruk is extraordinarily difficult to identify at night. We could never be sure of our bearings and nobody dared to show any lights or flash searchlights to help us. All we could do was to go on a dead reckoning as far as possible. The search for the harbour delayed things at times and you will remember the whole business was a fight against time. So eventually we felt we just could not risk the loss of valuable time and the garrison decided that they must show some sort of light to guide us. The light selected was a green oil lamp and the day before the destroyers were due to arrive, the garrison would set this lamp in position, and at the approved time they would light it. This was a great improvement, but eventually the Italians got wind of what was happening and used to sneak out and move the light to another position calculated to suit their ideas as to where the destroyers should go! However, we in our turn soon tumbled to their trick, but nonetheless the result was that our precious green light could not be trusted and was as much use to us as if it wasn't there at all.

Finally the beleaguered garrison would, at an appointed time, flash a searchlight about twice into the air. We were waiting for it and could take our bearings from it.

All vessels in the convoy would steal into the harbour together, creeping around the headland, edging carefully through the tranquil waters towards the last remaining unobstructed jetty. Wrecked vessels littered the seabed, some with masts and superstructure showing above the surface but just as many not. As the long months went by stories had been circulating around the garrison about their cargoes and turned into doggerel. One verse had it that all kinds of treasures lay deep under the water:

> They say there's a ship in the 'arbour, the 'arbour,
> They say it's all loaded with beer,
> But what is the use of a ship in the 'arbour,
> When we want the bloody stuff 'ere?

Through the thunderous display overhead, Private Leonard Passfield of 1st Essex heard a calm voice come over the ship's tannoy: 'Now will our soldier passengers please face the bow – that's the sharp end – and prepare to disembark. Good luck. God bless.' Magnetic and acoustic mines dropped by enemy aircraft added to the hazards that littered the water which the ships traversed, but all this was largely unknown to the newcomers. As HMS *Havock* came alongside in the darkness, Lieutenant Philip Brownless heard an Australian voice echo up from the dockside, 'Hurry up, Tommy. You're bloody lucky!'

Brownless and Passfield were taking part in Operation Cultivate, the final phase of the relief-in-place of Morshead's Australians. Their British colleagues in Tobruk had despaired of the news that the Diggers were to be withdrawn, and morale plummeted. 'The average Aussie is a poor soldier on the parade ground,' observed Leonard Tutt, 'but one hell of a fighter in action.' Widespread political pressure from Australia to ensure that the 2nd AIF fought together had resulted in Auchinleck's decision to withdrawn Morshead's troops. 'Whingeing bloody politicians,' was an oft-heard refrain from Tutt's Digger friends in Tobruk, but they were nevertheless not unhappy to leave when the opportunity came. Their British friends watched them depart with sorrow.

Wearing soft-soled Army-issue plimsolls rather than hobnailed boots, the men of 1st Essex quickly disembarked onto the quay, to be met by escorts from the Australian battalions they were relieving. They then walked up the long slope away from the harbour to the battered Ford, Chevrolet and captured Lancia trucks for their journey to the Blue Line. The Englishmen were heavily laden. Along with their fighting order – helmets, ammunition and grenade pouches, bayonets, Lee Enfield rifles, Bren machine guns and small fighting packs with blanket roll and waterproof – they also carried their kitbags, into which were stuffed spare clothing, private possessions, strategic reserves of tobacco and greatcoats.

Australian journalist Chester Wilmot, who had been in Tobruk since its capture in February, recalled watching the orderly disembarkation of the 2nd Battalion Leicestershire Regiment from 16th Brigade on 27 September: 'British Tommies began streaming down the narrow gangway, across the wreck and onto the jetty. There was no clank of iron heels on steel plates because they all wore rubber-soled desert boots. They needed them. The gangway was narrow and they were more heavily laden than any Arab mule. Nevertheless, 300 padded off in ten minutes.'

In Tobruk each man's kitbag would be held by his company quartermaster sergeant in a central point well to the rear of the front line, so as to provide a set of replacement clothing and small comforts when they became necessary. On the dockside the men were given whatever they could carry: crates of tinned food, unwieldy ammunition boxes, sacks of potatoes and boxes of unprimed grenades.

Five miles south-east along the rutted dirt track to King's Cross, the men of 1st Essex were deposited next to the old POW cage for their first night in Tobruk at the Sidi Mahmoud junction, the backstop in the desperate Easter battles where the RHA had fired their 25-pounders point blank and over open sights into the advancing panzers. The plan was that over the two following days their Australian hosts from the 2/17th Battalion would familiarize them with the ground, before taking them through the gun lines out to the outer perimeter – the Red Line – on the 21st. The Australians would then bid them farewell.

The evacuation procedures for Operations Treacle, Supercharge and Cultivate were fraught with danger. Bringing in and taking off large numbers of troops was an invitation to German and Italian air, artillery and submarine attack. But, through good planning and plenty of luck, all three phases of the evacuation of Morshead's division passed without incident. On the first night of Operation Treacle, during which the Polish 1st Carpathian Brigade was to be brought into Tobruk and the 18th Australian Brigade, 18th King Edward's Own Cavalry, Indian Army and the 152nd Heavy Anti-Aircraft Battery were to be evacuated, Captain Anthony Heckstall-Smith, a Royal Navy officer who spent most of 1941 on the Spud Run, sat on a bench outside Navy House on the northern side of the harbour. It was the first day of August's moonless period and had been unbearably hot. But the tension at the start of this critical operation was even worse. Would they be able to pull off the most audacious feat of the whole siege? The Germans knew full well that the Allies used every moonless night to smuggle men and supplies in and out of the vulnerable harbour. A thousand Poles and 200 tons of precious supplies had been crammed onto the minelayer HMS *Latona* and three destroyers. Treacle was a trial run for the remainder of the 9th Division. If it failed many men would die. Axis sea, air and long-range artillery units would do everything in their power to prevent the replacement of the Australian troops who had repeatedly denied them the port. Heckstall-Smith recalled that the departing Australians at the harbour waited patiently: 'They stood shoulder to shoulder on the only jetty, on the rusting hulks of two half-sunken hulks, packed like cattle in the cavernous holds of the A lighters, and on the decks of launches and tugs. On the quay below Navy House and at the edge of beaches, the lorries waited.'

As the men of the Australian 2/28th Battalion waited on the dockside HMS *Kimberley* came alongside out of the night gloom, carrying their replacements, the men of the 2nd Battalion the King's Own Regiment. 'You pretty little bastard,' breathed the man alongside Captain Vernon Northwood. 'His words expressed the feelings of us all,' said Northwood. When, after safely negotiating the Suicide Run, the ship came alongside in Alexandria, the soldiers were quiet, to the surprise of the Australian General Blamey, who expected to see much cheerful exuberance now that Tobruk lay far behind. But Northwood and his comrades were too tired for exuberance. The men 'were very thin, they were burned almost as dark as the local natives: but their eyes were so alert. It was most noticeable. They were on edge, they noticed everything. They were sharp, sharp as a razor – but so, so tired.' A young Royal Navy officer on HMS *Griffin*, Alec Dennis, had a slightly different experience. He recalled taking off a party of Australians from Tobruk:

> They came along the harbour all anyhow, tin mugs rattling on their knapsacks, as cool as you like, all swearing. We got them aboard and were about to cast off when we saw this chap shambling along on his own. We were all shouting: 'Come on, get a move on, we're just off!' Even then he didn't run, but just broke into this kind of casual trot.
>
> We put them all over the ship, got their officers down in the wardroom for a drink. On the mess deck the men carried on as if they were still in Tobruk, opening their tins of bully beef and fruit, chucking the empty tins on the floor. A frightful mess.
>
> As we were coming into Alex, this fusillade of shots broke out from the upper deck. We thought it must be an air attack and they were shooting at the planes. But not a bit of it – a seagull was perched on a buoy, and the Aussie soldiers were taking potshots at it.

Dennis nevertheless forgave his Aussie friends their untidiness and their moment of exuberance. Although 'a wild bunch' he recalled, they 'were fine warriors'.

As commander of the small flotilla of landing ships, Heckstall-Smith had been one of the few to know the plan for Treacle. He had been convinced it wouldn't work. The operation required seven separate convoys between Alexandria and Tobruk, between 19 and 29 August, to transport 5,065 Polish officers and other ranks. Heckstall-Smith could not believe that Rommel would allow it to happen. The moonless period was a giveaway – surely the Stukas and long-range artillery would be poised with everything they had.

It had been a day of unbearable suspense which the burning heat had intensified to a pitch almost beyond human endurance. The muscles in my neck and shoulders ached dully and my eyes smarted from staring into the glaring sun in search of enemy planes. My nerves were so stretched that they recoiled violently to the slightest sound. When a truck backfired on the quay below, I had jumped half out of my skin. Even the familiar roar of one of the landing crafts' engines starting up I had mistaken for a squadron of Stukas winging their way over the escarpment.

Military plans rarely survive intact but, incredibly, the operation had gone without a hitch. It had been planned down to the last detail. Every effort had been made to keep Axis aircraft out of the sky and Bardia Bill silent during the critical period of the exchange of troops in Tobruk. Hurricanes escorted the little convoy out of Alexandria. When they reached the limit of their endurance and were forced to return, RAF Wellington and Blenheim bombers had flown from their bases on the Nile to pound the Luftwaffe's desert airfields. As the convoy approached Tobruk and the critical run into harbour, one of the destroyers had joined the garrison artillery in a bombardment of known Axis artillery positions.

Masked by the din of the anti-aircraft barrage, hidden by dust clouds raised by shellfire and bombing, the ships of the Treacle convoy edged into their berths. Heckstall-Smith watched nervously:

Slowly, *Latona* glided up the harbour and lost way, and the onyx water sparkled with phosphorus as her anchor cracked its surface. Through my night-glasses I watched two of the destroyers until they vanished into the shadows of the wrecks crowded with waiting troops. The third nosed her way towards the quay, to come to rest alongside yet another wreck. I could see the soldiers lining her deck four deep and heard above the thunder of the bombardment the clatter of the gangways.

Almost before the shore parties had secured her lines, the Indians were aboard offloading boxes of ammunition, while down the narrow gangplanks the Poles came ashore. As the last of them landed, the Aussies swarmed aboard. There was no noise, no shouting, no flashing of torches, not even a lighted cigarette to be seen, and no confusion.

In less than ten minutes some 350 men had left her deck and another 350, including wounded on stretchers, had taken their places and the destroyer was going astern on her engines.

Within thirty minutes the four ships were heading for the harbour entrance. High overhead their masts screamed the salvoes from the 60- and 25-pounders as one by one they merged with the darkness.

Neither Bardia Bill, firing from Belgassem, nor 'Salient Sue' (the nickname for the German heavy-calibre gun, from El Adem), had fired a shot. The otherwise nightly visitations by squadrons of Stukas, Heinkels and Savoia 79s had not materialized. A fresh consignment of troops had arrived to inject mettle into Tobruk's defences. But for the departing Australians the danger was far from over: they now had to run the gauntlet of bombers and U-boats. Bombardier Ray Ellis recounted the loss of a friend:

During one the many battles in which we were engaged the gun next to ours received a direct hit. We saw the flash of the explosion and at the first opportunity we rushed over to help the gun crew who were all in a sorry state. Among those stricken men was another old pal, and he was in dire distress. Dear old Ginger Barker ... was lying there with his legs all shattered. I could see the splintered white bones protruding through the bloody tangled flesh, and knew that he would never walk again.

The wounded were taken back to the field hospital and we later heard that Arthur Barker had had both his legs amputated at the thigh. He survived the operation and when he was strong enough to be moved he was placed aboard a Royal Navy destroyer for evacuation to a place of safety in Egypt. During the passage to Alexandria the destroyer was attacked by enemy aircraft and sunk. I still shudder at the thought of my old friend's last moments. Lying below decks, with no legs, helpless and unable to move and knowing that he was on a sinking ship.

During the siege the sea between Tobruk and Alexandria was the graveyard of two destroyers, three sloops, seven anti-submarine vessels and minesweepers, together with many smaller craft. In total twenty-five warships and five merchantmen were lost, along with 539 lives. Even the faithful HMS *Latona* was sunk during the concluding phase of Operation Cultivate, falling victim to a German 100-kilogram bomb which sank her forty nautical miles north-west of Bardia on 25 October. This was a heavy price to pay, but an essential one without which the siege could never have been endured.

In June frequent losses were sustained as a result of German and Italian dive-bomber attacks. On the 24th HMS *Auckland* met her fate twenty miles north-east of Tobruk while escorting the tanker *Pass of Balmaha* carrying 750 tons of aviation fuel. Some time after 5 p.m. the convoy was attacked by several Italian Savoia 79 bombers of the 5th Air Fleet and later, and more heavily, by two formations of Italo-German planes: the first consisted of two Ju 88s and twenty-four Stukas commanded by Major Walter Ennecerus; the second was a mixed group of eight German and five Italian Stukas of the 239th Dive-bombing Squadron commanded by Captain Giuseppe Cenni. HMS *Auckland* was badly damaged and her crew abandoned ship. HMAS *Parramatta* closed in to rescue the 162 survivors, who were being machine-gunned in the water. On fire, *Auckland* then capsized and sank after an explosion. The *Pass of Balmaha* was damaged by near-misses but reached Tobruk escorted by the newly arrived HMAS *Waterhen*.

On 29 June 1941 Gunner Bill Lewis of 202 Coastal Defence Battery was shipped with his regiment up to Tobruk from Alexandria in HMAS *Waterhen* and HMS *Defender*. The decks of both ships were crammed with ammunition, mailbags and gun barrels. Leaving early in the morning, the destroyers were due to arrive in Tobruk at midnight. Most of the troops lazed about on deck, enjoying the sunshine. At 4 p.m. several planes were spotted high in the sky. 'This must be our air escort,' shouted out one voice, but suddenly a series of terrific bangs shock the destroyer as the anti-aircraft guns opened up. Action stations were sounded, sailors racing to their positions, the soldiers being told to find what cover they could. The Stukas began their dive, sirens wailing. HMS *Defender* zigzagged through the water, bombs falling on either side. At each turn waves splashed over the deck, soaking everyone. Peering from his hiding place underneath the torpedo tubes, Lewis could see the Stukas drop their bombs almost on top of the destroyer before heading away above the waves to gain height for another attack. Time and again the destroyer miraculously dodged the bombs, and after a while the planes disappeared. *Defender* had survived unscathed, but *Waterhen* had been badly hit and was listing at an alarming angle. Her crew were throwing whatever they could overboard in an attempt to rebalance the ship. HMS *Defender* went alongside and took off the crew and passengers – none had been killed although some were seriously injured – and attempted to tow *Waterhen* back to Alexandria. Shortly afterwards the ropes had to be cut and at 1.50 a.m. on 30 June 1941 the twenty-three-year-old 'Chook', as she was affectionately known to her crew, rolled over and sank, the first ship of the Royal Australian Navy to be lost by enemy action in the Second World War.

The return journey to Alexandria did not pass without incident. During the night a U-boat surfaced in the darkness ahead, apparently unaware of HMS *Defender*'s presence. Immediately fired on, the U-boat dived. For nearly an hour the destroyer circled the spot firing depth charges into the sea. Eventually an oil slick was spotted on the surface, and judging that the U-boat had been sent to its grave, the crowded HMS *Defender* made its way back to the safety of Alexandria harbour. Four days later the regiment left the bug-ridden Moustafa Barracks in Alexandria and travelled by rail to Mersa Matruh, from where, meeting up again with HMS *Defender*, once more they attempted to make the run into Tobruk. Again a U-boat was chased, but apart from this the journey was uneventful, and the troops disembarked before the nightly 'hate' began and the Tobruk Orchestra began its doleful cacophony.

In Tobruk harbour on 21 April 1941 Private John Parish and a small team went aboard the passenger ship SS *Bankura*, sinking after being attacked by dive-bombers. The captain had been killed along with eight others, and there were several wounded. Parish and his team helped off the wounded and recovered all the medical supplies on board. He was struck by the apparent normality. The wardroom was set for lunch – glistening silver and snowy-white linen, the smell of cooking from the galley, a book hurriedly put down on the arm of a chair with a still-warm pipe beside it. 'The sight of the black water slowly creeping up the staircase from the lounge to the deck was horrible but fascinating.'

Private Alex Franks and Lieutenant Alexander McGinlay witnessed, separately, the demise of the redoubtable Chinese river gunboat HMS *Ladybird* on 12 May 1941. *Ladybird* was a twenty-five-year-old *Insect*-class veteran of the Yangtze River which had reached Mediterranean waters in 1940. She was heavily armed for such a small vessel, boasting two 6-inch guns and two 12-pounders, and was used extensively to bombard shore positions, including the airfield at Gazala further up the coast. On 12 May McGinlay had been visiting one of his wounded soldiers in hospital in Tobruk town, and had just come out of the building when a Stuka attack began:

> I hid in a ditch which was very near the docks. Not more than a couple of hundred yards away lay the *Ladybird* at anchor. Then followed the most amazing fight. Every Stuka was hell-bent on sinking her, and they succeeded, after I don't know how many bombs. As the *Ladybird* settled in what was only a few feet of water, through all the smoke and spray I could clearly see the ack-ack and machine guns on the bridge ... blazing away. It was one of the most impressive sights I have ever seen.

The *Ladybird* was attacked by Italian-piloted Stukas, and caught fire, settling on an even keel in ten feet of water. For his actions during the attack Leading Seaman George Booker, in command of one of the anti-aircraft guns, was awarded the Conspicuous Gallantry Medal. In the words of the citation, 'a bomb struck the ship, killing all the gun's crew but him, wrecking the gun and wounding many other men. He himself was badly wounded in both arms but he at once set about rescuing the injured from a fire which had broken out near the magazine.' Seeing the attack, Alex Franks raced down to the harbour with his ancient Morris ambulance and helped several badly burned men to safety. The ship remained full of fight: until the end of the siege anti-aircraft gunners continued to use her anti-aircraft guns.

*

Though the Luftwaffe did not interfere with Operation Treacle, three days later, in the evening, they launched one of their fiercest aerial bombardments. Just as the last Australians of 18th Brigade were queuing to take their places on the departing ships, German Ju 88s and Italian Savoia 79s came over on a high-altitude raid. The harbour erupted in smoke and flame, the explosions reverberating around the low escarpment that fringed the semicircular area, geysers of water soaring skyward. The anti-aircraft gunners on the promontory and at Fort Solaro replied, the steady boom of the heavy guns accompanied by the short bursts of the single-barrelled Bofors, the sky criss-crossed by tracer and the probing fingers of searchlights. Shell fragments fell across Tobruk like rain, almost as threatening to life and limb as the planes above.

When the air attack rolled in from the sea at 8 p.m. Private John Rutherford of 18th Brigade was three miles north-west of Tobruk in Wadi Auda, waiting for orders to make his way to the harbour. Did the Germans know what was afoot or was this simply another raid? Either way, it might spell the end of the Australians' hopes of escaping their desert prison. Rutherford recalled:

Ack-ack guns bark furiously, there's an ominous crunch of bursting bombs and we watch anxiously as volumes of black billowing smoke bulge heavily over the port. Then, just as suddenly as it began, the raid is over . . .

Time mooches on. A convoy of trucks bumps noisily into sight. Orders are rapped out. Pick up packs . . . Put down packs . . . Pick up packs! She's on all right – the same old rigmarole! At last we move off in sections to our trucks and the order is given to embus.

After a slow bumpy journey the vehicles reached the top of the final escarpment above the harbour, where the troops debussed. The night was dark, cloudless and unusually quiet. In the distance flares danced madly on the horizon, searchlights flash in the sky, and we know that somewhere over there our patrols are out and giving the enemy merry hell.

We're led off in sections over the rough country in the general direction of the harbour. Men stumble under the load of their packs and curse softly as though scared that Jerry will hear them and wake up to what is doing.

A whispered order and we halt. An officer goes on ahead to find the way, then suddenly he returns and we are on the move again. We pause momentarily on the top of the escarpment and then commence a perilous climb in the inky blackness down the precipitous slope to the harbour below.

Curses are more numerous now as loose stones clatter noisily down the escarpment; troops lose their foothold and lurch violently into their neighbours. Then, at last, we have made the grade and are assembled near a swinging pontoon bridge leading out into the harbour where the hulk of the *Serenitas* lies derelict. This is to be our landing stage . . .

We shuffle warily over the heaving bridge to the *Serenitas*, slip thankfully out of our webbing, and squat patiently on our packs, prepared for a long wait. Away in the distance an artillery battery fires a few desultory rounds as though to warn Jerry that he is not to get up to any mischief. Jerry sends his regards with a few in return, just to let us know he is still there.

Then that brooding silence again – heavy and pregnant. We are not at ease. We are thinking of Bardia Bill. We are thinking also of the Luftwaffe. They must be about due again and this spot is no garden of roses. Surely they won't let us slide out as easily as all this? . . .

A light winks out at sea. We stir expectantly and stare fixedly in that direction in an effort to pierce the wall of darkness.

Maybe we imagined it. No, there it is again! A ship is signalling. It shouldn't be long now.

It's longer than we expect, however, and we are about to give it away as a bad job when, just on midnight, our ship arrives. Like a ghost she emerges from the darkness and glides gently yet confidently to her berth alongside the *Serenitas*. No sound of given orders, no hint of pulsating engines, not even a bump as she berths. No taxi could have pulled into the kerb as effortlessly as this.

One moment there is nothing and next, well, there she is! We are deeply impressed.

The ship comes to life. Sailors appear as though by magic. Orders are given quietly. Polish troops and stores come off from one end and we proceed to embark at the other. There is a minimum of fuss. Everything seems to be working smoothly to a prearranged plan.

Our ship is the British destroyer *Jervis*, a flotilla leader. We file along the deck, scramble down companionways and are ushered down below into the crew's quarters. Wherever there is space, there are we bedded down. I lose a little skin during the process as I discover that military boots were not designed for steel decks and companionways.

The whole operation is completed in almost exactly one hour and at 1 a.m. we steal slowly out of the harbour, gratefully acknowledging the forbearance of the enemy, who obligingly refrains from throwing a spanner into the works with his usual display of fireworks.

And so we say farewell to Tobruk – a sailor's farewell – and, as we make for the open sea, the troops settle down for the night.

Given the heavy air raid five hours before, Anthony Heckstall-Smith was hugely relieved to see Rutherford's ship depart. He recalled that 'as the throb of the last destroyer's engines faded away, a poignant "Coo-ee!" echoed back through the darkness.'

Finding the convoy at sea the next morning, the ever-alert Luftwaffe did its utmost. For the Diggers confined below decks, unable to see what was going on, the experience was unsettling. They knew that if the *Jervis* were hit and sunk, few would get out alive.

It is 6.15 a.m. and we have been unpleasantly awakened from our slumber. We think that we are back again in Tobruk because all hell has broken loose. The ship is vibrating madly. Her guns blaze desperately. A sickening thud hits her broadside on, dull and metallic. We heel over sharply.

We don't like this at all. Cooped up below as we are, we wonder what's going on. Expressions are strained – extremely so. As land-lubbers we are definitely out of our element. A sailor appears and informs us that there is an air raid on and that we must keep to our quarters . . . All's well that ends well, however, and before long the action is over. We are now allowed on deck and we discover that the worst that has happened is that we have suffered a near miss.

Thirteen hours after leaving Tobruk, the six-ship convoy finally reached Alexandria, but for Lieutenant Philip Brownless and his young platoon from 1st Essex, the departure of the Australians was the beginning of their story. Falling asleep in the weapon pits allocated to them, the warm night air and long journey sent them quickly to sleep. Awaking the next morning to survey their new surroundings, the first thing they did was scratch, as they were introduced to the Tobruk fleas. The Germans did not leave the new arrivals alone for long. Their new life began shortly after a breakfast of hard biscuits and salty tea, when a squadron of twelve Stukas screamed down on the position. The evil-looking aircraft made a habit of attacking out of the sun, and were often hard to detect. Philip Brownless had chosen that moment to pay his first visit to an Australian field latrine. The latrines were either deeply dug holes in the rock or ammunition boxes emptied every night. Brownless had barely sat down on the 'thunder box' before the Stukas arrived, but in a commendable display of sangfroid sat tight as the aircraft dropped their payload. Not content with bombing the newcomers, the aircraft returned to spray the area with machine-gun fire. The noise of the attack was its worst aspect. Nothing apart from the desert was hit – not even the conspicuous latrine – and no one was injured. With the drone of the departing engines growing weaker, Brownless sheepishly emerged with his pride intact. Other hazards immediately presented themselves. Walking to breakfast that first morning a member of A Company kicked away a red Italian 'post-box' hand grenade, which promptly exploded, wounding four men.

Later that first day the Essex moved up to their forward positions on foot, loaded like mules. Escorted by the Diggers of 2/17th Battalion, who would leave the positions that night for their return to

Alexandria, they were shown into the weapon pits and dugouts that would be their homes. Brownless noticed that every pit was surrounded by barbed wire and positioned to provide mutual support for its neighbours up to one hundred feet away. The Australians had been both industrious and ingenious. The weapon pits were well dug, carefully revetted and topped off with low walls built from rocks gathered from the desert floor. In the centre of a widely dispersed platoon position of twenty pits spread over an area some 300 yards across, Brownless found his command post. Platoon headquarters was a roofed weapon pit with living accommodation dug into the rock. It was here that the detailed business of the defence was conducted: orders, ammunition and casualty returns, rations and quartermaster indents, wiring, mining and patrols. Inside his bunker during this October day it was hot but by December it would be freezing.

Elsewhere the Australians had used pneumatic drills on the rock: company headquarters half a mile to the rear was deeply dug and well camouflaged. The one hot meal of the day was brought up at night, along with supplies of ammunition and cans of the brackish Tobruk water. Food remained scarce. Once a month, at full moon, Brownless would be ordered to explain to his men that rations would be short for the next ten days because supply ships could not enter harbour.

Forward of Brownless's platoon position ran the anti-tank ditch, which in addition to its primary purpose also served as a sunken road. Between his position and the anti-tank ditch stretched lines of barbed wire ten feet deep, staked between knee and waist height to catch those advancing at the walk or run. To the left of the El Adem road rows of coiled concertina wire lay in front of the anti-tank ditch, adding to the defensive barrier. It was to the area beyond this wire that the platoons dotted along the perimeter sent out their nightly standing patrols – groups of men who acted as the eyes and ears of Tobruk. Lying in the rocky sand and building what shelter they could around them, their task was to listen for sounds of enemy movement. If a pattern was discerned a much stronger fighting patrol would be sent out on another night to attack the enemy position or take prisoners for interrogation. Lightly armed and small, standing patrols would not engage the enemy if they could avoid it, but night encounters with enemy troops were frequent.

The night had its own dangers. 'Soldiers are taught that if aircraft drop parachute flares during the hours of darkness,' recalled Private Len Passfield of the 1st Essex, 'they must stand perfectly still with heads slightly bowed so that movement [and the light shining on their faces] doesn't give anything away.' One night Passfield was walking back from the latrines to his trench as the sound of a German aircraft approaching grew louder:

> The blackness of the night was suddenly pierced and then completely dispersed by a large white light bathing the whole desert in its brilliance and revealing all to the pilot above. I stood still with head bowed. Despite the fact that I was in close proximity to a few hundred men I felt terribly and utterly alone. Rocks, dispersed tanks, guns and odd pieces of war debris cast shadows that weaved and danced as the flare drifted all too slowly downwards. The feeling that the pilot was searching for me alone was strong. Hours later it seemed the light started to lose some of its brilliance until the tiny parachute, tired of hanging about, landed gently on the desert and the light died its death.

It was easy to get lost at night. Lieutenant Geoffrey Fearnside recounted the occasion when an unarmed Australian ration party became disorientated and bumped into an equally unarmed Italian ration party. The Australians pretended to have weapons but their bluff was called. Both parties were uncertain what to do in the semi-darkness of the desert night. The impasse was resolved by the arrival of an Australian patrol. The Italians were taken prisoner:

> As they moved towards the Australian forward defended localities, [an] Italian, who had resigned himself to his fate, now that the issue was indisputably decided, touched Bardsley [one of the ration party] on the arm. 'I am glad we did not fight, my friend,' he said. 'I have the instincts of a gentleman. I am ... the welterweight champion of Sicily.'
>
> 'Your misgivings were quite unjustified,' replied Bardsley with shameful mendacity. 'I am the heavyweight champion of Australia.' Together they laughed.

Sergeant Harold Harper of 426th Battery Royal Horse Artillery had a similar experience in his artillery OP on the perimeter. One night a sandstorm was raging and he and some colleagues were playing cards by the light of a hurricane lamp.

[Suddenly] the flap of the tarpaulin came back and a pair of legs descended. We thought, Well who the dickens can this be at this time of night? The next thing was a dixie full of stew and then this German lad came down, a very young boy, seventeen or eighteen at the very most. He was in the cookhouse and he'd strayed in this sandstorm, lost his way, seen a chink of light we'd left uncovered, thought it was his own crowd and appeared in our dugout.

After eating the boy's stew, Harper pointed out the German lines and let him go.

Wandering about at night held other dangers since the ground was liberally mined. Minefields dotted the whole Tobruk area. By October it was difficult to know with certainty where all the mines were. People were constantly coming across the old Italian fields, and Major General Morshead's far-sighted decision to defend Tobruk in depth meant that minefields were not a hazard confined to the perimeter. When gaps were required to allow for the departure of a patrol outside the wire mines would be carefully lifted and laid aside to await replanting on the patrol's return. It was a mark of nocturnal desert navigation of the highest order to find the gap in the wire on one's return from a patrol. Departure points were usually marked with white mine tape, but in time the whole perimeter became littered with tape, and reliance on this alone could be fatal.

Brownless took a good look at his kingdom on the morning of 21 October 1941. To the front of his platoon position lay the enemy. The forward German and Italian posts were a mile into the desert, gathered in defensive clumps ahead of the Trigh Capuzzo, the vital artery that ran between Benghazi and Bardia. The Axis gun lines and tank parks lay further back. When Brownless asked the Australian platoon commander whose position he was taking over whether he had any maps of the minefields he shook his head and pointed to the forward right of the position on the enemy side of the anti-tank ditch and said, 'You want to be careful over there, Tommy. We've set some of our Aussie specials.' These were Italian anti-tank box mines normally immune to anything but the weight of a tank or armoured car. The Australians had replaced the large coil springs in them with tiny ones taken from grenades, making them apt to detonate at the slightest movement. Private Richard Grimsey of the Bedfordshire and Hertfordshire Regiment (the 'Beds and Herts') was at a training session on German landmines soon after his arrival. The corporal instructor was showing the group a particular mine that, he said, 'would not go off even if you stand on it'. To demonstrate his point he stood on it. The mine went off, killing him instantly, deafening his class and leaving them stunned and spattered with gore.

Because of the sun and heat little fighting took place during the day; apart from the set-piece battles for Tobruk, which raged both day and night, most infantry actions occurred at night. Small standing patrols, nerve-racking affairs, would carefully push forward to protect positions from sudden attack. Fighting patrols, sometimes the best part of a whole platoon, carried Thompson sub-machine guns and hessian sandbags full of grenades – perfect weapons for the night, when aimed fire from rifles was less effective – together with knives or bayonets. Many men on fighting patrol also took their rifles with them, bayonets attached. In good hands the bayonet was a formidable weapon and a silent killer. The Australians were past masters of the bayonet and grenade patrol.

The men of the British 70th Division had much to learn from the Australians, and little time to do it. The 2nd Battalion King's Own Royal Regiment arrived in Tobruk on the night of 21 September after an uneventful run into Tobruk on HMS *Napier* and HMS *Kingston*. After three days in reserve they moved forward to relieve the 2/13th Australians. Sergeant Harry Atkins was Platoon Sergeant of 14 Platoon, C Company, based at R65 on the south-east corner of the perimeter. Seven hundred yards to his right was 13 Platoon, and a further 700 yards to the left was a platoon of D Company. On the night of his arrival he went out on a familiarization patrol with the Australians from whom they were taking over. After getting across the anti-tank ditch and through the minefield, he learned that 1,000 paces south-east would take him to the enemy outpost known as Tugun, while after 1,000 paces south-west he would arrive at the position code-named Bondi. To get through the minefield he had to hold on to a telephone wire secured to the ground by a metal stake and follow this out to another metal stake beyond the minefield, the men following in single file.

Most patrols went out in a diamond formation and followed a triangular route. 'We were normally briefed to proceed on a compass bearing for a distance of 1,000 paces, change compass bearing and proceed along the enemy front for another 1,000 paces, before returning on the third leg of the patrol back to the place where we had started,' recalled Atkins. This was easier said than done, Atkins admitting, 'I only managed to get back exactly where I started once during the whole time I was there.' Second Lieutenant Ben Thomas of the Beds and Herts also went on patrol under the supervision of an Australian officer on his first night in Tobruk, exiting through one of the several gaps or 'gates' in the wire. In general, the object of each patrol, the route to be followed both out and return, and the arms to be taken were specified, but the time of return was a bit more open and depended on developments. A patrol map or sketch would be given to everyone by the Patrol Commander and off they slipped into the darkness. The direction followed was entirely dependent on compass bearing and distance was measured in paces. Thomas's plan that night was:

Patrol: B Company

Exit: B Gate

Composition: 1 officer, 1 sergeant, 10 men and 4 sappers

Arms: 8 riflemen, 24 hand grenades

Object: Protect sapper party to lay mines across gap in enemy minefield.

Route: Bacon to Wrecked Plane bearing 105° distance 2,400 yards (2,880 paces). Wrecked Plane to enemy minefield bearing 55°, distance 500 yards (600 paces). Patrol will then follow a gap believed to be approximately 300 yards further along. Patrol commander will then dispose of patrol so as to afford maximum protection to the sappers, who will proceed to lay booby traps across the gap. Special care will be taken to ensure that a small gap is left for our own patrols and that the position of this small gap is carefully noted. The patrol will withdraw and return to the Wrecked Plane when the sappers have finished. Wrecked Plane to Eggs bearing 346°, distance 2,850 yards (3,420 paces) to be met by patrol from A Company.

That night Thomas led with two men close by, one responsible for the compass bearing, the other counting the paces. While making their way across the rocky terrain an enemy patrol was spotted in the gloom ahead. Everyone hit the ground and waited. They were not spotted, but rather than risk a confrontation (they were not a fighting patrol and hence had only personal weapons with them – rifles, grenades and pistols) they crawled back the way they had come for some 200 yards, not easy to do on one's belly, and then retraced their steps back to the starting point.

Mistakes were made. Atkins, new to the job, was on patrol one night when two of his men developed hiccups. They had to go back as they would have compromised the patrol. Instead of abandoning his mission, Atkins sent the two men back with a corporal, and gave them the compass. On the return journey he became lost, and wandered into the minefield in front of A Company, far off his path. He set off a trip wire and was forced to lie low and wait for dawn, for A Company to let him through the minefield and back to safety.

The Australians had become proficient at navigating by the stars. Lieutenant Anthony Laing of the Beds and Herts recalled going on a patrol with two Australian guides shortly after he had arrived to booby-trap a prominent tank wreck beyond the wire that a German sniper was using during the day to cause a nuisance along that stretch of the Red Line:

We had been very well briefed as to the route which we should take, with bearings and distances which I tried to memorize, thinking that in the event of casualties I might become responsible for getting the patrol back to our lines. After a while it became clear to me that we were not following the route which we had been given at our briefing. I made my way forward to the English subaltern. But he was just as lost as I was. I caught up with the two Australians.

'This isn't the route we were given! Where are we?' Laing asked.

'Where are we?' the Digger asked incredulously. 'Why, just look at the stars!'

Disgusted by the Pommie officer's ignorance, he turned and walked on. Shortly afterwards the patrol arrived at its objective.

The enemy counter-patrolled, pushing patrols forward at night against Tobruk's defensive perimeter to dig weapon pits or build low stone sangars, leaving snipers or small groups of men with machine guns to catch the defenders off guard the next day. These ad hoc positions took a steady toll on lives and morale. If prepared well they blended perfectly into the desert floor, the tricks played by the sun and heat rendering them almost invisible to the naked eye. There were two ways to deal with them. The first was by counter-patrolling in daylight, a difficult and dangerous task. The second was for the artillery observers, if they could spot them, to call in artillery or machine-gun fire. Bombardier Ray Ellis explained the effects of the heat:

By the middle of the morning, as the heat of the day became more intense, you could walk about without compunction. They [the enemy] could see you – but only in a distorted way. They did the same thing, and we could see them walking about – but you'd see a man walking upside down fifteen foot in the air – distorted visions – but you couldn't aim at him because you didn't know where he really was. Sometimes by a trick of the light . . . it would all revert back to normal again in a second and they had a complete view of the front again, maybe for quarter of an hour, and then it would go again.

Following the departure of the Australians (save for the unfortunate 2/13th Battalion who remained in Tobruk until December 1941), the 70th British Division rapidly adapted to the ways of their predecessors, and the pattern of the day continued very much as it had done under the previous regime. At about 5.30 each morning whispered orders would herald reveille for any sleeping soldiers (night was the busiest time of the day and few men would actually be asleep) to join their comrades on sentry duty, watching for any sign of enemy activity at this most vulnerable of moments, the breaking dawn. The last fighting or wiring patrol would have re-entered the perimeter wire an hour or so before. Slowly the rising sun would thaw cold hands, drying out battledress jackets and greatcoats dampened by dew. Under the gaze of the whole platoon standing patrols would be called in one by one, the men moving in that expectant crouching posture unique to soldiers close to the enemy. Quietly, the barbed wire would be pulled aside, the dinner-plate-sized Italian anti-tank mines gently replaced and covered with sand. Stand-to would last an hour, after which the troops would resume their underground existence.

Sentries stood alert on their revetments, bayonets pointed towards the desert, while a brew was boiled up in billycans. By 7 a.m. the first machine guns of the day would rattle out and, because the heat haze would not rise for another two hours, this was an ideal time for sniping. Extra vigilance was always required in the early mornings. Long hard searches with binoculars of the desert floor would be carried out to see if any changes had taken place. Had any enemy patrols been inserted overnight? Long bursts of machine-gun fire played over suspect ground.

A few days after Brownless and his men took over, a German patrol managed to slip past their position, cut through the outer perimeter wire and bring up machine guns. Philip Brownless was inside his own wire conducting the late-evening check of his men's positions before they settled into the night routine of sentry rosters, trench repair and patrolling. As he and his platoon sergeant returned to their command post, suddenly:

> six machine guns started firing right over where we were. We lay flat, with bullets hitting the ground round us and why we weren't hit I never understood. The moment the fire lifted we rushed . . . into our weapon pits. We exchanged fire and one young soldier was hit through the back of the head but the enemy got into the anti-tank ditch and got away.

Though close, the Germans were nevertheless firing blind, and that saved their lives. Sniping by machine gun on fixed lines was used by both sides. It could have a detrimental effect on morale, as Brownless was to discover.

After a week or two I was asked to take over the platoon next door, where morale was bad, and I soon discovered they were scared stiff by the enemy machine-gunning over their position, which happened every single morning. In addition to our light machine guns we had an Italian medium machine gun mounted on its tripod. Corporal Skinner and his mate who manned the gun were a reliable couple: they thoroughly cleaned and oiled it and next morning, as it grew light and before the heat haze got up, we were ready. One of the enemy machine guns opened up and I spotted through my binoculars the white puffs of smoke from it and told Skinner to fire two bursts. I saw where these kicked up the sand and said, 'Up fifty [yards]: two bursts, fire.' The enemy machine gun started to reply but after only three rounds it sputtered and stopped so we knew we had hit something. We put another thirty or forty rounds over that position without them retaliating. Then I picked out some other enemy movement and we shot at that. Every morning at first light we machine-gunned anything I could pick out, and from that day onwards we were never machine-gunned in the morning again. Morale improved! We never lacked ammunition as the troops were always digging up more boxes the Italians had left behind.

The interminable days would stretch out, enlivened only by unfriendly visits from the sky. Those men not involved in sentry or air raid duty would catch up on the sleep denied them by the night's activities. The day would end as it had begun, with the daily fireworks display far in the distance over the harbour, after which – if it was dark enough – the ships would again rush in. Along the Red Line the murderous business of the night would once more get under way.

8 » ED DUDA

With the onset of the cold season in early October rumours swept the garrison that a 'big push' was soon to take place from Egypt in another attempt to break the siege. Rumours, observed Ray Ellis of the South Notts Hussars, were part of life in Tobruk and mostly spurious, but 'this one persisted and it began to have the ring of truth about it'. This time the 70th British Division inside Tobruk would break out and join up with the men of the advancing 8th Army in a battle confidently expected to last three days. In fact, it was to last three long weeks. Meanwhile, aware that the British would attempt at some stage to repeat Battleaxe, Rommel was determined once and for all to crush Tobruk, preparing for an assault through the south-eastern defences (where the British and Australians had attacked in February 1941) in mid-November. He had only been prevented from doing this earlier because of devastating losses to his convoys in the Mediterranean. It was clear to the Allies that Rommel was up to something: for weeks German and Italian troops pressed forward in this sector, building up wired and mined positions and gradually venturing closer to the perimeter defences.

Captain John Marriott, adjutant of the 2nd Battalion, Royal Leicestershire Regiment, observed the telltale signs. German and Italian shelling was increasingly heavy, as was their patrolling, and the Stukas even neglected the harbour for periods to concentrate on infantry and artillery positions along the south-eastern sector of the Red Line. During one attack Marriott looked up to see a flock of Stukas gathering in a predatory circle high above B Company's position. Calling up the company signaller on the telephone, Marriott asked Private Fretwell for a running commentary to take the signaller's mind off the danger.

Fretwell chatted away unconcernedly until he yelled, 'I think this bastard's coming for company HQ; he's opening his crooked feet and there's a dirty great bomb coming screaming down – he's pulled out of sight – it is coming at us!' Marriott heard an enormous crash and saw smoke and dust billow from the position. As the Stukas flew off an ominous silence fell over the battlefield, but a few minutes later Fretwell called up: 'Sorry, sir, the instrument was blown out of my hand!' 'Are there any casualties?' Marriott asked. 'Not sure yet,' came the calm reply. 'The protective wire is hit, the overhead covering has partly gone and the four lads who were asleep in the dugout are awake and coughing, and my ears are ringing with the blast. The sentry's been hurt on the shoulder.'

In the area of the Ras el Medawar salient, now defended by the Polish Carpathian Brigade, the three German infantry battalions were relieved by Italian troops and in the east and south-east their patrols pushed back no-man's-land, eliminating the forward British outposts. This aggressive encroachment resulted in the loss of two Australian posts well forward of the wire in the El Adem area – Plonk and Bondi, some 700 yards south of the Red Line – but despite two attempts to recover these positions by the garrison using Matildas of 4th RTR they remained in Axis hands. Then in late October the forward British posts on Jack and Jill in the east both fell to German night attack and no-man's-land shrank from four to one thousand yards. Enemy troops were now clearly seen every day, and Boys anti-tank rifles, useless for their original purpose, were used to snipe at human targets at up to 1,500 yards. 'There were fresh diggings appearing every morning,' recalled Leonard Tutt, watching from the top of one of the artillery observation towers in the eastern sector, and 'track marks of troop carriers coming much nearer the wire. The sight of a man, carelessly unaware that he had wandered from the dead ground into our view, gave a lot of thought.'

On 9 November the enemy-held pimple at Plonk was once again attacked, this time by Major Hugh Vaux's D Company of the Durham Light Infantry. Plonk was by now even more strongly defended, however, and ringed by three separate barriers of barbed wire, and the Durhams' attack failed even to penetrate the wire. Every day an old

Heinkel traversed the skies above the Red Line, clearly mapping and photographing and too high to be concerned by machine-gun fire. Every night enemy patrols were more ambitious, seeking the locations of crossing points over the anti-tank ditch, and on 15 November rubber dinghies were found, to much alarm, on a beach inside the wire. On 17 November it rained hard – the heaviest and most sustained rainfall in memory – which had the advantage of keeping enemy aircraft out of the air, although temperatures were low.

Rommel's plan to break into Tobruk using the 90th Light and Bologna Divisions coincided almost exactly, in terms of both time and geography, with the plan prepared by Major General Reginald Scobie (Morshead's successor) to break out in conjunction with the British 8th Army's offensive from Egypt (Operation Crusader). Extraordinarily, both sides decided upon the same day for their respective operations: 20 November 1941. Rommel moved the 90th into position opposite the south-eastern defences under conditions of great secrecy, the subterfuge extending to the wearing by German troops of Italian helmets, lent by the Bologna Division. Heading straight for them, Scobie planned a phased advance with his newly arrived division – and his armoured vehicles – to the Ed Duda escarpment south-east of the perimeter. This escarpment, along which ran the relief road Rommel had built to bypass the port, dominated the terrain north-west to Tobruk, and also south-east, where two miles further on the desert rose to the escarpment above Sidi Rezegh.

Operation Crusader involved advancing the 8th Army (118,000 troops with 723 tanks) into Libya, with the 30th Corps under Lieutenant General Norrie tasked to undertake an armoured sweep to destroy Rommel's armour in the desert south and south-east of Tobruk before heading to the coast to relieve the port, and the slower, infantry-based 13th Corps under Lieutenant General Godwin-Austen (with 123 'infantry' tanks – Matildas and Valentines) rolling up the enemy frontier posts at Halfaya, Sollum, Sidi Omar and Fort Capuzzo. Numerically, the British tank force was formidable: 210 were Matildas, and the remainder the faster tanks of each of the armoured brigades. However, the 158 new A15 Crusaders, which had performed badly during Battleaxe, remained a maintenance nightmare and the bulk of the rest were old cruisers and 165 of the new American Stuarts – nicknamed 'Honeys'. Most of the troops were new to their equipment and poorly trained.

Rommel boasted a similar number of men, with about 560 tanks of which two-thirds were German panzers. The Italian 21st Corps (Brescia, Trento, Bologna and Pavia Divisions) was besieging Tobruk, the Trieste Division was at Bir Hacheim and the Ariete Armoured Division was dug in behind a massive minefield at Bir el Gubi. In his newly formed *Panzergruppe Afrika* Rommel had the experienced Afrika Korps consisting of the 90th Light Division, and the 15th and 21st Panzer Divisions, the latter previously known as the 5th Light Division, and re-equipped with new medium Mark III panzers mounting 50-millimetre guns. Also in the Axis armoury were the 88-millimetre anti-aircraft gun employed in the anti-tank role, and the powerful 50-millimetre anti-tank gun. It was to be these hugely effective weapons (only twelve of the former and 108 of the latter) that time and again negated any numerical advantage enjoyed by the British, by repeatedly bringing their armoured thrusts to abrupt, fiery ends.

*

Operation Crusader began on 18 November, with 30th Corps (7th Armoured Division, 22nd Guards Motorized Brigade, 4th Armoured Brigade and the 1st South African Division) crossing the wire and advancing deep into Libya, hoping to find, engage and destroy the German armour in the desert vastness far to the south of Tobruk. The offensive came as a surprise to Rommel but any advantage was soon squandered by the British. Lieutenant General Sir Alan Cunningham, the 8th Army commander, had not yet learned the secret of Rommel's success – concentration of strength – and made the usual British mistake of dispersing his force, weakening his otherwise formidable thrust from the outset. By the second day of the operation the corps was widely separated, and although the airfield at Sidi Rezegh, only twenty miles south-east of Tobruk had been captured, its dispersal meant the force was not strong enough to deliver the knockout blow. Inside Tobruk the garrison awaited the code word Pop, which would indicate that the panzer divisions had been smashed and their breakout towards the Ed Duda escarpment was imminent. By the evening of 20 November, following much confusion across a widely disparate battlefield, the centre of gravity for 30th Corps had moved to Sidi Rezegh. 'Pop' came through that evening, and amid entirely misplaced optimism that the Germans were on the run, the Tobruk garrison was ordered to attack for the first time in nine months.

Early the following morning a diversionary attack was launched by the Polish Carpathian Brigade in the western area, while the three infantry battalions leading the breakout – 2nd Black Watch, 2nd King's Own and 1st Beds and Herts – came up into the sector of the line (centred on R66) manned by the 2nd Leicesters, who worked feverishly to prepare the front for the breakout. A special machine-gun group in the Leicesters, under the command of Major Jack Bryant comprising fifty Brens plus captured Spandaus and Bredas, had been created to provide fire support to the troops of the King's Own (attacking Butch) and the Black Watch (assaulting Jill and Tiger). In the cold and gloom of the morning the men of the King's Own under Lieutenant Colonel 'Crackers' Creedon trudged grimly through the position, the tanks of 7th RTR creaking and squealing slowly after them.

The Tobruk Tanks had 158 armoured vehicles (69 Matildas, 32 old cruisers, 25 Mark VIs and 32 armoured cars) at the start of that first day of what was predicted to be a three-day battle. The troops had lain out on the desert all night, provided with blankets brought up specially and fortified with a slug of rum. A whispered reveille was sounded at 5.15 a.m. At 6.20 a.m. precisely, H Hour, one hundred guns of the garrison's artillery – having hoarded ammunition for weeks and moved to new firing positions during the night – opened fire. Sergeant Ray Ellis was commanding No.1 Gun in A Troop of 425 Battery, South Notts Hussars, and had spent most of the night in the cold and wet getting ready for the bombardment. There was no shelter from the wind and rain, and only the constant activity during that day prevented the men from dwelling on the fact that they were soaking wet, muddy and miserable. During the first day of the battle each of the sixteen British 25-pounders (Rommel, in contrast, had over 200 guns in Böttcher's Artillery Group ready to attack Tobruk) fired over 900 shells. The physical demands of loading and dragging the gun out of the ground (into which it embedded itself after each shot) were huge, and when there was no firing the gunners had to try to sleep in waterlogged trenches, it being too dangerous to remain above ground. The Italians had perfected the art of firing their Bredas at such an angle that the dangerous little shell was easily able to take a man's head off or would descend almost vertically without any warning to explode in trenches or gun positions. Their favourite targets were gunners, who were forced to operate in largely fixed locations and to man their guns without the protection an infantryman would have when fighting from his trench, or a cavalryman would have in his tank.

At 6.30 a.m. – Z Hour – on the left flank of the breakout A and D Companies of the King's Own Regiment led the attack on Butch, while the Black Watch prepared to attack on the right. Each section of the King's Own was armed with a Bren gun and thirteen Bren magazines; each rifleman carried a hundred rounds in bandoliers and three grenades; each platoon had two Thompson sub-machine guns and one anti-tank rifle. The enemy retaliated immediately with a tremendous artillery barrage but most shells fell behind the attacking troops. Ten Matildas of 7th RTR also moved forward, followed by Bren carriers, but most were immediately disabled by mines. Despite this, D Company moved forward steadily and with a final rush captured Butch at the point of the bayonet. It was a desperate and bloody – albeit mercifully short-lived – fight. The position – held to British surprise by German rather than Italian infantry – fell in ten minutes, but at the cost of thirty dead and over seventy other casualties. An even greater surprise was that two of the German infantry battalions (the 155th and 200th) were from the 361st Afrika Regiment, made up entirely of Germans who had served in the French Foreign Legion. Many had fifteen years experience of fighting in North Africa and Indochina and were formidable troops.

With Butch secure, the remainder of the King's Own turned their attention to the well-wired and heavily mined Jill, which they attacked from the left while B Company of the Black Watch advanced with bayonets fixed from the front. In this attack things went wrong from the start. The 7th RTR Matildas that had supported the King's Own attack on Butch should in fact have gone forward with the Highlanders against Jill. Unwilling to delay their attack, the Black Watch advanced without waiting for the promised armour. For several hundred yards the widely dispersed company, the pipes of Pipe Major Rab Roy skirling 'Highland Laddie', 'Lawson's Men' and 'The Black Bear' through the dark dawn, moved forward. Suddenly, the enemy trenches opened up with a barrage of fire and flame. German machine guns hidden in the camel thorn devastated the advancing Highlanders: all five company officers and seven of thirteen NCOs were hit. Given the slaughter there seemed no choice for the remnants but to charge. Led by the bayonet, inspired by the pipes, the remaining Highlanders surged forward. The position was taken, but only ten men were left standing as the last Germans raised their hands in surrender.

'In due course,' wrote a watching journalist, William Forrest of London's *News Chronicle*, who had been bottled up in Tobruk for three months, 'Jack fell down and Jill came tumbling after.' One watching gunner officer, staggered by the bayonet charge he had just witnessed, could only say of the Jocks, 'They were absolutely terrific; I've never seen anything like it.' One Black Watch officer, lying badly wounded in the arm and leg, came round to the sound of 'Highland Laddie' wafting across the battlefield and promptly got to his feet, straightened his webbing, picked up his Webley revolver and began to advance again towards the sound of the fighting. D Company then rushed through the survivors of B Company on Jill, still without the promised tanks, in the direction of Tiger, where lay entrenched an entire German machine-gun battalion. Meanwhile the Vickers machine guns of the Northumberland Fusiliers were brought up to Butch to play their deadly music.

During the previous night the Germans had laid an anti-tank minefield running from Jill on the left to the positions known as Tugun on the right. All that morning the British tanks, first of 7th and then 1st RTR, stumbled into this minefield, were immobilized and came under infantry fire from the watching German positions. Four Matildas from Captain Walter Benzie's C Squadron were brought to a stop, their crews sniped at and several men killed. Until they were cleared by hand, these mines almost brought the tank support to a complete halt. Brigadier Willison, commander of the Tobruk Tanks since September and in overall command of the breakout, ordered both 1st and 4th RTR to skirt the minefield as best they could and make their way to Tiger. In the meantime the Black Watch again advanced without support

In the assault on Tiger, Pipe-Major Roy was twice wounded but continued to play. It was a fearsome, Somme-like battle, the Highlanders marching forward into the German fire as steadily as the Argylls had at Sidi Barrani the year before, the constant whine of bullets, the rapid staccato of machine-gun fire, the crump of mortar and artillery shells and the crack of exploding anti-personnel mines leaving a crumpled patchwork of bodies on the desert floor. 'Isn't this the Black Watch?' shouted Captain Mungo Stirling, the adjutant, already wounded in the leg, when machine-gun bullets scythed through the advancing ranks and tempted men to seek the sanctuary of the ground. 'Then charge!' Waving his men on with his blackthorn stick, he was shot down and killed. Where they could, comrades would thrust a bayoneted rifle into the ground to guide the stretcher bearers following up. The path to Jill and then Tiger became a forest of inverted rifles.

Only now did the Matildas arrive from the direction of Butch to the north, Colonel Rusk of the Black Watch, having chased all over the battlefield for these errant beasts, standing up in one to provide direction to the tank commanders and leadership to his men. Pipe Sergeant McNicol, with Pipe Major Roy wounded now for the third time, played the remainder of the battalion forward on to Tiger, which was by now entirely covered in a layer of dust and smoke. By 10.15 a.m. it had been taken, but at a horrendous cost. In the hardest battle the Black Watch had fought since Loos in 1915, only eight officers and 160 men from the 632 that had started out that morning remained. Four hundred and sixty-four Highlanders lay in bloody heaps all the way back to Jill and the Tobruk perimeter. Some survived the long wait for stretcher bearers; many did not.

In order to protect his right flank, Willison ordered A Company of the Beds and Herts and B Company of the 2nd Battalion Queens Regiment, together with the remaining Matildas of 7th RTR, to attack the enemy position at Tugun. If this flank remained insecure the advance on Ed Duda, when it was ordered, would be especially vulnerable. The initial attack on Tugun was completely successful, 185

Italians being captured. It was only later that the jubilant infantrymen realized that they had not taken the whole position, but only the outer edge of an extensive series of fortifications. Nevertheless a foothold had been established.

Tiger and the margins of Tugun were the limits of the British advance that day. A wedge four miles deep and two wide had been driven into the enemy positions in the direction of the Ed Duda escarpment. This high ground overlooked the desert all the way back to the Tobruk perimeter and controlled the route of the Trigh Capuzzo in the shallow valley further south. But the cost had been high, not just in infantry but also tanks. By the end of the day 1st RTR had only eight cruisers and thirteen Mark VIs left from an original twenty-six cruisers and nineteen light tanks, and had lost twenty-two crew. O'Carroll's 4th RTR was down to twenty-five Matildas.

Meanwhile, out in the desert, the 8th Army's plans were in complete disarray. Late on the 19th the 7th Armoured Brigade had captured the airfield at Sidi Rezegh, which sat on a slight escarpment above the Trigh Capuzzo, but an attempt to push on to Ed Duda by 6th RTR was halted personally by Rommel, who took command of a battery of 88s. Although the Allied plan was to reinforce the Sidi Rezegh position as soon as possible with the South African Division, after which a link-up with the Tobruk garrison could be achieved, this never happened as the South Africans were mauled by the Ariete Division at Bir Gubi and made no further progress north. The 21st Panzer Division retook the airfield on 21 November while the 15th Panzer Division all but destroyed the 4th Armoured Brigade. Operation Crusader now began to unravel. Sunday 23 November – *Totensonntag* – German remembrance day for the victims of the Great War, resulted in considerable losses of British armour across a confusing desert battlescape. By the end of the day the 8th Army had only 44 runners left from its tank force, although urgent efforts were being made to recover and repair damaged vehicles. Only the New Zealand 6th Infantry Brigade seemed to have had had any success, seizing Point 175 some seven miles east of Sidi Rezegh and capturing a sizeable part of the Afrika Korps HQ. Norrie's 13th Corps was ordered to take over what had been the 30th Corps offensive, with instructions to take Sidi

Rezegh and Ed Duda 'at all costs'. Scobie's 70th Division and the salient from Tobruk, now five miles long and four miles wide, also came under Norrie's command.

In the salient Brigadier Willison's troops worked hard to consolidate their positions and to prepare for the next and final stage of the breakout: to meet up with the advancing 8th Army on the Ed Duda ridge. The plan was for the salient to form the corridor into Tobruk for the relieving 8th Army approaching from the direction of Sidi Rezegh. On 24 November the Leicesters advanced from the perimeter and took responsibility for the northern edge of the salient, which at 2,000 yards long was easily covered by fire during the day but more porous at night. On the right was A Company, in the old Jack position, and D Company on the left occupied the enemy's old posts opposite the perimeter, which comprised mutually supporting platoon areas surrounded by mines and wire, each with three triangular-shaped section posts. The 70th Division now worked hard to expand the salient both north and south-west, as it was under constant enemy observation and fire from machine guns, artillery and a single 88. Lethal against vehicles, the 88's high-velocity flat-trajectory shell had limited effect against entrenched troops.

On the night of 25/26 November C Company advanced north, with the support of tanks, to attack a position around a wrecked plane. The tanks were stopped by mines although the Leicesters pressed on regardless. No 13 Platoon, taking 50 per cent casualties, succeeded in cutting through the enemy wire and capturing the position. Protecting the newly won post, Sergeant Forrester of the Leicesters encountered an enemy patrol, into which he instantly charged, cutting down two enemy soldiers with the bayonet and forcing the other nine to surrender.

On the right, southern flank of the salient successful though costly efforts were made to eject the enemy from positions south of Tugun known as Dalby Square by both 1st and 4th RTR and the 2nd Battalion the York and Lancaster Regiment. An attempt had been made on the night of 24/25 November to take the remainder of Tugun. It was not a success, the weight of fire being so severe that the men were forced to the ground, where they remained throughout the night, unable to move. Then, on the afternoon of the 25th, an extraordinary display of courage unnerved the defenders. Second Lieutenant Ben Thomas watched a second attack by forty-five men under the command of Second Lieutenant Teddy Ablett set out in broad daylight with 1,000 yards of open ground to cover without any tank or air support.

> These forty-five men just walked slowly towards Tugun armed only with rifles, a Bren gun or two and some hand grenades. One hundred yards, 200 onwards up to about 300 yards from the enemy before they let loose. Here and there a man went down, hit or taking temporary cover. But Teddy strode on and Sergeant Major Kemp with him, until they hit the defence wire which they bashed down or found a gap.
>
> They disappeared from sight and it seemed that about eight or nine men followed in. Then there seemed an interminable lull when one couldn't tell what had happened, but all firing ceased on both sides. Then suddenly figures appeared signalling success – then more and more figures and some eighty Italians had given themselves up and were straggling back over the ground covered in the attack to surrender. In fact, they gave in when face to face with the first few of our men to get in ... Unfortunately Teddy, first man in, had a hand-to-hand struggle for a moment or two and lost an eye in the process: neither he nor anyone else knows quite how.

With the Beds and Herts now in Tugun, it was left to the 2nd Battalion Queens Regiment to launch a night attack westward on Bondi from Tugun during the night of 24/25 November. It proved a disaster for the Queen's Own, and Bondi was not evacuated by the enemy until their general withdrawal began two weeks later. 'One of the Bren carriers carrying the mortar platoon was blown up on a minefield,' recalled Sergeant Harry Atkins:

> The driver, Hurst, was badly injured. CSM Fred Jode and I lifted him from the wreck, but it was obvious that he was beyond help and he died. Georgie Poole, a North Country lad, was then badly wounded. Captain Armstrong, the company second-in-command and a new arrival, was in conference with the company commander, Captain

P.R.H. Kealey, when a mortar bomb landed among them and Captain Armstrong was killed, and Corporal North, one of my section commanders, was shot dead as he lay close to me.

Heroism such as that displayed by Teddy Ablett was not unusual within the salient. On Sunday 23 November, as preparations were under way for the attack on Dalby Square, Private Frank Harrison, working the radio sets in the back of Brigadier Willison's command vehicle, heard news of the fate of two of the King's Dragoon Guards armoured cars sent out to search for the South Africans, who were thought (wrongly as it transpired) to be trying to make their way from the Sidi Rezegh escarpment north across the Trigh Capuzzo to the Ed Duda ridge. Instead of the 8th Army, they had run into heavy fire in the area of Wolf, which was still strongly defended by the enemy. Lieutenant Beames's armoured car was hit first and his driver killed. Beames managed to get out of the vehicle, but was wounded in the arm and both legs. The second vehicle, under the command of Lieutenant Franks, was also hit, and all four members of the crew killed.

When news of this contact came over the radio, Lieutenant Colonel O'Carroll, CO of 4th RTR, ordered two of his Matildas preparing for the assault on Dalby Square to change direction south-east to rescue the unfortunate cavalrymen. One of these Matildas was commanded by Captain Philip 'Pips' Gardner. Finding the stricken vehicles still under heavy fire, Gardner instructed the second tank to provide covering fire while he tried to recover the wounded from Lieutenant Beames's car. When he reached it, he decided to try to tow the vehicle back, but to do so required getting out of his tank. Frank Harrison listened in over the command radio:

> Then his problems began. He found that he couldn't budge the tow rope fixed along the side of the tank. He went to the rear of the tank and tried the one attached there. This came free, but in order for him to be able to use it, driver Trooper Robertson had to turn the tank round. Gardner signalled to him through the tank visor to do this, and he began the manoeuvre. The men inside the tank turret had no idea what was happening and Lance Corporal McTier, who was firing the Besa [machine-gun], suddenly found himself

being turned off his target. Trooper Richards, the wireless operator, who was now acting as loader, put his head out of the turret to find out what was happening and was killed immediately and fell back inside the tank.

McTier pulled Richards's body away, and despite the enemy fire stuck his head out of the turret so that he could hear Captain Gardner's instructions. Gardner managed to attach the rope to the stricken armoured car but then saw Beames lying wounded on the ground. Picking the wounded officer up, he signalled to McTier to take the strain and back up, but at that moment Gardner was himself struck in the leg by a bullet and knocked off his feet, and the tow rope snapped. Fortunately the bullet had not broken Gardner's leg and he managed to pick himself up and half-drag, half-carry Beames to the tank. Lifting Beames onto the side of his Matilda, Gardner then pulled himself up and ordered McTier to reverse. As the Matilda began backing away the gallant Gardner was hit again, this time in the arm.

By this time the second Matilda was alongside pouring Besa fire into the enemy positions, and the batteries of 1st RHA were also laying down heavy fire to cover their withdrawal. With both Matildas now moving away from the fray McTier climbed out of the turret and helped the wounded Gardner hold on to Beames. Willison, in his command vehicle listening to these extraordinary events on the command radio net, turned to Harrison and said of Pip Gardner, 'That man is going to get the Victoria Cross.' As the tank crawled back past his HQ Willison marched out and saluted its gallant crew. For extraordinary bravery and perseverance in the face of overwhelming odds, Gardner was indeed awarded Britain's highest award for gallantry.

Despite the expansion of the salient, it nevertheless remained vulnerable on its three flanks. Two nights after the initial attack on the area of the wrecked plane to the north of the corridor, the Leicesters mounted a full battalion attack, with four companies, again supported by tanks of 7th RTR and the guns of the Essex Yeomanry, to clear German positions firing into the corridor and hindering British freedom of movement. Again the toughness and determination of the infantry brought about success. With 800 yards to go before the enemy positions were reached, the tanks hit an old enemy defensive minefield and could not get through. They maintained heavy fire for a while on the enemy positions in a dazzling display of noise and light but were forced to stop as the infantry neared its objective. The yeomanry 25-pounders also provided heavy fire at the start of the attack, but were then switched to support other operations.

Held up initially on the enemy's forward positions, Second Lieutenant Dane Vanderspar managed to insert his platoon over the enemy wire and into two of their four posts. By now the attackers had virtually exhausted their supplies of ammunition and grenades, and in the words of John Marriott 'the battle developed into a shouting match of broken English and German, each side calling on the other to surrender'. Fortunately for the Leicesters, the Germans decided to give up, abandoning their positions soon after. The Leicesters, with the loss of eighteen men, had succeeded in widening the corridor by 800 yards.

*

Out in the southern desert the battle between Rommel's *Panzergruppe Afrika* and the 8th Army raged confusedly. On the 25th Rommel launched an armoured thrust to the Egyptian border at Sidi Omar, in an attempt to destabilize the British entirely and panic Cunningham into a precipitate withdrawal. It very nearly worked, but in the end Rommel's drive ran out of steam (and fuel), although it added yet more complexity to an already complicated battle. General Auchinleck replaced Cunningham with Ritchie, and demanded that the 8th Army stand and fight to the last tank. The New Zealanders were ordered to advance to the long ridge skirting the southern fringe of the Tobruk perimeter to capture the escarpment with Belhamed to the east and Ed Duda two miles to the west, and to recapture Sidi Rezegh from the three German battalions Rommel had left to defend this vital location. After this, the long-anticipated link-up with the Tobruk garrison could be achieved. By the 25th, however, it was clear that this was not going to happen any time soon; instead, Scobie took the initiative, ordering his men onto the Ed Duda escarpment on 26 November.

This time, unlike during the breakout itself, Willison ensured that cooperation between infantry, artillery and armour was faultless. The Matildas moved first, accompanied by Z Company of the Royal Northumberland Fusiliers, with their Vickers heavy machine guns in Bren carriers under the command of Captain J.J.B. Jackman. Their task was to get onto the escarpment in order to allow the following infantry – 1st Essex – to secure it. By 1 p.m. the Matildas and Northumberland Fusiliers had made it to the base of the escarpment, the 1st Essex waiting four miles back in trucks, ready to move up to occupy the position. The struggle for the ridge was heavy and sustained, and for a time it was not thought that the tanks and the Fusiliers would be able to hold it against the weight of fire they were receiving.

On the Tobruk side of the escarpment David Prosser, a Movietone cameraman, was filming the distant battle. He could see artillery shells bursting among the tanks and the fearsome explosions as the hit Matildas 'brewed up'. Even where he was the desert was a dangerous place. 'Sometimes a man would be struck down beside you by a stray splinter from a burst,' he wrote. 'The difficulty with these shells was that the splinters went such a very long way, so that you might stand up a few seconds after a burst in the distance, thinking that they would have settled by then, only to hear a heavy smack on the ground alongside seeing a splinter as big as your fist drop at your feet.'

Then the attack reached the crest of the escarpment and with it a portion of the relief road which ran across the top. With the Matilda tanks now in hull-down positions firing as rapidly as possible to suppress the enemy artillery and machine-gun fire, the Fusiliers were able to site their weapons on the ridge and began engaging targets in the shallow valley beyond, where the enemy had camps and gun batteries. The Northumberland Fusiliers and their machine guns were distinctly vulnerable. Captain Jackman rushed from post to post, coordinating fire. One of his soldiers, Fusilier Richard Dishman, recalled that the company commander came up to his Vickers position and 'lay down on the gun line, and began to observe through his binoculars. He then gave us the order to fire on a truck and cyclist [on the Trigh Capuzzo]. "Give them a burst," he said, and just as these words were said a mortar bomb dropped just in front of our left-hand gun, wounding three and killing Captain Jackman and Corporal Gare instantly.' For his inspirational leadership during this battle, which was decisive in the capture of the Ed Duda ridge, Jackman was awarded a posthumous Victoria Cross.

At 1.45 p.m., with the Matildas and Northumberland Fusiliers holding their own on the northern edge of the escarpment, the order for the main infantry advance was given, and 1st Essex moved off to follow the armour, Bren gun carriers leading the way. The tanks had done their job well in spite of intense artillery and mortar fire, but as the carriers drew closer to the escarpment they too came under direct artillery fire. Half of the carriers were destroyed with the loss of nearly forty men. The Reverend John Quinn, regimental chaplain, went forward with the troops during the attack on Ed Duda. He got more than he bargained for:

> Finding a Bren carrier going forward to bring back another damaged carrier, I got a lift forward. But I got a bit alarmed how far forward we were going, far further than I should ever have wished. First we passed the Matilda tanks, which had stopped, then we passed through the infantry advancing with fixed bayonets through a tornado of enemy shelling.
>
> Suddenly there was a terrific explosion, and we were enveloped in a cloud of smoke, and we were half-blown, half-scrambled out of the carrier and fell on the ground. I was surprised to see that I was still alive and later that all my limbs were all complete apart from a pain on the knee.

The driver and his companion had both been killed; soldiers of the Northumberland Fusiliers helped the padre to safety in a slit trench.

The RAF, after months absent from the skies over Tobruk, had reappeared in force to support the garrison and take on the clouds of Stukas that could otherwise have prevented the breakout, but as the Essex advanced, tragedy struck. A flight of South African Air Force Maryland bombers called up by the New Zealanders on Belhamed, unaware of what Willison was doing on the Ed Duda front, dropped their bombs with devastating effect on the carriers of D Company, leading the Essex charge. Eighteen men including the company commander, Major Robinson, were killed. Lieutenant Philip Brownless, heading forward in a truck with his men of C Company, was shocked to see a curtain of flame and smoke descend upon the carriers only 200 yards ahead. But within seconds they were through the carnage and moving on to their objective, the left side of the Ed Duda escarpment, undeterred despite the shells falling among the bouncing column of dust-churning trucks. Eventually the tank line was reached. Passing the hull-down vehicles at the escarpment, Brownless and his men leapt from their vehicles.

I put two sections forward, and one following twenty yards behind, all in extended order, and started moving east, along the bottom of the escarpment. The shelling was extremely heavy. Shells were landing all around us. I kept them moving as hard as I could. We kept lying down as the salvos started to land, but the men were marvellous the way they were up as I shouted, 'Up' . . . One of my men fell, hit in the crutch.

As we advanced over the top, shells were bursting everywhere. The road was 150 yards in front, with a continuous storm of shells bursting down its length, and knocking the telegraph poles about like pea-sticks. I kept shouting to the sections to keep well spaced. We reached the road, which was our objective. There were some deafening explosions as shells landed right amongst the platoon. I was blown over, and so were some others. I felt myself and was surprised to find that I was all right. I could not see a thing. The dust cleared. It was obvious that if we remained in the area they were shelling on that rocky ridge there would not be many of us left . . . I shouted, 'Advance!' and moved a hundred yards forward of the road, made the platoon get down, and placed my sections, one covering the road and the other two forward.

Despite the fire, the Essex quickly occupied the ridge in support of the lone company of Northumberland Fusiliers, who were firing on a rich selection of targets in the broad valley ahead of them, through the centre of which ran the Trigh Capuzzo. In spite of the battle raging on the ridge, German and Italian vehicles continued to use the road. The men lay down and quickly built stone sangars – or reused now-empty German ones – to prepare for the inevitable counter-attack, while fifty German prisoners were sent to the rear. The 1st Essex did not have to wait long for Rommel's reply. Immediately ahead of his position Brownless saw three German panzers crawling up the bare rise towards him. A number of D Company men who had gone further forward came running back: Brownless and Lieutenant Browne, the company second-in-command, collared these men and distributed them among the company before calling up battalion HQ at the base of the escarpment behind them for tank support. The Essex had no anti-tank weapons. To Brownless's great relief a light tank then appeared behind him and courageously engaged the panzers single-handedly. Perhaps assuming that the lone tank was the harbinger of many more, the panzers backed off.

By 3 p.m. the threat to the front of the position had reduced, but at the cost of Lieutenant Parry, the young stand-in company commander from C Company, who was killed. In the confusion of the fighting enemy vehicles still tried to use the relief road, which now ran through the battalion position. A German staff car came careering up the road from the direction of Belhamed to the east: two bursts of Bren gun fire killed the driver and sent the vehicle crashing off the road. As the day developed, the bag included three trucks and three more cars.

Furious that they had been pushed off this vital ridge – which not only dominated the desert into Tobruk but also carried the relief road – the Germans were determined to recover it at all costs, and desperate counter-attacks were thrown against the point of the British salient. Artillery in the shallow valley between the Ed Duda escarpment and the Sidi Rezegh ridge further to the south continued to drop shells onto the newly acquired Essex positions, where the men were feverishly trying to dig themselves into the solid rock with shovels, helmets and bayonets. Brownless recalled that the mortar fire was continuous and intensely frightening: 'The Germans used about eight mortars at a time, and divided the area into quarters, each of which they concentrated on in turn, and always fired rapidly. How I remember lying flat in the bottom of my weapon pit with my batman, terrified as we listened to the swish of bombs as they came down, and then the deadening crash as they landed all around us.'

Immediately after the attack on the front of the position of the sorely depleted D Company – which numbered forty men at the end of the day, down from 120 at the start – an attack on the right flank, following the road leading from El Adem, was launched on B Company. This was held, and a spirited counter-attack produced a bag of eighty German prisoners, who were sent trudging to the rear. At the same time the battalion's left flank was struck, from the direction of Belhamed, but this too was repulsed.

During that first night on the escarpment enemy forces closed in on the thin British perimeter. Meanwhile, following days of desperate fighting, the first exhausted elements of the 8th Army arrived inside the salient: the 19th New Zealand Infantry Battalion and a Squadron of the 44th RTR managed to link up with Willison's Tobruk Tanks at Belhamed. The first, albeit tenuous, link had been established, but it was a psychological achievement rather than a practical one. The Kiwis were delighted to have reached what they mistakenly thought was the sanctuary of Tobruk. 'We soon realized,' recalled Captain John Marriott of the Leicesters, 'that they were looking on Tobruk as a haven of refuge, and that they were far from a relieving force.' Indeed, General Godwin-Austen announced the link-up of the Tobruk garrison and the New Zealanders with the signal 'Tobruk and I both relieved.'

The battle was far from won, however, and much remained in the balance. Control of Sidi Rezegh, which dominated the Trigh Capuzzo in the valley below the Ed Duda escarpment, would be fiercely contested by Axis and British armour for several days to come. Rommel had been persuaded that Sidi Rezegh was vulnerable to a pincer movement from the Tobruk garrison breakout in the north and the 8th Army in the south, and ordered that it be reinforced, at the same time withdrawing his forces from the speculative and wasteful sally towards the Egyptian frontier. As it moved west the 15th Panzer Division overwhelmed and destroyed the 5th New Zealand Brigade at Sidi Azeiz. Unable to fight tanks with rifles and grenades, the Kiwis were forced to surrender, and 800 were taken prisoner including the brigade commander.

The days which followed were ones of constant though confusing and disparate battles across the desert. It was often difficult to tell friend from foe and to understand exactly what the enemy intended. The Germans and Italians, however, had mastered the art of killing British tanks, using panzers in concentrated forces and the deadly 88s to maximum effect in ambushes. The fighting swirled about the breakout corridor and over and around the Sidi Rezegh escarpment.

At the front end of the 70th Division salient lay the exposed 1st Essex on the Ed Duda ridge, upon whom artillery fell like rain, or so it felt to the men, who spent their days trying to improve their inadequate holes in the rock. 'We were shelled with everything,' recalled Brownless, 'from small-bore high-velocity guns to 9-inch howitzers. Quite a few of the 9-inch shells were duds. It was a remarkable sight to see such massive projectiles bounce off the ground, and travel for another 200 or 300 yards, making a queer jerky noise as they spun askew through the air, and then rolling over and over as they hit the ground.' Most of the incoming shells, however, exploded. The day after they seized the ridge Brownless was twenty yards from the company commander, Captain 'Jock' Nelson, and his second-in-command, Lieutenant Browne, when a shell landed among them. When the dust cleared, Nelson ran over to a body prostrate on the ground. 'It was Browne, his limbs twisted horribly, but his face untouched, looking lifelike, except for the eyes, which were still. The shell had landed at his feet as he was talking, and blown him thirty yards away . . . So died one of the youngest and bravest soldiers I had known.'

On 27 November a D Company patrol pushed 2,000 yards across the Trigh Capuzzo to the heights on the southern side of the valley in the hope of contacting the advancing 8th Army. They found only parties of enemy infantry, however, and no sign of the tanks of 30th Corps. Through the valley and along the Trigh Capuzzo German and Italian forces surged, first east and then west, flowing back and forth like the tide, all the while bumping up against the jagged salient thrust out at Ed Duda by the Tobruk garrison. Tutt recalled:

At times the situation was so confused that we did not know what the next few hours would bring. Sometimes we were asked to bring down fire on positions in the rear of our forward troops, indicating that they had been encircled. A tank skirmish took place behind one of our gun positions and we were unable to fire for fear of hitting our own men. We worked out fire tasks in the command post, only to tear them up half-completed as our axis of fire swung through ninety degrees because the battle had changed direction. The sky was permanently darkened by the smoke of burning vehicles and tanks. There were explosions all around us and no fixed base that we could safely call our own. At times we were without food or water and practically out of ammunition because our supply trucks could not thread their way between friend and foe. Often the command post telephone rang to report another casualty to be shuttled down to the hospital. For a number it was too late. Their silent, blanket-wrapped bodies were carried away, all of them good companions, four of them close friends.

Just forward of Ed Duda, on the southern side of the valley, the fleeing Germans had left a battery of medium artillery. These guns were now in the middle of no-man's-land, and the enemy were expected to make an attempt to recover them. Sergeant Ray Ellis volunteered – he was never sure why – to attempt to salvage the guns and bring them into the British lines. The plan was for Ellis to go out to the battery to prepare the guns for recovery, and for Private Jim Martin to rush out in a truck to tow them in one at a time. After the Royal Engineers had made a gap in the wire to allow him through, Ellis started towards the guns:

> There was almost continuous mortar fire coming over at the time and also a great deal of shellfire, which became so heavy at one point that I had to dive for cover . . . My main concern at the time was finding any available cover as I dodged across the windswept ground towards those horribly exposed guns, wishing all the time that I had not been so foolhardy as to volunteer for such an escapade.
>
> The ground was littered with the bodies of men who had fallen in the attack and I felt very vulnerable imagining that every soldier in the German army had me in his sights. When I eventually reached the guns it seemed strange to be among these German guns. There were eight of them in a staggered line, each one surrounded by the usual equipment found on a gun site: ammunition, gun stores, men's equipment, empty cartridges and, in this particular situation, dead bodies . . .
>
> I went first towards the gun at the right of the line, and after a quick inspection of the piece and the gun carriage, I was able to make a start in lowering and centring the gun barrel, fastening the

clamps, releasing the brakes and generally preparing it for movement. This done, I hurriedly made my way towards a pile of rocks which lay in front of the guns ... I threw myself down behind them to wait for the truck, and found myself in company with the body of a British soldier ... He was a private soldier from the Beds and Herts, and had been badly wounded in the lower abdomen. Someone had tied a shell dressing over his wound and dragged him into the cover of the pile of rocks during the battle. There he had been left to die all alone in this bleak, godforsaken desolation. He had bled to death.

Private Jim Martin then sped across the rocky ground in his truck and hitched up the first gun. German artillery was by now firing at the vehicle, but the pair managed to hitch up four guns, each taking about an hour to recover. Then the Germans switched targets to the guns themselves, Ellis risking the whirring shrapnel as he dashed about, seeking cover in the dust beside his silent companion after each effort. 'The noise alone was above imagination,' he recorded, 'the whine of bullets, the scream and crash of shellfire, the roar of aircraft engines overhead, and from time to time the shriek of Stukas as they dived to unload their bombs onto our positions.' By the end of the day Martin had collected the last gun and made it safely back through the wire on the top of Ed Duda. 'Darkness had now fallen,' recalled Ellis, 'but there was no difficulty in finding our way because the sky seemed to be alive with flares.' Back in the gun position the exhausted Ellis was given a swig of rum. Not having eaten all day, it had an immediate effect: rolling himself into a wet blanket, he curled up in his soggy slit trench and fell into a deep sleep.

All the while steady improvements were made to the battalion's defences, but even these were nearly of no avail on the early afternoon of the 29th, when a major German tank and infantry attack by the 15th Panzer Division began on the right. B Company were targeted in an attempt to roll up the British defenders from the western flank. Philip Brownless watched the attack unfold:

German tanks were standing 1,000 yards off our position and shelling us. They started closing in. It was late in the afternoon, and the sun was behind them. Three of our [Matilda] tanks came up on the side of our position, later joined by a fourth ... They started withdrawing in pairs, firing as they went. As the heavy tanks got nearer the position, the German light Mk IIs moved up on our flank, and swept the area with machine-gun fire.

The flimsy stone sangars proved no match for the German tanks, and were destroyed piecemeal, the British anti-tank guns being knocked out one by one. By early evening some twenty-five Panzers had penetrated to the heart of the battalion position and were within 400 yards of Lieutenant Colonel 'Crasher' Nichols's HQ, most of B and A Companies having been killed, wounded or taken prisoner. 'You could plainly see German infantry with our prisoners behind those tanks,' recalled Brownless. The situation was plainly serious, although Nichols remained confident that all was not lost, and that fresh troops with armoured support could drive the enemy from their newly won positions. D Company was managing to hold off infantry attacks on the southern front, and C Company, on the left-hand edge of the escarpment, remained intact. Counter-fire by Matilda tanks was unable to make any headway against the Mark IVs on B Company's old position, however, and a number of Matildas were in flames. But it was now getting dark, and although Brownless feared that the Germans were about to sweep across the rest of the escarpment, they held off, deterred perhaps by the four Matildas which were now to the rear of Brownless's platoon position, firing hull-down over the top of the deafened infantry.

At this critical moment Lieutenant Colonel Nichols asked for the support of two companies of the Australian 2/13th Battalion, those unfortunates left behind when the remainder of Morshead's division were shipped out in October. The Essex Battalion HQ received a warning from Headquarters 70th Division inside Tobruk, running the battle, that it was feared that Ed Duda might very shortly become untenable, and to prepare for a withdrawal back to Tobruk. But this was not how Crasher Nichols saw the situation, and he immediately drafted a signal back to Major General Scobie: 'Ed Duda growing stronger every hour, feel confident we can resist attack from any quarter. Strongly deplore any suggestion of withdrawal.' What Nichols did not know was that the newly appointed commander of the 8th Army –Lieutenant General Ritchie, who had replaced the sacked Cunningham on 26 November – recorded on the same day the view 'if our troops can continue to hold Ed Duda the battle will be won'. Scobie immediately accepted Nichols's assessment and asked the Australians whether they would assist. 'Whatever happens,' Scobie told Lieutenant Colonel 'Bull' Burrows of the 2/13th, 'we must hold Ed Duda.'

While the Australians were being brought up from Tobruk by truck, every British tank that could be spared was rushed to the western edge of the escarpment as fast as their eight miles per hour could manage, and a tank-versus-tank duel then got under way. Philip Brownless had a grandstand view from his weapon pit:

> We could hear our tanks coming up behind us, their engines groaning as they manoeuvred into formation. Suddenly our guns started shelling very accurately just behind the German tanks ... The shellfire stopped, and our tanks started moving through our positions towards the Germans. There were about twelve of them. As soon as their lumbering forms were sighted by the Germans, the area broke into a blaze of fire. White-lighted tracer shells scorched the air. The German light tanks, with their heavy machine guns, were blazing strings of tracer bullets at the tanks. Our tanks deployed. They too were firing furiously. There was confused firing for some time. The Germans showed no sign of withdrawing. One of their tanks had flames pouring from it.

The Matildas (from O'Carroll's 4th RTR) then withdrew to the Essex position.

By 10 p.m. the Diggers had quietly arrived and formed up, facing west. Then, following the Matildas, they launched a counter-attack against the intruders. Nichols offered Lieutenant Colonel Burrows the use of a carrier, but the Australian replied, 'No thanks, Colonel. I'll go in with the boys.' The tanks drove directly into the German armour, and a furious battle again ensued, with tanks manoeuvring across the escarpment. The night was bright with the light of repeated explosions, and bullets cut the parapet of Brownless's trench. In the confusion a panzer 'crashed up to our weapon pits', he recalled, 'went straight over two of the only three pits in my platoon which could be dug down into the ground, wheeled round just in front of my hole, and trundled off in another direction'. Then, with a wild yell the Australians ran in with the bayonet. The attack was spectacularly successful, the entire right wing of the escarpment being recovered, the tanks driven off and most of the German infantry taken prisoner, undoubtedly surprised at the sudden reappearance of the Australians on the battlefield. Captain Walsoe of the 2/13th described this attack, the last Australian action of the siege:

> Suddenly we were away. I remember calling out 'Come on Aussies' and seeing the long line of steadily advancing men on either side of me. Up the slope we went and as we neared the top we heard the jabber of a foreign tongue in which we could soon distinguish '*Englander kommen*'. I fired a green Very light and with a wild roar our chaps charged down upon them. The sight and sound of us must have been too much for the Germans. A few desultory bursts of fire and then they cracked. Some broke and ran; some, cowering in their weapon pits, held up their hands.

Lieutenant Geoffrey Fearnside recalled men:

> . . . running everywhere, whooping like savages. Moonlight gleams and ripples restlessly upon naked bayonets . . . The Germans are yelling confusedly . . . We have surprised them: some have raised their hands and are running in; others stand where they are, uncertain . . .
>
> It is all very confused. We come upon a German lying on the ground. His face is a black shadow underneath his steel helmet . . . A burst of machine-gun fire had disembowelled him and his intestines are hanging from his body. He salutes us frantically with a bleeding arm. '*Bitte!*' he whispers hoarsely, '*Schiesst mich, Kameraden!*'
>
> There is a movement in a sangar just ahead. I go towards it and come face to face with a German soldier. He is bare-headed and his hair is closely cropped. He just stands there, unable to collect his wits . . . I shoot him down like a dog and watch him fall queerly to earth. Even in the moonlight his blood flows vividly red.

The Australians swept over the German position in disciplined fury. By dawn resistance had ceased. The 2/13th had captured 167 prisoners, more than the number of Diggers involved. Later that morning an attempted German counter-attack got no closer than 800 yards before being beaten back. The Diggers, whose arrival had undoubtedly turned the situation on the right flank of the Ed Duda position, remained with the Essex until 3 December, when their Antipodean brethren, the 19th New Zealand Infantry Battalion, who had set out for Tobruk expecting to be welcomed as liberators but instead had reached the salient exhausted on 26 November, replaced them. The situation around the escarpment remained extremely fluid, as German and Italian troops were forced against the sides of the corridor by the pressure of battle. On the morning after the Diggers arrived the Germans launched an assault from the north against the positions held by C Company. A German infantry battalion, supported by artillery and mortar fire, hurled itself against the Essex positions, but the steadiness of the troops, now in their shallow holes for a week under constant attack, turned the tide, and a counter-attack by the New Zealanders broke up the enemy assault. That day – 30 November – Rommel launched a strong attack across the Trigh Capuzzo on Sidi Rezegh, taking prisoner most of what remained of the 24th and 26th New Zealand Brigades.

German attacks were launched repeatedly against the northern side of the corridor. By 30 November there were signs of westward movement by the Germans and Italians, and a battery of 1st RHA fired hard all day against them. Retaliation was not long in coming. The next morning, as the usual cold clammy mist hugged the ground in the pre-dawn darkness, shapes advancing in attack formation were seen by alert sentries forward of the Royal Leicesters' position. A troop of tanks that happened to be resting to the rear of the battalion was alerted, and before long enemy anti-tank guns opened fire and the assault began in a cacophony of noise. Three of the Leicesters' carriers, with captured Spandaus instead of the normal Bren guns, managed to catch the enemy infantry in the flank and caused them heavy damage. Within the hour the assault foundered, at the cost of thirty German dead, twenty wounded and fifty-two sullen prisoners, as well as two captured 50-millimetre anti-tank guns, which had been brought up to deal with the British 25-pounders that had caused such havoc the previous day.

On the extreme left of the escarpment, however, at Belhamed, the 4th New Zealand Brigade was attacked by elements of the 15th Panzer Division, and forced to relinquish its positions. Scobie, desperate to stop the panzers, called up the Polish Carpathian Brigade's anti-tank guns. Two batteries under the command of Lieutenant Colonel Dolega-Cieszkowski arrived on the forward slopes of Belhamed on the afternoon of 30 November, and a third battery was brought up the following day. They arrived with no time to spare. Private Grimsey of the Beds and Herts was dug in on the forward slope of Belhamed when on the early morning of 1 December another German attack came in:

> German infantrymen were swarming towards us. I kept wondering when our captain was going to give the order to fire. We hadn't much ammunition – every bullet must count. As they came towards us the waiting was unbearable. It was a relief when the order to fire came. We halted them to such an extent that some Germans started setting off their smoke canisters to enable them to retreat, taking their casualties with them. We were all jubilant. I got hold of the muzzle of my rifle and burnt my hand; it was so hot from firing.
>
> Our joy didn't last long. Several German tanks appeared on the scene. We had no anti-tank guns, but a Polish unit behind us had one ... The tanks approached steadily and when we had given up hope the Polish gun opened up with tracers. He stopped three tanks with three shells. The others retreated: they must have thought that we had a number of anti-tank guns.

On the western side of the Ed Duda escarpment on the relief road in the direction of El Adem the Axis held positions at Points 157 and 162. (The fact that Ed Duda itself is 158 feet above sea level gives some indication of how minor the variations in height are.) In order to consolidate the British hold on the Ed Duda ridge it was important to take these positions. The Durham Light Infantry were ordered to attack first against Point 157. Once this was taken, the 4th Battalion Border Regiment was to advance through them to capture Point 162.

At 8.30 p.m. on the evening of 5 December the Durhams began their three-and-a-half-mile advance from the Essex Battalion's position on Ed Duda, the only noise being the swish of boots in the sand. A Company advanced on the left, C on the right, with B and D Companies behind. 'Just like training,' observed the adjutant, Captain 'Topper' Browne, to the CO, Lieutenant Colonel Eustace Arderne.

After two hours, singing could be heard in the distance – to keep their spirits up the Italians always sang at night. But then the Durhams were spotted. The singing abruptly stopped and a murderous fire was opened on the advancing troops. The fire was so fierce that both A and B companies came to an immediate halt, the men burrowing into the sand and taking shelter where they could behind rocks as the Italians reacted with machine guns, rifles and 75-millimetre guns, the latter firing over open sights. Casualties quickly mounted, and Arderne realized the foolishness of advancing without tank cover. On previous experience, it had not been worth the trouble, with the tanks falling easy victim to mines in the darkness, and the noise giving their presence away long before they arrived. But the element of surprise was now lost anyway, and Arderne sent back for armour.

While the tanks were being mustered men of C Company managed to infiltrate the Italian positions on the right flank, but then the Matildas rumbled up. The tanks deployed and advanced on the Italian positions, machine guns spewing fire with the Durhams advancing at the double with fixed bayonets behind them, led by the redoubtable Arderne. Fighting through the position – the Italian artillerymen fought valiantly – the CO's party came across a bunker. 'Sergeant Blenkinsop was with me,' Arderne was later to write, 'he had just seen his company commander [Major Adrian Keith] killed [by an Italian grenade] and was out for blood. Down he went [into the bunker] and after a good deal of noise there was silence and out came Blenkinsop.' 'Well?' Arderne asked. Blenkinsop looked a bit sheepish and replied, 'They offered me chocolates, sir, and I hadn't the heart to kill them.' The action was over by 2.30 a.m., Point 157 falling for the loss of thirty-eight Durham casualties. Four 75-millimetre artillery pieces, some anti-tank and machine guns, together with five officers and 125 Italians, were captured. One officer was taken prisoner attempting to escape on a motorcycle on the back of which was strapped a large suitcase.

This was very nearly the final action of the siege: the 4th Borders occupied Point 157 against no opposition, and by 10 December Rommel's army was in full retreat. In fact, for some days large quantities of German and Italian transport had been flooding west along the Trigh Capuzzo and the southern escarpment in an effort to evacuate to a new line west of Tobruk. The British seemed unable to do anything about these struggling dusty columns, either from the air or with artillery fire. The long and confused battles for eastern Cyrenaica, which had focused on Sidi Rezegh in the final fortnight of Operation Crusader, were drawing to a close, Rommel now certain that with only forty of the 558 tanks with which he had started three weeks before, he could not win this battle, at least.

However, none of this was apparent to the exhausted men on the Ed Duda escarpment. They had seen these tidal waves of men and equipment move east and west and back again many times during the previous fortnight. Indeed for two days the enemy had been pressing a company against the base of the southern escarpment, harassing the Essex mens' position atop the ridge with machine-gun and mortar fire. But now artillery shells from the south began landing amid the Axis columns – fire from the advancing 8th Army – and the spirits of the tired Tobruk garrison desperately defending the corridor began to lift. At 7 a.m. on 6 December Rommel ordered the Afrika Korps to withdraw to the north-west to cover the withdrawal of all German and Italian forces from Cyrenaica. Early the following day Crasher Nichols instructed Brownless to take a strong patrol out to the base of the forward escarpment to clear the German company position. At 11 a.m., just as he was leading his men out, a hailstorm of mortar shells fell across the position, and Brownless's patrol was forced to seek sanctuary in the D Company trenches on the forward slope. Horrified at the extent of his task – his patrol comprised fifteen men against potentially a hundred Germans – Brownless nevertheless obediently edged his way down a wadi towards the German position. To his surprise, it was empty:

> The Germans had left, and probably under cover of the mortar fire, half an hour earlier. This was too good to be true. I decided to have a look round some of the tents. We found a store of food in one of

them ... There was nothing very interesting, but we helped our-selves to a few tins of food and some black bread, which we had learnt was rather palatable. There were a lot of empty beer bottles round the tents. We failed to discover any full ones. In one store tent, though, we found some band instruments and drums ...

I thought we really ought to go back and report the valley clear, though the temptation to stay and look through more tents was strong, for I love looting. We returned in correct formation, but carrying three bugles, two drums, three flutes, a ukulele, and our pockets and equipment bulging with food.

When Brownless returned to his own position Jock Nelson told him that Nichols was going to inspect the battalion. It was their first parade for many months, certainly the first in Tobruk, and it meant only one thing: the battle – and therefore the siege – was over. In fact the salient in the south-west corner at Ras el Medawar would not be recovered by the Poles until the night of 9 December, but on the 7th a mass of 8th Army transport finally made it through the corridor and into Tobruk. The reality did not immediately sink in. Brownless formed up his severely depleted platoon. In operations between 26 November and 9 December the Essex battalion had lost 240 men, a third of its fighting strength. It was their fourteenth day on Ed Duda, and the nineteenth since the breakout. The men had been counter-attacked six times and had on at least one occasion been completely overrun by enemy tanks, to the extent that General Scobie had been prepared to order the evacuation of the ridge. But the battalion – reinforced throughout by a company of the Northumberland Fusiliers and for two days by two companies of the Australian 2/13th Battalion, themselves relieved by the Kiwis of the 19th Infantry Battalion – had managed not merely to survive at the point of the Tobruk salient, but to overcome everything Rommel could throw against them. They had won. Looking at the men drawn up in front of him, Brownless could feel only two things: exhaustion and pride. 'Never before had I seen such a scruffy, dirty-looking lot of bodies in the King's uniform. I must have looked as bad myself, but we could not help it. The colonel strode up, walked quickly round the ranks, and asked one or two of the men questions. He then turned to me and said, "Excellent! Well done.

Excellent." I saluted, and as he walked off turned round and dismissed a platoon of which I was very proud.'

On the same day Rommel wrote to his wife from his headquarters off the Derna Road:

Dearest Lu

You will no doubt have seen how we're doing from the *Wehrmacht* communiqués. I've had to break off the action outside Tobruk on account of the Italian formations and also the badly exhausted German troops. I'm hoping we'll succeed in escaping enemy encirclement and holding on to Cyrenaica. I'm keeping well. You can imagine what I'm going through and what anxieties I have. It doesn't look as though we'll get any Christmas this year.

And in London that afternoon Winston Churchill told a packed House of Commons, to whooping cheers, 'It may definitely be said that Tobruk has been disengaged.'

*

The longest siege in the history of the British empire was finally over. The end had come quickly and as something of an anticlimax. With the enemy gone for the moment (Rommel would be back again in 1942), the constant pressure of encirclement lifted and, as Brownless discovered, military routine inexorably reasserted itself. The detritus of battle needed to be dealt with, and the dead had to be collected and buried, but almost overnight the peculiar features of siege life quietly disappeared. Troops not required for the pursuit of Rommel, which in the main was conducted by the 8th Army, were sent back to Egypt, some by way of a bumpy three-day journey in the backs of trucks, some via the quicker but still dangerous sea route to Alexandria. For many of the Tobruk garrison their first baths and proper meals in many months came only when Cairo or Alex was reached.

The defence of Tobruk had begun with inexperienced Australian citizen-infantrymen in Italian-built perimeter posts, supported by British artillerymen and tanks swept together from the chaos of defeat. These heterogeneous forces had melded together quickly and completely, to withstand and repel everything which an increasingly frustrated German and Italian high command could throw at them. They withstood the enemy in the skies and on the ground, and they survived the physical challenges of a North African desert summer with little water, poor food and the constant irritations of rats, flies and fleas. They had triumphed. They knew it too. They knew that without Tobruk Rommel would be unable to advance with confidence into Egypt. The triumph of the siege of Tobruk in 1941 was that a handful of dusty Australians, Britons, Indians, Poles and Czechs no more than 24,000 strong had prevented Rommel from securing Egypt and possibly the entire Middle East. In vanquishing an arrogant enemy never before defeated in battle and exulting in its omnipotence, they had also smashed the myth of German invincibility.

When the bulk of Morshead's Australians left in October 1941 the Britons left behind had feared for the future. They need not have done, for the men of the incoming British 70th Division measured up in every respect to the standards set by the departing Diggers. When the Leicestershire Regiment finally left Tobruk on 18 December Captain John Marriott declared, 'The spirit of defiance that the Australians had bred in Tobruk had passed into them, and we felt that they had not let them down.' How right he was. They were all, now, Rats of Tobruk.

The cost could be counted then, as now, by the neat rows of headstones in Tobruk and Acroma cemeteries. Five thousand, nine hundred and eighty-nine men died during those 242 days of death, and today many lie buried beneath the Libyan sands. A further 539 members of the Royal and Royal Australian Navies, together with their compatriots in the Merchant Navy, found their watery graves along the route of the Suicide Run between Tobruk and Alexandria. Major General Leslie Morshead provided the words which grace the entrance to the Tobruk cemetery and which remember all those Rats who failed to return home:

> THIS IS HALLOWED GROUND FOR HERE LIE THOSE
> WHO DIED FOR THEIR COUNTRY.

Epilogue

With Rommel pushed out of Cyrenaica in December 1941 Tobruk's defences were allowed to crumble. But in 1942 the tide of war in North Africa swept back, and this time carried the Axis army all the way into Egypt, swamping Tobruk and only coming to a stop in August 1942 at the small town of El Alamein, where General Auchinleck's 8th Army brought Rommel's second North African blitzkrieg to a halt. There, in October and November 1942, the tide turned once more. Decisively defeated by the 8th Army, now under the command of Lieutenant General Bernard Montgomery, the Germans and Italians began a fighting withdrawal westward.

For Rudolf Schneider and his comrades of the Afrika Korps the war in North Africa ended with surrender in May 1943 in Homs, Tunisia. Transported as POWs to Canada, they were not to return to Germany until 1947. But at least they returned. Of the 386 men in Schneider's company in November 1941 only thirty remained eighteen months later.

For the Australians of the 9th Division the war turned in an entirely different direction in December 1941 with the Japanese invasion of Malaya. The 2nd AIF was ordered by an understandably nervous Australian government back to defend shores nearer home. Those who had fought through the heat and dust of the Libyan summer now found themselves in the humid jungle battlefields of south-east Asia. And so too did the men of the British 70th Division. Shipped to India, Lieutenant Philip Brownless and his comrades were absorbed into a new formation under the command of a young major general by the name of Orde Wingate. Known as the Chindits, they were to fight deep behind enemy lines in the heart of Burma. But that is another story.

The battlefields of Tobruk, handed back to nature on the departure of the combatants and ignored by all but passing Bedouin for years, were cleared of large quantities of detritus in the 1950s and 1960s. But much remains: considerable quantities of munitions still remain near the surface of the desert and retain their capacity to maim and kill. Scores of Libyans die every year as a result of the siege of Tobruk. The sun continues to beat down on the combatants of many nationalities – German, Australian, Briton, Czech, Pole, New Zealander, South African, Frenchman and Italian – who never left Tobruk and whose silent graves bear witness to the war fought here over six decades ago.

Standing in Knightsbridge Cemetery in October 2007, the Libyan sun warming my face and the desert wind prickling my skin with sand, I closed my eyes and could almost see those Diggers of Len Tutt's memory, particularly the 'tall Australian with his battered bush hat, a finger on the trigger of his Bren'. I could almost hear what he was saying to his Number Two: 'Come on, Bluey, let's give the buggers a couple of magazines full – let 'em know we're still here.'

Appendix

MAJOR MILITARY UNITS INVOLVED IN THE
SIEGE OF TOBRUK, 1941

AUSTRALIAN (April–October)

9TH DIVISION

18th Infantry Brigade (attached)
2/9th Battalion, 2/10th Battalion, 2/12th Battalion, 16th Anti-Tank Company

20th Infantry Brigade
*2/13th Battalion (April–December), 2/15th Battalion, 2/17th Battalion,
20th Anti-Tank Company*

24th Infantry Brigade
2/28th Battalion, 2/32nd Battalion, 2/43rd Battalion, 24th Anti-Tank Company

26th Infantry Brigade
2/23rd Battalion, 2/24th Battalion, 2/48th Battalion, 26th Anti-Tank Company

ROYAL AUSTRALIAN ARTILLERY

*2/12th Field Regiment, 3rd Anti-Tank Regiment,
8th Light Anti-Aircraft Regiment*

BRITISH (April–December)

3rd Armoured Brigade (Tobruk Tanks)
*1st RTR, 4th RTR, D Squadron 7th RTR, 1st King's Dragoon Guards,
3rd Queen's Own Hussars, 1st Royal Northumberland Fusiliers*

ROYAL ARTILLERY

*51st Field Regiment, 1st RHA, 104th RHA (Essex Yeomanry),
107th RHA (South Nottinghamshire Yeomanry), 3rd RHA (Anti-Tanks)*

4th Anti-Aircraft Brigade
*51st Heavy Anti-Aircraft Regiment (152, 153, 235 Batteries),
13th Light Anti-Aircraft Regiment (1, 37, 38 Batteries),
14th Light Anti-Aircraft Regiment (39, 40, 57 Batteries)*

BRITISH (October–December)

70TH DIVISION

14th Infantry Brigade
*2nd Battalion Black Watch,
1st Battalion Bedfordshire and Hertfordshire Regiment,
2nd Battalion York and Lancaster Regiment*

16th Infantry Brigade
*2nd Battalion King's Own Royal Regiment, 2nd Battalion Leicestershire Regiment,
2nd Battalion Queen's Regiment*

23rd Infantry Brigade
*1st Battalion Durham Light Infantry, 4th Battalion Border Regiment,
1st Battalion Essex Regiment*

INDIAN ARMY (April–August)

18th King Edward's Own Cavalry, Indian Army

FREE POLISH ARMY (August–December)

1st Carpathian Brigade

1st and 2nd Anti-Tank Companies, Carpathian Artillery Regiment,
Machine-Gun Battalion, Carpathian Lancers Regiment (Reconnaissance),
1st 2nd and 3rd Rifle Battalions, 11th Czechoslovak Infantry Battalion

GERMAN (across the entire Western Desert)

AFRIKA KORPS

5TH LIGHT DIVISION (later 21st Panzer Division)

5th Panzer Regiment, 3rd Reconnaissance Battalion,
104th Motorized Infantry Regiment (also known as 104th Panzer Grenadier Regt
and the 104th Rifle Regiment), 155th Armoured Artillery Regiment,
200th Anti-Tank Battalion, 39th Anti-Tank Battalion,
200th Motorized Signals Battalion, 200th Armoured Supply Battalion,
200th Armoured Engineer Battalion, 605th Anti-Tank Battalion,
2nd Machine-Gun Battalion, 8th Machine-Gun Battalion

15TH PANZER DIVISION

8th Panzer Regiment, 115th Infantry Regiment,
33rd Armoured Artillery Regiment, 33rd Armoured Reconnaissance Battalion,
33rd Anti-Tank Battalion, 15th Motorized Infantry Battalion,
33rd Armoured Supply Battalion, 33rd Armoured Engineer Battalion,
33rd Anti-Aircraft Battalion, 200th Motor Rifle Regiment

CORPS UNITS

1st Battalion 18th Anti-Aircraft Regiment, 576th Anti-Tank Regiment,
1st Battalion 33rd Anti-Aircraft Regiment, Logistical Units

90TH LIGHT DIVISION

155th Infantry Regiment, 361st Afrika Regiment,
288th Sonderverband (Special Unit), 580th Reconnaissance Battalion

ITALIAN

21ST CORPS

Bologna Division

Brescia Division

Pavia Division

Sacona Division

Trento Division

BÖTTCHER ARTILLERY GROUP

MANOEUVRE GROUP

Ariete Armoured Division

132nd Armoured Regiment, 8th Bersaglieri Regiment,
132nd Artillery Regiment

Trieste Armoured Division

65th and 66th Infantry Regiments, 9th Bersaglieri Regiment

Select Bibliography

Max Arthur, *Forgotten Voices of the Second World War* (London: Ted Smart, 2004)

Claude Auchinleck, *London Gazette Supplement, Operations in the Middle East, 5 July 1941–31 October 1941* (London: London Gazette, 1942)

Pietro Badoglio, *Italy in the Second World War* (Greenwood Press, 1976)

C.N. Barclay, *History of the Royal Northumberland Fusiliers* (London: William Clowes and Sons, 1952)

Corelli Barnett, *The Desert Generals* (London: Allen and Unwin, 1960)

John Bierman and Colin Smith, *War Without Hate: The Desert Campaign of 1940–1943* (New York: Penguin USA, 2004)

Paul Carell, *The Foxes of the Desert* (New York: Bantam, 1960)

Michael Carver, *Dilemmas of the Desert War* (London: Batsford, 1986)

Winston Churchill, *The Second World War Volume Two Their Finest Hour* (London: Cassell, 1949)

Richard Collier, *War in the Desert* (London: Time Life, 1997)

R.J. Collins, *Lord Wavell* (London: Hodder and Stoughton, 1948)

John Connell, *Auchinleck* (London: Cassell, 1959)

John Connell, *Wavell: Scholar and Soldier* (London: Collins, 1964)

Geoffrey Cox, *A Tale Of Two Battles: A Personal Memoir of Crete and the Western Desert, 1941* (London: Kimber, 1987)

Brian Cull and Don Minterne, *Hurricanes over Tobruk* (London: Grub Street, 1999)

John Cumpston, *Rats Remain: Tobruk Siege, 1941* (Melbourne: Grayflower, 1966)

T.B. Davis, *The Surrey and Sussex Yeomanry in the Second World War* (Ditchling, Sussex: Ditchling Press, 1980)

Lawrence Durrell, *Spirit of the Place* (Faber and Faber 1969)

Roy Farran, *Winged Dagger* (London: Collins, 1948)

George Forty, *Afrika Korps at War, Vol. 1: The Road to Alexandria* (New York: Scribner, 1978)

David Fraser, *Knight's Cross: A Life of Field Marshal Erwin Rommel* (London: HarperCollins, 1993)

Rudolfo Graziani, *Africa Settentrionale 1940–41* (Durasie, 1948)

Jack Greene and Alessandro Massignani, *Rommel's North Africa Campaign, September 1940–November 1942* (Conshohocken, Pa.: Combined Books, 1994)

Frank Harrison, *Tobruk: The Great Siege Reassessed* (London: Brockhampton Press, 1999)

Peter Hart, *To the Last Round: The South Notts Hussars* (Pen and Sword, 1996)

Anthony Heckstall-Smith, *Tobruk: Story of a Siege* (New York: Norton, 1960)

Christopher Hibbert, *Benito Mussolini* (Penguin, 1975)

F.H. Hinsley, *British Intelligence in the Second World War* Volume 1 (London: HMSO, 1979)

David Irving, *The Trail of the Fox* (New York: Dutton, 1977)

W.G.F. Jackson, *The Battle for North Africa, 1940–43* (New York: Mason/ Charter, 1975)

Cyril Jolly, *Take These Men* (London: Constable, 1955)

Volkmar Kühn, *Rommel in the Desert* (West Chester, Pa.: Schiffer Publishing, 1991)

Jon Latimer, *Alamein* (London: John Murray, 2002)

Jon Latimer, *Tobruk 1941: Rommel's Opening Move* (Westport, Conn.: Praeger Publishing, 2004)

John Laffin, *Digger* (London: Cassell, 1959)

Rea Leakey, *Leakey's Luck: A Tank Commander with Nine Lives* (Stroud; Sutton Publishing, 1999)

Ronald Lewin, *Life and Death of the Afrika Korps* (New York: Quadrangle, 1977)

Ronald Lewin, *Ultra Goes to War* (London: Hutchinson, 1978)

B.H. Liddell Hart, *The Tanks* (London: Cassell, 1959)

B.H. Liddell Hart (ed.), *The Rommel Papers* (London: Collins, 1953)

Gavin Long, *To Benghazi* (Sydney: Collins, 1986)

James Lucas, *Panzer Army Afrika* (Novato, Calif.: Presidio Press, 1977).

James Lucas, *Rommel's Year of Victory* (Mechanicsburg, Pa.: Stackpole Books, 1998)

Barton Maughan, *Australia in the War of 1939–1945, Series I, Volume III. Tobruk and el Alamein* (Canberra: Australian War Memorial, 1966)

Dal McGuirk, *Rommel's Army in Africa* (Osceola, Wis.: Motorbooks International, 1987).

Ministero della Difesa, *Italian Official History. Seconda Offensiva Britannica in Africa Settentrionale e Ripiegamento Italo-Tedesco nella Sirtica Orientale, 18 Novembre 1941–17 Gennaio 1942* (Rome: Ufficio Storico, 1949)

Ministero della Difesa, *Italian Official History. La Prima Controffensiva Italo-Tedesca in Africa Settentrionale* (Rome: Ufficio Storico, 1974)

Mario Montanari, *Le Operazioni in Africa Settentrionale* (Rome: Stato Maggiore dell'Esercito, 1985–1993).

W.E. Murphy, *Official History of New Zealand in the Second World War, 1939–45. The Relief of Tobruk* (Wellington: War History Branch, 1961)

Barrie Pitt, *Crucible of War, Volume 2. Auchinleck's Command* (London: Cassell & Co., 2001)

I.S.O. Playfair, *History of the Second World War. The Mediterranean and Middle East, Volume 2: The Germans Come to the Help of Their Ally, 1941* (London: HMSO, 1956)

I.S.O Playfair, *History of the Second World War. The Mediterranean and Middle East, Volume 3: British Fortunes Reach Their Lowest Ebb* (London: HMSO, 1960)

Kenneth Rankin, *Top-Hats in Tobruk* (Odiham, privately published, 1983)

David Rissik, *The Durham Light Infantry at War* (Eastbourne: Anthony Rowe, 1952)

J. C. Salter, *A Padre with the Rats of Tobruk* (Hobart: 1946)

O.F. Sheffield, *The York and Lancaster Regiment, Volume 3: 1919–1953* (Aldershot: Gale and Polden, 1956)

Christopher Somerville, *Our War: How the British Commonwealth Fought the Second World War* (London: Weidenfeld and Nicolson, 1999)

Lieutenant Colonel G.R. Stevens, *Fourth Indian Division* (printed for the division, 1948)

James Stock, *Tobruk: The Siege* (New York: Ballantine, 1973)

John Strawson, *The Battle for North Africa* (London: Batsford, 1969)

Susan Travers, *Tomorrow to be Brave* (London: Bantam Press, 2000)

W.E. Underhill, *The Royal Leicestershire Regiment* (Eastbourne: Anthony Rowe, 1957)

SELECT BIBLIOGRAPHY

G.L. Verney, *Desert Rats: The 7th Armoured Division in World War II* (London: Hutchinson, 1954)

Archibald Wavell, *Operations in the Middle East from 7 Feb 1941 to 15 July 1941* (London: *London Gazette*, 1941).

Don West, *Warriors in the Know* (two volumes), (Colchester: Warrior Press, 1996)

Lewis M. White (ed.), *On All Fronts: Czechs and Slovaks in World War II* (Boulder, Colo.: East European Monographs, 1991)

Desmond Young, *Rommel* (London: Collins, 1953)

Index

Index

Cirener, Lt 170

Clark, Lt James 'Nobby' 74, 91–2

Cleere, Sergeant Patrick 7, 8

Cochrane 2nd Lt Peter 29–30, 34, 36, 37–8, 39, 48, 50, 122

Collins, Bombardier Mick 197, 207

Collishaw, Air Commodore Raymond 6, 15

Combe, Lt Col John 21–2, 51, 70

Compass, Operation 31–2, 33–75
  attack on Bardia 55–6, 57–63
  attack on Derna 68
  attack on Mechili 68
  attack on Nibeiwa 37–9
  attack on Sidi Barrani 42–50
  attack on Sidi Omar 54–5
  attack on Tobruk 63, 64–7
  attack on Tummar camps 39–40
  destruction of Italian 10th Army 68–74
  impact of success of 53–4
  Italian retreat 54
  scale of Italian surrender 61–2, 66, 74
  success of 75
  unexpected success of 56

Cona, General 74

Cooper, Reginald 198, 219

Copland, Lt 65

Cowles, Corporal 'Bunny' 193, 196, 202–3, 219, 221, 222, 229, 235

Creedon, Lt Col 'Crackers' 263

Crusader, Operation 261–3, 267, 272, 287

Cugnasca, Carlo 152

Cultivate, Operation 237, 239

Cunningham, Admiral Andrew 56, 200

Cunningham, Lt Gen Sir Alan 262, 272

Cyrene 69, 101

Dainty, Bill 228–9

Daniel, Gunner Jack 179, 206

Daniell, Betty 220–1

Daniell, Major Robert 126, 155, 156, 203

D'Avanzo, Lt Col 9

Dennis, Alec 240

Derna 2, 3, 68, 98, 100, 101, 106, 107

Devine, Major John 77, 78, 79, 101, 106–7, 110–11, 137, 138, 140–1, 163, 168, 195–6, 203–4, 209, 219, 225

Dill, General Sir John 56, 225

Dishman, Fusilier Richard 273

dive-bombers
  German 19, 75, 93, 98, 138–40, 164–5,

175, 178–9, 205–7, 209, 211, 249, 259–60
  Italian 39

Dolega-Cieszkowski, Lt Col 285

Dorman-Smith, Brigadier Eric 88

Douglas, Lt Col 161

Drew, Lt Col Henry 89, 121, 132, 133, 147

Drysdale, Captain Walter 46–7

Ed Duda 3, 186, 261
  Allied break-out from Tobruk 261, 263–88

Eden, Anthony 31, 52–3, 75

Edmondson, Corporal Jack 143–4

Eggert, Corporal 162

Egypt
  British military weakness 4, 5–6
  Italian invasion 26–8
  Mussolini orders invasion 2

Ehlert, Maj 103

El Adem 12, 111, 113, 115, 123, 126
  German attack 130–6, 141–57

El Agheila 91

El Alamein 291

El Gubbi airfield 120, 136, 137, 147

Ellis, Bombardier (later Sgt) Ray 125, 126–7, 129–30, 136–7, 142, 145, 146, 152, 155, 178, 194, 200, 229, 230, 242, 256, 259, 263, 279–80

Enba Gap 33, 41

Ennecerus, Major Walter 243

Esebeck, Baron von 104

Evans, Lt Col 212

Fabris, Lt Col 99

Faltenbacher, Major 170

Farran 2nd Lt Roy 35–6, 39, 49, 54, 64, 68, 89, 93, 96, 97, 98, 106, 135, 140

Fearnside, Lt Geoffrey 207–8, 251, 283

Fellers, Colonel Bonner 35, 53

Felton, Pte 91

Folliot, Commandant 33, 89

food 218–21, 250

Forrest, William 265

Forrester, Sgt 268

Francis, Pte 38

Franks, Lt 270

Franks, Pte Alex 164, 197, 203, 205–6, 223, 228, 245

Free French 33, 57, 89, 92, 97

Index